Classifying Psychopathology

Philosophical Psychopathology

Jennifer Radden and Jeffrey Poland, editors

Classifying Psychopathology

Mental Kinds and Natural Kinds

edited by Harold Kincaid and Jacqueline Sullivan

The MIT Press
Cambridge, Massachusetts
London, England

MIT Press books may be purchased at special quantity discounts for business or sales promotional use. For information, email special_sales@mitpress.mit.edu.

Set in Stone Serif Std and Stone Sans Std 9/13 pt by Toppan Best-set Premedia Limited. Printed and bound in the United States of America.

Library of Congress Cataloging-in-Publication Data

Classifying psychopathology : mental kinds and natural kinds / edited by Harold Kincaid and Jacqueline A. Sullivan.
    pages cm. — (Philosophical psychopathology)
Includes bibliographical references and index.
ISBN 978-0-262-02705-2 (hardcover : alk. paper) 1. Mental illness—Classification. 2. Psychology, Pathological. I. Kincaid, Harold, 1952–editor of compilation. II. Sullivan, Jacqueline A., editor of compilation.
RC455.2.C4C58   2014
616.89—dc23
2013031918

10 9 8 7 6 5 4 3 2 1

for Scott Kincaid and Kathryn Sullivan

Contents

Preface

This volume brings together a number of perspectives on the issue of whether mental disorders are natural kinds. Some of the contributors presented papers at a workshop on Natural Kinds and Classification in Psychopathology held at the University of Alabama at Birmingham in April of 2009. The workshop generated enough interest that some of the participants enthusiastically agreed to contribute to a volume. Philosophers who had been active participants in debates about natural kinds in philosophy of psychiatry were also invited to contribute.

1 Classifying Psychopathology: Mental Kinds and Natural Kinds

Harold Kincaid and Jacqueline Sullivan

According to the *Mental Health Atlas* (World Health Organization 2011, p. 13), "neuropsychiatric disorders are estimated to contribute to 13% of the global burden of disease"—that is, more than 450 million people suffer from neuropsychiatric disorders. They are leading causes of disability-adjusted life years, accounting for 37 percent of the healthy years lost from all non-communicable diseases. Depression alone accounts for one-third of this (Insel 2011).

The global cost of mental illness is estimated at 2.5 trillion US dollars and is expected to increase to more than 6 trillion dollars by 2030 (World Health Organization 2011). In the United States alone, estimates indicate that mental-health disorders account for 59 percent of the economic costs that stem from injury or illness-related loss of productivity (ibid.). Perhaps surprisingly, the economic burden of mental-health disorders stems less from the cost of care than from loss of income due to unemployment, expenses for social supports, and a range of indirect costs due to chronic disability that begins early in life (Insel 2011). According to the director of the National Institutes for Mental Health, "considering that those with mental illness are at high risk for developing cardiovascular disease, respiratory disease, and diabetes, the true costs of mental illness must be even higher" (ibid.).

While awareness of the cost of mental disorders is increasing, doubts about overmedicalization—about treating what really are problems in living as if they were medical diseases calling for pharmacological treatment—are also increasing. For example, there is evidence that certain sociological and economic pressures on the development of manuals such as the *Diagnostic and Statistical Manual of Mental Disorders* have eroded historically preserved distinctions between categories differentiating "normal" types of human suffering from mental disorder and dysfunction. A classic case in point, analyzed by Allan Horwitz and Jerome Wakefield in their 2007 book *The Loss of Sadness*, is the late-twentieth-century erosion of the boundaries between sadness and depression. (See chapter 11 below.) At one time, the two categories were kept distinct. However, the operationalization of depressive disorder put forward in the fourth edition of *Diagnostic and Statistical Manual of Mental Disorders* (referred to as *DSM*-IV) included conditions that served to broaden the kinds of phenomena picked out by the concept to the extent that what was previously considered sadness came to be lumped together with what was previously considered major depression. As the class of persons picked out by the category became more heterogeneous, the number of persons diagnosed as "depressed" increased, as did the number of prescriptions for anti-depressants. The removal of the grief and bereavement clause from the fifth edition of the *DSM* (2013) further broadens the category of major depression by allowing doctors to diagnose individuals suffering from sustained grief due to loss of a loved one as having major depression. This move is likely to impede the search for the causes of depression further and to result in an increase in the overuse of psychotropic drugs.

This volume asks whether psychiatry as a science may better position itself to cure mental-health disorders by considering whether improvements to the current criteria for classifying mental disorders are warranted or whether the classification schemes are fine as they stand. Either directly or indirectly, the authors take up the question of whether mental disorders are natural kinds. The basic idea behind the concept of natural kinds is that science identifies the most fundamental entities of nature and shows how they are interrelated. In the case of mental disorders, psychiatric categories ought to group together phenomena in such a way that those phenomena are subject to the same type of causal explanation (see, e.g., Craver 2009) and respond similarly to the same kinds of causal interventions (see, e.g., Woodward 2003). If psychiatric categories do not find such groupings, then there is reason to revise and/or eliminate existing classifications.

This volume is thus organized around the scientific ideal of natural kinds and the extent to which psychiatry can and currently does identify them. The notion of natural kinds can be read in multiple ways. It will be useful to set out some of the main variants of the concept of natural kind here.

All senses of natural kinds assume that there is something out there in the world that grounds classifications. The open questions are "What is that something like?" and "What kinds of classifications can it ground?" The strongest sense of natural kinds, often called "essentialism," thinks that there are sets of individually necessary and jointly sufficient properties for a given kind that entail a strict in or out classification of all individuals. The weakest sense asserts only that some properties are statistically associated; it allows for no sharp, non-arbitrary categorizing of individuals who lie on a continuum. Various other notions fall between these two poles. Pragmatic approaches might agree with the weak continuum picture but think that practical reasons such as cost effectiveness might allow for drawing motivated boundaries. The view adopted most often in this volume allows for natural kinds without a single set of necessary and sufficient conditions but instead with multiple different property combinations with family resemblance similarity relations.

These are some main contours of different views of natural kinds. There are further sophistications possible beyond these basic views, and some of them are explored in this volume. The chapters are generally united, however, in the belief that it is important for practice and scientific inquiry to get clear about what sense of natural kinds is at work in any particular classification of psychopathology.

Many of those who have participated in the natural-kinds debate about psychiatry are realists about mental disorders and would like it to be the case that psychiatric classification systems such as that of the *DSM* did a better job of tracking natural kinds. There are optimists; there are also pessimists. However, the *validity* of categories of mental disorder has never been, and continues not to be, the main aim of the task forces involved in the development of the *DSM*. Rather, the primary aims are *intra-rater reliability* and *inter-rater reliability*. The result is a classification system in which the necessary and sufficient conditions associated with a given category of mental disorder pick out a heterogeneous rather than a homogeneous class of individuals. In addition, boundaries between the categories fail to be robust to the extent that there is significant comorbidity between categories. These shortcomings may be regarded as rendering the classification system poorly poised to serve as a basis for identifying the causes of mental disorders and locating effective strategies for intervening in them. However, current categories *are* used as the primary basis for research into the causes of mental disorders, because they are the best classification schemes available. This may soon be changing, insofar as the National Institutes of Mental Health have recently "launched the Research Domain Criteria (RDoC) project to transform diagnosis by incorporating genetics, imaging, cognitive science, and other levels of information to lay the foundation for a new classification system" (Insel 2013).

Two primary themes emerge from the chapters that follow: that current classification systems of mental disorders are insufficient for the purposes of successful diagnosis, treatment, and research and that the assumptions on which these classification systems are based are problematic. However, the contributors provide different answers as to why the current classification systems fail, different ideas on how the failures might be overcome, and different suggestions as to how the assumptions on which the systems are based might be revised.

Nick Haslam begins his chapter by laying out the useful set of different senses of "natural kind." He argues that there probably are no cases of mental disorders that meet the strict essentialist requirements, and that different conceptions of natural kind may be appropriate for different disorders. Haslam then discusses taxometric methods for identifying natural kinds. He notes that taxometric analyses of artificial data sets with a subset of individuals that only share family resemblances conclude that there is positive evidence for a taxon. Thus, when taxometric analyses do find positive evidence for a discreet class, that evidence may be only evidence for a family-resemblance kind, not for a discrete or essentialist kind. Haslam's second point is that taxometric studies have found positive evidence for treating mental disorders as taxons in a small minority of possible disorders. Haslam concludes his chapter by describing some empirical evidence that essentialist concepts of mental disorders promote stigmatization, contrary to the widespread notion that treating mental disorders as disease will make persons diagnosed with them less prone to social discrimination.

Jeffrey Poland argues that contemporary treatment and research on mental disorders is dominated by "conventional psychiatric practice" (CPP), which is ordered around the *DSM*: individuals are diagnosed on the basis of the *DSM*, treatment and research studies are based on it, and the *DSM* is strongly embedded in the financial and educational sides of psychiatry. Poland claims that the empirical evidence shows that the *DSM* categories are a scientific failure in that none of them have been found to have predictive validity and in that they have multiple defects as a basis for treatment decisions and approaches. (See chapter 8 for a dissenting opinion.) The reason for these failures, Poland suggests, is that the assumptions of CPP and the *DSM* are inconsistent with the essential nature of mental phenomena and mental disorders. There is no sharp difference between normal mental functioning and the process involved in mental disorders. All mental phenomena are hierarchically organized, multidimensional, context sensitive, and so on—characteristics that don't fit well with the medical model of *DSM*-based practice. Unfortunately, that model is deeply embedded in current practices and institutions, and Poland doubts that the latest revisions in the *DSM* will change its basic character. Poland makes some suggestions for reform.

Dan Stein begins his chapter by pointing out that for some time it was widely believed that psychotropic drugs, insofar as they acted on different neurobiological substrates, could be used to distinguish different mental disorders from one another and even to differentiate abnormal from normal behavior. However, the fact that the action of specific psychotropic drugs is fairly diffuse and the fact that mild depression responds to placebo alone suggest that psychotropic drugs cannot be used to "carve nature at her joints" when it comes to psychiatric kinds. Stein further demonstrates the limitations of this view by pointing out that there are multiple ways to differentiate mental disorders. For example, from the "classical perspective" the correct way to individuate mental disorders is by appeal to necessary and sufficient conditions, whereas a "critical perspective" acknowledges that classification systems may change over time and may vary across cultures. In contrast, an "integrative perspective" acknowledges that, even though the categories are in part socially constructed, this does not mean that they aren't amenable to being understood scientifically and explained mechanistically, but it may indeed rule out the possibility that psychotropic agents will be sufficient for differentiating normal behavior from pathological behavior. Stein argues for this integrative perspective, and claims that it is instantiated in what he refers to as "the naturalistic approach." According to Stein, insights from cognitive psychology suggests that ordinary folk universally agree that certain kinds of phenomena may be classified as normal and others cannot be so classified. Neuroscience provides us with good reasons to believe that the mental phenomena we take to be indicative of a mental disorder correspond to or are caused by abnormal brain processes, and anthropology teaches us that social constructions influence the categories, but neither neuroscience nor anthropology rules out the possibility that psychopharmacological interventions may be used to treat the disorders corresponding to the categories. It just turns out that in instances in which a condition is deemed psychiatric yet not attributable to underlying abnormalities in the brain, and is spoken of using moral metaphors, it will probably not be subject to medical intervention, but rather to social intervention. How one regards a particular psychiatric disorder and how one thinks it is best to be treated will vary, depending on one's perspective.

Like Haslam, Peter Zachar notes that there are different senses attached to the term "natural kinds" and that the different senses may be more or less demanding. Zachar's own previous work on "practical kinds" is partial motivation for Haslam's framework. On Zachar's view, "being out there"—not being merely a subjective fact about how we like to talk, but being something in the world—is a central feature of most notions of natural kinds. Fitting into laws, supporting induction, and identifying discrete entities are further criteria, and the strong essentialist version requires underlying causal properties that are necessary and sufficient for classification. Zachar identifies several different weaker notions of natural kinds, most of which involve some kind of objective similarity that grounds predictions. He notes that one motivation for identifying natural kinds in the study of mental disorders is scientific legitimacy. However, he denies that scientific legitimacy requires the full-fledged essentialist notion. There are useful generalizations about depression, for example, even if it is not well captured as an essentialist natural kind.

Dominic Murphy asserts at the outset of his chapter that the categories of psychiatric disorders found in the *DSM* are informed by folk psychology. This prompts the question of whether current taxonomic schemes in psychiatry actually track natural kinds. Specifically, Murphy has in mind Richard Boyd's (1991) view of natural kinds as homeostatic property clusters that group together phenomena that are similar enough to be subject to explanation in terms of the same underlying causal properties. In order to broach the question of whether classification systems based on folk-psychological distinctions are capable of yielding Boydian natural kinds, Murphy considers the case of delusional beliefs. The category of *delusion*, according to Murphy, is based on folk-epistemological considerations of what constitutes good and bad outputs of our knowledge-producing processes. While delusions are regarded as abnormal outputs, it is a separate question whether the kinds of phenomena that are grouped together under the heading of "delusion" may be used to track one or several common belief-producing mechanisms that go awry. On an optimistic interpretation of what folk-psychological thought may accomplish, we might be inclined to think that the category of delusion is an example of a Boydian homeostatic property cluster. However, on the skeptical interpretation that Murphy advocates, it is likely that the category groups together such disparate and heterogeneous phenomena that a whole host of causal processes will have to be posited in order to accommodate them. Furthermore, the same may be said for any psychiatric classification system that is informed by folk psychology.

George Graham raises the question of whether mental disorders are real. As he rightly notes, answering this question requires that we first specify what a mental disorder is, and that we then identify the evidentiary standards required for attributing mental disorders to persons. Graham's aim is to argue for a realist position about mental disorders by answering these two questions and demonstrating that mental disorders are both "act-of-classification-independent" and "inherent" conditions of persons. According to Graham, mental disorders are real insofar as they are psychologically incapacitated conditions in the world that inhere in persons, are independent of our actively classifying them, are harmful to the persons in whom they inhere, and are sometimes harmful to other persons. These features are true of these conditions irrespective of whether they are natural kinds or brain disorders.

Harold Kincaid defends the view that there are some categorical groupings that support objective predictive and explanatory accounts of psychopathology, though he shares the views of Haslam and Zachar that there need be no one right notion of natural kinds for psychopathology and indeed argues that many alleged psychopathologies may not be natural kinds in any sense. His notion of natural kinds is in the same genre as Boyd's concept of a homeostatic property, Haslam's discrete and prototype groups, and Zachar's variants-based ability to predict. However, he is more explicit in discussing what the ability to predict involves and in defending categorical accounts against dimensional accounts. The latter approach is favored by the dominant psychometric practice and is a serious threat to a categorical conception of natural kinds of psychopathology. Kincaid finishes by making a case that major depression is a categorical grouping that supports prediction and explanation. He agrees with Horwitz that current criteria and current screens for depression mislead, and he provides taxometric, behavioral, and neurobiological evidence that major depressive disorder constitutes a distinct set of individuals.

Nancy Nyquist Potter, Don Ross, and Allan Horwitz take up specific mental disorders and examine the complexities involved in classifying them. Potter focuses on oppositional defiant disorder and its application to African Americans, especially young men. She argues that the legacy of racism and inequality is a powerful presence in the everyday lives of African Americans, and that labeling the behavior of black boys in school as Oppositional Defiant Disorder can be regarded as a misclassification based on failure to understand the social context constituted by a society in which racism is widespread. What teachers take to be disordered defiance can be an understandable expression of self-worth in the face of preexisting racial stereotypes. Failure to show deference to teachers may be a reflection of the fact that at home teenagers and adults relate in a nondeferential way. Medical models of disorders downplay social context, but understanding social context is essential to differentiating real mental disorder from culturally based behavior. Like Horwitz, Potter wants socio-logical understanding to be used to improve classification practices. If misapplication of depression to ordinary sadness causes inappropriate treatment, so does misapplication of ODD—it may even contribute to the perpetuation of racism.

Ross surveys recent progress in delineating problem and pathological gambling. He notes at the start that this distinction is based on an analogy to the popular distinction between problem drinking and alcoholism and that how these categories are applied is a function of social norms. The task for those interested in studying and treating gambling disorders is to turn folk-psychological notions into something scientifically and clinically useful. Clinicians do not give equal weight to the various symptoms listed in the *DSM*, and clinical screens by design minimize false negatives and thus produce false positives. Nonetheless, different screens applied across quite different populations have reached similar conclusions about the prevalence of pathological gambling. A major open question is whether these screens are getting at qualitatively different phenomena from ordi-nary gambling or whether gambling problems are best regarded as situated along a continuum. (For a discussion of this issue in general for psycho-pathology, see chapter 8.) Evidence from neurobiology and from molecular genetics suggests that pathological gambling is a qualitatively distinct phenomenon. Those with the most serious gambling problems show dis-turbances in the dopamine reward system, and in the neuroadapted hypo-activity of serotonergic circuits that normally inhibit impulsive behavior, that are similar to those of drug addicts. Ross also cites the literature showing that drug addicts exhibit distinct genetic differences. One impor-tant moral is that standard screens for psychopathology are weak instru-ments for detecting natural kinds if they exist.

Horwitz uses a sociological understanding to point out flaws in current criteria while defending the prospect for an objective disorder. He defends the idea that depression might be a natural kind, but argues that the current *DSM* criteria fail to pick it out. He believes depression is a distinct naturally occurring entity because the historical record clearly identifies it across millennia. Not until the 1970s did the *DSM* conception take root, and the result was an explosion in the number of individuals described as suffering from depression. *DSM*-III put in place the current *DSM* depression criteria, which include a poor appetite, inability to sleep, and low energy for two weeks. The criteria are sufficiently far from serious melancholia and of such short duration that a diagnosis of major depression now comes much easier. Understandable reactions to life events such as job loss, divorce, and bereavement (on bereavement see *DSM*-5) become cases of major depression. Horwitz traces the various professional and financial interests that made the change in classification happen and sustain it today.

Şerife Tekin aims to establish that Ian Hacking's looping effects are far more complex than Hacking himself has indicated and his critics have appreciated. Tekin's primary criticism of Hacking is that although changes in an individual's "self-concept" are one of the main components of Hacking's looping effects, Hacking himself never puts forward a concept of the self (only a concept of "a classified person"), and that this has left him open to attacks by critics who argue that mental disorders are on a par with kinds in other areas of science. Tekin argues persuasively that Hacking's account of looping effects needs to be buttressed by an account of how an individual's "self-concept" changes in response to receiving a diagnosis of a mental disorder and changes further in response to the individual's experiencing himself as someone having a mental disorder. To this end, Tekin puts forward what she refers to as a model of "the multitudinous self," which she uses to provide a much more detailed understanding of the nature of Hacking's looping effects.

Jacqueline Sullivan concludes the volume with an investigation of the changes that psychiatric kinds undergo when they become explanatory targets of areas of sciences that are not "mature" (see, e.g., Hacking 1988, 1992) and are in the early stages of discovering mechanisms (see, e.g., Bechtel and Richardson 1993; Bechtel 2008; Craver 2007). She focuses on two such areas of science involved in the investigation of the mechanisms of mental disorders: cognitive neuroscience and cognitive neurobiology. Neuroscientists have recently come to understand mental disorders as disorders of cognition (see, e.g., Carter et al. 2009 and Insel 2013), and a number of intra-disciplinary and inter-disciplinary research initiatives have emerged to study their mechanisms. Sullivan evaluates one such research initiative and uses it to show that even if scientific research were to begin with somewhat "stable" psychiatric and cognitive kinds, the kinds have the potential to become wildly unstable because the areas of science studying them are relatively new and the methods put forward for individuating them are not standardized across research contexts. Sullivan argues, via an analysis of the case study, that although such instability can be ameliorated if investigators impose intra-disciplinary and inter-disciplinary "strategies of stabilization," such "unifying measures" also have certain unpalatable consequences such as potentially impeding important scientific discoveries. She concludes by suggesting that this tension be overcome by striking a balance between standardizing research methods and allowing for a modest pluralism.

References

Bechtel, W. 2008. *Mental Mechanisms: Philosophical Perspectives on Cognitive Neuroscience*. Erlbaum.

Bechtel, W., and R. Richardson. [1993] 2010. *Discovering Complexity: Decomposition and Localization as Strategies in Scientific Research*. MIT Press.

Boyd, R. 1991. Realism, antifoundationalism, and the enthusiasm for natural kinds. *Philosophical Studies* 61: 127–148.

Carter, C., J. Kerns, and J. Cohen. 2009. Cognitive neuroscience: Bridging thinking and feeling to the brain, and its implications for psychiatry. In *Neurobiology of Mental Illness*, third edition, ed. D. Charney and E. Nestler. Oxford University Press.

Craver, C. 2007. *Explaining the Brain: Mechanisms and the Mosaic Unity of Neuroscience*. Oxford University Press.

Craver, C. 2009. Mechanisms and natural kinds. *Philosophical Psychology* 22: 575–594.

Hacking, I. 1988. On the stability of the laboratory sciences. *Journal of Philosophy* 85 (10): 507–514.

Hacking, I. 1992. The self-vindication of the laboratory sciences. In *Science as Practice and Culture*, ed. A. Pickering. University of Chicago Press.

Horwitz, A., and J. Wakefield. 2007. *The Loss of Sadness: How Psychiatry Transformed Normal Sorrow into Depressive Disorder*. Oxford University Press.

Insel, T. 2011. The global cost of mental illness. At http://www.nimh.nih.gov.

Insel, T. 2013. Transforming diagnosis. At http://www.nimh.nih.gov.

Woodward, J. 2003. *Making Things Happen*. Oxford University Press.

World Health Organization. 2011. *Mental Health Atlas*.

2   Natural Kinds in Psychiatry: Conceptually Implausible, Empirically Questionable, and Stigmatizing

Nick Haslam

Psychiatric classification would be a great deal easier if its diagnostic entities were like biological species. Taxonomists of spiders, snails, or slime molds can be reasonably certain that nature contains an assortment of distinct types, that each type has an identity-fixing genetic signature, and that the diversity of types can be organized into hierarchies that tell the story of their evolutionary origins. The process of locating, characterizing, and systematizing biological taxa is no picnic, but it can at least rest on a scientifically impeccable confidence that naturally occurring biological kinds exist.

The taxonomic situation in psychiatry is different, as mental disorders are fundamentally unlike biological species. Mental disorders do not pick out distinct, reproductively isolated, spatially concentrated populations. Individual persons can manifest more than one disorder, but an organism belongs to only one species. Disorders may be transient afflictions, but species membership is a life sentence. Disorders are generally less defining of individuals than species—more attributes than deep-seated identities.

Many of the differences between psychiatric taxa and biological taxa reflect the special challenges of classifying persons. Biological species are generally "indifferent kinds," impervious to the classificatory concepts, labels, systems, and theories that taxonomists develop about them. In contrast, at least some mental disorders are "interactive kinds" (Hacking 1999); people may become aware of the diagnostic labels and practices that attempt to capture them and alter their behavior and experience of self in response. Disorders may become moving targets (Hacking 2007) as these "looping effects" change the characteristic properties of the disorder and lead to revisions in the system of classification. Kinds of persons also tend to differ from biological species in their causal origins, being at least partly shaped by social processes rather than determined by biology. Even the most heritable mental disorders are heavily influenced by the social environment in their symptoms and course. In particular, it is rarely clear that individuals with a particular mental disorder all share a single, defining causal mechanism in the same way that all members of a biological species share genetic commonalities. Finally, the hierarchical structure of psychiatric categories primarily reflects phenotypic resemblance, not a history of genotypic divergences. Anxiety disorders are grouped together because they all are characterized by anxiety and fear, not because they share mechanisms or because they all speciated from a primordial angst. Metaphorically speaking, psychiatric classifications class bats with birds and fish with dolphins.

The differences between psychiatric kinds and biological taxa are structurally and causally stark. For this reason, some have argued that attempts to classify mental disorders as if they were distinct species of human misery are mistaken. On this view, psychiatric classifications can only reflect agreed-upon conventions, and should be developed to serve pragmatic clinical ends rather than to mirror an underlying psychopathological reality. Any suggestion that classifications might carve psychiatric nature at its joints would therefore be foolish. However, the desire to locate and name these joints persists, supported by a belief that real, biologically grounded entities exist independent of our efforts to describe them. The quest for psychiatric natural kinds is a continuing one, and to dismiss it out of hand on the basis of apparent differences between mental disorders and biological species would be premature.

In this chapter I examine whether the natural-kind view of mental disorders has any merit. In the first section, I present a pluralistic account of the structure of psychiatric kinds according to which some are more natural than others. Five kinds of kinds are presented, which satisfy progressively more stringent criteria. In principle, each kind of kind could be exemplified by certain disorders. I propose that only the most restrictive of these kinds of kinds can be properly described as natural. In the second section, I review one line of classification research that attempts to clarify the structure of mental disorders empirically, rather than assuming that all disorders are of the same type. On the basis of this review, I draw conclusions about the frequency of natural kinds in the field of psychopathology. In the third section, I turn from the actual structure of mental disorders to people's beliefs about them. In particular, I examine the tendency of laypeople to think about some disorders as if they were natural kinds and to hold essentialist beliefs about them. The consequences of this tendency are damaging, and constitute a strong but rarely considered argument against the use of natural-kind concepts in psychiatry.

Kinds of Kinds

Many accounts of mental disorders imply or assume that all disorders have a particular kind of structure. Advocates of the so-called disease model conceptualize disorders as categories whose outward signs and symptoms derive from an underlying neural or genetic abnormality. Proponents of dimensional models of psychopathology understand disorders as quantitative elevations on underlying symptom or personality dimensions. Prototype models represent disorders as having a family-resemblance structure, such that mental disorders are ideal types that individual cases may approximate to a greater or lesser degree along gradients of similarity. Some critics of psychiatric classifications see disorders as arbitrarily or conventionally defined forms of deviance that reflect the interests and values of classifiers rather than any underlying reality.

In an earlier work (Haslam 2002) I argued that there is little reason to believe that any one of these alternative accounts of the structure of psychiatric kinds is most adequate across the board. Instead, different accounts may suit different disorders. Some psychiatric conditions may be well described by the disease model, others by dimensional models, others by prototype models, and so on. I proposed a series of five different kinds of kinds that satisfy increasingly stringent structural criteria. These kinds represent a hierarchically ordered ladder, each successive kind having to meet one more requirement than the kind below it. This account is presented schematically in table 2.1.

Table 2.1
Schematic account of the kinds-of-kinds model

Kind type	Criterion				
	Clustered properties	Non-arbitrary cutpoint	Discontinuity	Category boundary	Category essence
Dimension	✓	✗	✗	✗	✗
Practical kind	✓	✓	✗	✗	✗
Fuzzy kind	✓	✓	✓	✗	✗
Discrete kind	✓	✓	✓	✓	✗
Natural kind	✓	✓	✓	✓	✓

Dimensions

According to the kinds-of-kinds account, dimensions are the least demand-ing structure. All that is required for a form of psychopathology to qualify as a dimension is that there be a set of correlated properties (e.g., symp-toms). Individuals may differ by degree along a dimension by possessing greater or lesser numbers or degrees of these properties. Variation along a dimension is continuous and seamless, so there is no naturally occurring break separating individuals who are affected with a condition from those who are not. Therefore, stating that a form of psychopathology is dimen-sional in this sense is not merely acknowledging that affected individuals differ in the severity of their condition; it is acknowledging that there is not a delimited condition at all. For the sake of convenience, a cutpoint may be defined on the dimension so that the quantitative variation is simplified into a dichotomous diagnosis. However, its placement is arbi-trary, much as 6 feet is a convenient but arbitrary cutpoint for deciding who is "tall" on the height continuum. Strictly, dimensions do not con-stitute kinds, as they do not define delimited categories. Proponents of dimensional models of psychopathology hold that the distribution of variation on psychopathology-related dimensions is continuous in this sense.

Practical Kinds

People may differ along a dimension, and yet it is sometimes possible to define a cutpoint on the continuum that is not arbitrary. By doing so, a meaningful kind of person may be defined in the absence of any underly-ing discontinuity on the dimension. The meaningfulness of this kind of kind depends on its relationship to some external criterion that is prag-matically relevant in the clinical context. For example, it might be that at some point along a dimension (perhaps defined as a particular test score or population percentile) the severity of the relevant symptoms becomes clinically significant or a source of functional impairment. Medical exam-ples of non-arbitrary cutpoints on continuous dimensions include blood-pressure values for diagnosing hypertension and body-mass-index values for diagnosing obesity. In both cases, the values have been selected because they roughly correspond to levels at which adverse health consequences become more likely or health risks begin to accelerate. These kinds are defined on the basis of pragmatic and external considerations rather than on the basis of internal discontinuities. This kind of kind corresponds roughly to Zachar's (2000) concept of "practical kind," after which it is named.

Fuzzy Kinds

Dimensions and practical kinds both represent forms of continuous variation between people. Such variation becomes categorical in a sense that goes beyond the merely pragmatic when some sort of internal discontinuity exists. Such a discontinuity involves a break on the underlying continuum, which produces a qualitative distinction between people who fall above the discontinuity and those who fall below it. An example is a threshold effect, in which a qualitative change of state occurs at a certain point on an underlying continuum (e.g., a liquid turning to a gas at a certain temperature, or a spring losing its tension beyond its elastic limit). Importantly, discontinuities need not be sharp. Rather than a precise categorical joint to carve, there may be a gradual inflexion or bend; if that is the case, there will be a penumbra of intermediate cases between those that are clearly on one side of the discontinuity or the other. The intermediate cases may vary along a gradient of category membership, between those that clearly don't belong to the category and those that unambiguously do. Such category-membership gradients are staples of fuzzy-set theory and of prototype models of categorization, which propose category structures that have degrees of membership or prototypicality. A hypothetical example in the domain of psychopathology might be the mania spectrum, on which full-blown mania is a qualitatively distinct emotional state from normal mood and hypomania varies by degrees in between these states.

Discrete Kinds

A discrete kind is one that has a sharp rather than graded or fuzzy discontinuity. Membership in such a kind is a step function rather than a gradient, so that any individual either belongs to the kind or doesn't. A sharp categorical discontinuity of this sort can be described metaphorically as a category boundary. Discrete kinds may have a variety of possible causal underpinnings, as numerous causal explanations can yield category boundaries. These causal explanation types include sharp threshold effects (where the qualitative change of state is abrupt), dynamic interactions of multiple causal factors, and explanations that invoke centripetal tendencies within categories (e.g., conscious identification with a group or label) and/or differentiating tendencies between them (e.g., boundary-reinforcing effects that punish transgressions of category norms). Existing psychiatric classifications generally represent mental disorders as discrete kinds in this sense: mental disorders are laid out as distinct categories, and diagnoses are made in a dichotomous, present-or-absent fashion.

Natural Kinds

Various causal stories can give rise to discrete categories, but only some causal stories can produce categories that might qualify as natural kinds in the classic, essentialist sense. Discrete categories whose origins are in threshold effects or complex multifactorial interactions, or whose boundaries are socially shaped in the manner of the looping kinds discussed by Hacking (2007) and others, cannot qualify as natural kinds in this demanding sense. Instead, natural kinds are the subset of discrete kinds whose basis is a single cause that is common to all category members and that directly gives rise to the kind's properties. In the psychiatric domain, for example, a discrete disorder whose clinical features ultimately derived from a specific neural or genetic dysfunction that was shared by all afflicted individuals would qualify as a natural kind in the sense intended here. For example, if it could be shown that all people suffering from a particular cluster of symptoms share a specific etiological factor (perhaps a gene mutation or a localized brain abnormality), and that that factor is causally responsible for those symptoms, we might be justified in calling the condition a natural kind.

These five kinds of kinds—or, more strictly, four kinds of kinds and one kind of non-kind (dimensions)—meet progressively more stringent criteria. A higher-level kind must meet the criteria for all lower-level kinds and at least one additional criterion. A natural kind, for example, must have a cluster of correlated properties and must have a non-arbitrary way of distinguishing members from non-members that is based on a sharp (not fuzzy) internal discontinuity and is caused by an underlying biological essence. To qualify as a natural kind, that is, a psychiatric condition must climb many demanding steps on our structural ladder. Each kind of kind corresponds to a prominent way of conceptualizing the structure of mental disorders, from the dimensional, to the practical or pragmatic, to the fuzzy-set-based or prototype-based, to the traditional categorical, and on to the disease model. In the absence of strong evidence for the exclusive validity of one conceptualization, I suggest, it is appropriate to adopt a pluralistic approach such that any one of these alternatives might best characterize a particular psychiatric condition. Deciding which conceptualization is most appropriate for each condition should be an empirical matter, and getting that decision wrong may have problematic consequences for psychiatric classification and diagnosis.

The subtle conceptual distinctions implicated in this classification of kind types may refine some of the coarser distinctions that are commonly drawn by writers on psychiatric taxonomy. Theorists and researchers often adopt simple binaries in this field, and the five-way classification helps to challenge these and to clarify how they conflate different kinds of kinds.

One example of an oversimplifying dichotomy is the popular distinction between categorical and dimensional models of psychopathology. This distinction is commonly represented as a division between discrete, bounded categories and continua, and can therefore be located in the kinds-of-kinds schema at the distinction between discrete and fuzzy kinds, which lack the required sharp boundaries. The categorical/dimensional distinction groups discrete kinds and natural kinds together, on the one hand, and fuzzy kinds, practical kinds, and dimensions, on the other; consequently it risks eliding the important differences among them. For instance, the "categorical" view is sometimes claimed to represent mental disorders as naturally occurring types, or as embodying a biomedical view of psychopathology, when these claims are only true of natural kinds. Discrete kinds are categories, but there is no reason to infer that they have a naturalistic basis or that the causal mechanisms responsible for them are biomedical or essentialist in nature. The *DSM* classification, for example, embodies a categorical view of mental disorders; however, it would be wrong to claim that it reflects a natural-kind model of mental disorder, because it has no commitment to underlying causal essences or to the idea that its diagnostic entities are discovered natural entities that are indifferent to shaping by the social environment.

The same potential for conflation exists on the dimensional side of the categorical/dimensional distinction. Proponents of dimensional models sometimes suppose that any attempt to draw categorical distinctions on the underlying continuum must be entirely arbitrary. If a condition appears to vary by degrees, they argue, the imposition of diagnostic cutpoints is purely subjective and indefensible. However, as my discussion of practical kinds indicates, there can be principled, non-arbitrary, and empirically justified ways to draw categorical distinctions on underlying dimensions. For this reason, evidence that a mental disorder falls on an underlying continuum is not sufficient grounds for refusing to draw diagnostic cutpoints on that continuum or for rejecting efforts to make categorical diagnoses. The kinds-of-kinds approach refines some of these judgments and reveals the crudeness of the categorical/dimensional distinction.

Another issue that the kinds-of-kinds schema clarifies is the nature of natural kinds. The schema understands the concept of "natural kind" in a particular way: as a naturally existing (i.e., objectively occurring, discovered rather than fabricated) discrete category whose causal basis is a shared, biological essence (Haslam 2000). This reflects an essentialist account of natural kinds that has been challenged in recent years. Less restrictive understandings of the natural-kind concept have been advanced in its place, the most prominent of which is Boyd's (1999) account of natural kinds as "homeostatic property clusters" (the HPC account). On this account, natural kinds are "real divisions in the structure of the world" (Craver 2009), but rather than having necessary features or causal essences they are simply clusters of properties with a similarity-generating mechanism that explains their co-occurrence. This mechanism may or may not be "underlying" and it may or may not involve the antecedent cause of the property cluster (ibid.). In all these respects, the HPC account of natural kinds differs from the essentialist account.

How, then, does the less stringent but arguably more plausible account of natural kinds as HPCs fit into the kinds-of-kinds schema? By not insisting on necessary properties or a single, essential cause, and by not specifying that such a cause be biological, the HPC account is clearly broader than the essentialist account of natural kinds. It also appears to be broader than discrete kinds, because similarity-generating mechanisms need not generate either-or category boundaries. Such mechanisms merely produce correlations among properties and resemblance among entities that possess those properties. There is no reason to believe that similarity-generating mechanisms invariably yield sharp, qualitative breaks between entities that possess sufficient levels or numbers of those properties and entities that don't. Indeed, Craver (2009) has argued that HPC kinds have a prototype or family-resemblance structure. The HPC concept therefore appears to correspond to fuzzy or higher-level kinds in our schema.

The HPC account of natural kinds is markedly more liberal than the essentialist account. It requires the existence of some sort of actual discontinuity "in nature," so it is more restrictive than our account of practical kinds, in which a categorical distinction is imposed on grounds that are pragmatic and external to the underlying structure of the kind. But it is less restrictive than our account of discrete kinds, the common-sense way of thinking about latent categories within psychopathology research, as it does not entail a discrete category boundary. A psychiatric condition could satisfy the requirements of an HPC natural kind even if the boundary separating the affected individuals from the unaffected was fundamentally ambiguous and the affected individuals fell on a gradient of prototypicality.

Figure 2.1 illustrates where the HPC distinction stands on our ladder of increasingly stringent kinds of kinds. HPC kinds are more structurally demanding than dimensions and practical kinds, but can include fuzzy

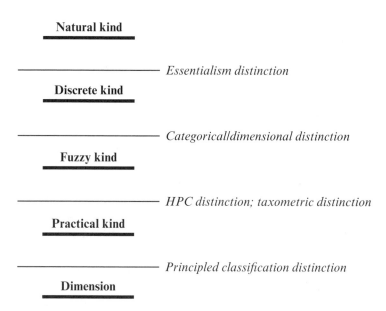

Figure 2.1
Location of critical conceptual distinctions on the kinds-of-kinds ladder.

kinds and higher-level kinds. For example, a subset of HPC kinds would also qualify as essentialist natural kinds if their similarity-generating mechanisms were of a particular sort (i.e., biological essences common to all kind members, causally responsible for the relationship among the relevant properties, and yielding a crisp category boundary). Figure 2.1 also shows the locations of several other important conceptual distinctions. The essentialism distinction contrasts natural kinds in the non-HPC sense with all other kinds of kinds. The standard categorical/dimensional distinction in psychopathology research and theory, as I noted above, contrasts discrete and natural kinds with the remainder. What I have referred to as the "principled classification distinction" contrasts all kinds of kinds where a non-arbitrary categorical distinction (e.g., a psychiatric diagnosis) can be drawn in a rigorous way, either by carving nature at an underlying discontinuity or by drawing a pragmatically grounded cutpoint on an underlying continuum, with the purely dimensional structure in which diagnosis is arbitrary. (The "taxometric distinction" will be discussed in the next section.) Figure 2.1 reveals that the structural forms that psychiatric conditions might take are diverse, and many of the distinctions that have been employed to make sense of this diversity are subtly but importantly different from one another.

Classification Research: The Case of Taxometrics

Determining the structure of mental disorders has been a major enterprise for psychopathology researchers. One of the more prominent approaches to classification in recent decades has been the use of taxometric analysis, a family of quantitative methods originally developed by Paul Meehl and colleagues. (See, e.g., Meehl 1995.) Taxometrics examines patterns of covariation among clinical properties, much as other forms of classification research in psychiatry do, but it reaches beyond them by investigating whether differences between individuals are better understood as matters of degree or as matters of kind. Most of its alternatives involve the inductive scanning of multiple properties (e.g., symptoms, signs, psychological test scores) for evidence of underlying clusters or dimensions, using quantitative methods that presume the appropriateness of one kind of structure or another. Cluster analyses invariably find clusters or "types," and factor analyses invariably find dimensions, whether or not the data structure being analyzed is truly categorical or dimensional. Taxometric analyses, in contrast, ask whether a particular latent variable, such as a mental disorder, is better modeled as a category (a "taxon") or as a dimension. (Even if a taxon exists, its members may vary along one or more dimensions.) The findings of these analyses are therefore conventionally described as "taxonic" or "nontaxonic." (For further discussion of these methods, see Ruscio, Haslam, and Ruscio 2006.)

Taxometric research has been animated by the category/dimension distinction, and researchers have rendered binary judgments on a large number of psychopathology-related variables. However, Meehl had a highly differentiated understanding of the diversity of latent structures, and was careful to clarify that the concept of "taxon"—the kind of latent category that can be inferred on the basis of a taxonic finding—is not the same as the essentialist concept of "natural kind." First, he acknowledged that taxa can be generated by a variety of causal structures, rather than only those that involve a single dichotomous (i.e., essential) cause, which in the psychiatric realm he referred to as a "specific etiology" (Meehl 1977). A variety of less strong forms of etiology (involving thresholds, interactions of multiple causal factors, and so on) can also generate discrete, bounded categories. Second, tightly clustered discrete categories can arise from social and other environmental influences rather than from biogenetic causes only. Meehl's favored example of such an "environment-mold taxon" was Trotskyite political ideology, which has an equally dichotomous structure as Down syndrome, but an entirely different, socially mediated causal basis. (See, e.g., Meehl 1992.) "Taxon" is therefore a much broader concept than "natural kind" in the essentialist sense, although some taxometric researchers persist in arguing that taxonic research findings support the existence of "naturally occurring" types and frame taxometric research as an exercise in "carving nature at its joints."

Although there has been a tendency to misunderstand taxometrics as a tool for detecting natural kinds, there is considerable ambiguity surrounding what kind of kind taxonic research findings support. If natural kinds in the essentialist sense cannot be inferred from such findings, as I have argued and as Meehl acknowledged, it might seem reasonable to suppose that a taxonic finding supports an inference one rung lower on our ladder: the discrete kind. This is the most common interpretation of taxonic findings, which are commonly discussed in terms of discrete categories and sharp category boundaries. However, even the inference of discrete kinds may not be warranted. There is evidence from simulation research (Haslam and Cleland 2002) that taxometric analyses yield taxonic findings for fuzzy data sets in which a substantial minority of cases have ambiguous or intermediate membership of a latent category. It appears that taxometric analyses detect the existence of latent discontinuities even when these are not sharp and binary. If data structures that lack discrete boundaries can "look" taxonic, then it is not appropriate to infer the existence of discrete kinds, let alone natural kinds, when taxometric research finds a taxon (Haslam 2009). In short, taxometric research adjudicates the distinction between practical and fuzzy kinds, and, contrary to most accounts, it cannot provide conclusive evidence for the existence of discrete category boundaries.

Meehl (1995) claimed that taxometrics could "solve" the classification problem in psychopathology. This extravagant promise has not been realized, but more than 180 published studies have employed taxometric research methods. The majority of studies have examined an assortment of psychopathologies and personality attributes, and a small minority have explored other variables (e.g., emotions, handedness, relationship types). What can we conclude about the distribution and frequency of taxa in the domain of psychopathology from this rapidly growing body of work? Haslam, Holland, and Kuppens (2012) conducted a systematic quantitative review of 311 taxometric research findings drawn from 177 studies that had been published or were in press as of April 2011, updating previous qualitative reviews (Haslam 2003, 2011b). Study findings were classified as taxonic or dimensional according to the researchers' conclusions, and an assortment of methodological and substantive factors that might be associated with these findings were examined (e.g., study sample size, type of mental disorder). Haslam et al. found that an overwhelming majority (86 percent) of taxometric research findings supported a dimensional latent structure when a variety of confounds were statistically controlled. There was very little replicated evidence for psychiatric categories within the small minority of robust taxonic findings (14 percent), the sole exceptions being in the domains of autism and substance use.

This systematic review of a large corpus of research offers a view of the psychopathological landscape that is highly pertinent to my discussion of psychiatric kinds in the first section. Taxonic findings indicate that some form of discontinuity exists in a variable of interest, not that the discontinuity is crisp and binary. Such findings only allow us to infer that kinds of the fuzzy type exist, although they could have been generated by discrete or natural kinds. Only a tiny minority of psychopathology-related variables show evidence of such a discontinuity when taxometric analyses are conducted. If very few psychopathology-related phenomena show evidence of even a minimal form of discontinuity, and if these few phenomena would have to meet stringent additional requirements to justify being considered as natural kinds in the essentialist sense, it is reasonable to conclude that such kinds are vanishingly rare within psychiatry. This empirically informed conclusion accords with the conclusions made on theoretical grounds by Zachar (2000) and others.

However, the essentialist account of natural kinds is not the only one available. If we adopt the most liberal account—the HPC concept of natural kinds as fuzzy prototype or family-resemblance structures—our conclusion about the prevalence of natural kinds changes somewhat. As we have seen in figure 2.1, the HPC concept corresponds to the distinction between fuzzy and practical kinds, the same distinction that taxometric research adjudicates. Thus, the accumulated evidence of taxometric research indicates that natural kinds of the HPC type may be a small minority of psychopathology-related phenomena, and that dimensions and practical kinds constitute the dominant majority. In noting this possibility, it is important to remember how weak a sense of "natural kind" this is. If an HPC natural kind is simply a property cluster associated with a similarity-generating mechanism, then some such kinds might have extremely unnatural bases. If we consider the case of alcohol dependency, which has received some mixed evidence for taxonic structure and therefore meets structural requirements for an HPC natural kind, then the similarity-generating mechanism is likely to involve a socially mediated history of excessive drinking, as the profound cross-cultural differences in rates of alcoholism would suggest. The relevant similarity-generating process might even involve conscious identification with the label "alcoholic" and centripetal molding of behavior to expectations of how to be an alcoholic, as in Hacking's discussions of interactive kinds (Khalidi 2010). If all that is needed to qualify as an HPC is a plausible similarity-generating mechanism, there is little reason to believe such a mechanism must be something "in nature" separate from social processes. In view of the evidence of extensive sociocultural shaping of many psychiatric phenomena, accounts of similarity-generating mechanisms will have to appeal to something beyond what we normally consider to be aspects of nature.

In short, it seems very likely that natural kinds of an essentialist sort are rare or non-existent within the domain of psychopathology. It is also likely that a small minority of psychopathology-related phenomena meet minimal structural requirements for a looser sense of natural kinds as HPCs, namely having at least a fuzzy discontinuity. However, if we are to accept such phenomena as natural kinds, we much recognize that they may be natural only in a very weak sense, and that the factors that are causally responsible for their coherence as property clusters may be highly social.

Risks of the Natural-Kind Approach: Perceptions of Disorder

Many writers have challenged the essentialist natural-kind view of psychiatric conditions on a variety of philosophical, scientific, and clinical grounds, focusing on the failings of the natural-kind concept in the discourse of mental-health professionals. However, the adverse consequences of essentialist thinking about mental disorders among laypeople are another neglected reason to be wary of these ways of conceptualizing psychiatric phenomena. Understandings of mental disorders as natural kinds with biogenetic essences that originate in professional discourse may spread into everyday language and thought, often in a vulgarized form, and there is now considerable evidence that the implications for lay conceptions of mental disorders are troubling.

It is increasingly clear that people hold essentialist beliefs about a wide variety of categories that they encounter in everyday life, including living kinds and social groups (Gelman 2003). For example, people tend to believe that some social categories—especially those based on gender, race, and ethnicity—have defining properties and are biologically based, discrete, historically invariant, and immutable (Haslam, Rothschild, and Ernst 2000). Crucially, thinking of social groups as natural kinds appears to have a variety of destructive implications for social perception. For instance, greater tendencies to essentialize are associated with race-based and gender-based prejudice (e.g., Keller 2005), endorsement of social stereotypes (Bastian and Haslam 2006), and a reluctance to cross the boundaries of social categories and interact with outgroup members (Williams and Eberhardt 2008). Thinking of social groups as essentialized natural kinds deepens social divides and promotes antagonistic, distancing, and hierarchical attitudes toward people who fall on the other side of them.

Essentialist thinking also attaches to psychiatric kinds. Ahn, Flanagan, Marsh, and Sanislow (2006) showed that beliefs that mental disorders are discrete, are biologically based, and have inhering causes and defining properties cohere among both laypeople and clinicians, although they tend to be weaker than for medical conditions. Ahn and colleagues found that essentialist beliefs were endorsed more strongly by laypeople than by experts, although one-third of the clinicians consistently endorsed a categorical view of psychopathology. Haslam and Ernst (2002) further showed that natural-kind concepts guide laypeople's reasoning about mental disorders, so that when they were given bogus scientific evidence that a disorder had a biological basis they inferred that it was also discrete and historically invariant. There is now substantial evidence that an essentialist mode of thinking is part of laypeople's "folk psychiatry" (Haslam 2005), and that it dovetails with a biomedical approach to mental disorder. For example, biologically essentialist beliefs about disorders are strongly associated with beliefs about the appropriateness and the efficacy of medical rather than psychotherapeutic forms of intervention (Ahn, Proctor, and Flanagan 2009).

Just as essentialist thinking about other social categories is associated with prejudice and social avoidance, it is becoming increasingly clear that essentialist views of mental disorders are linked to psychiatric stigma (Haslam 2011a). Numerous surveys and experimental studies have found that endorsement of biogenetic explanations of mental disorders tends to be associated with a desire for greater social distance from people experiencing those disorders, greater perceived unpredictability and dangerousness of them, lower expectations that they will recover, and more punitive behavior toward them. (See, e.g., Mehta and Farina 1997; Lam, Salkovskis, and Warwick 2005; Phelan 2005; Read and Harré 2001.) Although it may seem intuitive that attributing mental disorder to a biological aberration would reduce moral blame and increase sympathy, Phelan's work, for example, indicates that it increases the perceived seriousness and persistence of the disorder, and its perceived likelihood of spreading to others. Conceptualizing mental disorders as natural kinds, or as "illnesses like any others" (Read, Haslam, Sayce, and Davies 2006), is likely to encourage stigma because it represents sufferers as categorically abnormal, immutably afflicted, and essentially different.

In sum, representations of mental disorders as essentialist natural kinds that circulate in the professional discourse of psychiatry resonate with an existing mode of social cognition among laypeople. As Adriaens and De Block (2013) argue, existing psychiatric classifications have "boosted the already existing lay essentialism in psychiatry." The implications of this mode of thinking for attitudes and actions toward people with mental disorders are consistently negative. These implications provide another reason for taking a critical approach to the issue of psychiatric natural kinds. Projecting a critical voice amid the growing chorus of "neuro-essentialism" in the news media (Racine, Waldman, Rosenberg, and Illes 2010) and the institutional power of biological psychiatry may be a significant challenge.

Conclusions

In this chapter I have presented a critical examination of the idea of natural kinds in psychiatry, informed by research findings from clinical and social psychology. I began by arguing that a psychiatric condition would have to satisfy a very stringent set of requirements to justify being considered a natural kind in the essentialist sense. These requirements go well beyond those needed to establish that the condition has its basis in some kind of discontinuity or that it is a discrete category, and they may be prohibitively difficult to meet. If the concept of natural kind is relaxed to incorporate homeostatic property clusters, the structural requirements become easier to satisfy and the existence of psychiatric natural kinds becomes more plausible. However, the HPC view of natural kinds is so inclusive that the "naturalness" of any such kinds may be questionable: the mechanisms that may generate similarities among people experiencing a particular disorder need not be biological or otherwise "natural" and can include social mechanisms. I suggested, on the basis of a review of taxometric research, that a small minority of psychopathological phenomena may satisfy structural requirements for HPC natural kinds, although the great majority are probably dimensional or pragmatically based. There is no justification for inferring the existence of essentialist natural kinds from existing taxometric research. Despite the lack of the scientific evidence for psychiatric natural kinds, I noted, laypeople sometimes think about mental disorders in an essentialist fashion, and that this promotes psychiatric stigma. As psychiatry and its classifications continue to evolve, it will be important to recognize the scientific limitations, the conceptual ambiguities, and the social costs of natural-kind concepts.

References

Adriaens, P., and A. De Block. 2013. Why we essentialize mental disorders. *Journal of Medicine and Philosophy* 38: 107–127.

Ahn, W., E. Flanagan, J. Marsh, and C. Sanislow. 2006. Belief about essences and the reality of mental disorders. *Psychological Science* 17: 759–766.

Ahn, W., C. Proctor, and E. Flanagan. 2009. Mental health clinicians' beliefs about the biological, psychological, and environmental bases of mental disorders. *Cognitive Science* 33: 147–182.

Bastian, B., and N. Haslam. 2006. Psychological essentialism and stereotype endorsement. *Journal of Experimental Social Psychology* 42: 228–235.

Boyd, R. 1999. Homeostasis, species, and higher taxa. In *Species: New Interdisciplinary Essays*, ed. R. Wilson. MIT Press.

Craver, C. 2009. Mechanisms and natural kinds. *Philosophical Psychology* 22: 575–594.

Gelman, S. 2003. *The Essential Child: Origins of Essentialism in Everyday Thought.* Oxford University Press.

Hacking, I. 1999. *The Social Construction of What?* Harvard University Press.

Hacking, I. 2007. Kinds of people: Moving targets. *Proceedings of the British Academy* 151: 285–318.

Haslam, N. 2000a. Psychiatric categories as natural kinds: Essentialist thinking about mental disorders. *Social Research* 67: 1031–1058.

Haslam, N. 2002b. Kinds of kinds: A conceptual taxonomy of psychiatric categories. *Philosophy, Psychiatry, & Psychology* 9: 203–217.

Haslam, N. 2003. Categorical vs. dimensional models of mental disorder: The taxometric evidence. *Australian and New Zealand Journal of Psychiatry* 37: 696–704.

Haslam, N. 2005. Dimensions of folk psychiatry. *Review of General Psychology* 9: 35–47.

Haslam, N. 2009. The taxon concept is not taxonic: Response to Grove (2008). *Psychological Reports* 104: 784–786.

Haslam, N. 2011a. Genetic essentialism, neuroessentialism, and stigma: Comment on Dar-Nimrod and Heine (2011). *Psychological Bulletin* 17: 819–824.

Haslam, N. 2011b. The latent structure of personality and psychopathology: A review of trends in taxometric research. *Scientific Review of Mental Health Practice* 8: 17–29.

Haslam, N., and C. Cleland. 2002. Taxometric analysis of fuzzy categories: A Monte Carlo study. *Psychological Reports* 90: 401–404.

Haslam, N., and D. Ernst. 2002. Essentialist beliefs about mental disorders. *Journal of Social and Clinical Psychology* 21: 628–644.

Haslam, N., E. Holland, and P. Kuppens. 2012. Categories versus dimensions in personality and psychopathology: A quantitative review of taxometric research. *Psychological Medicine* 42: 903–920.

Haslam, N., L. Rothschild, and D. Ernst. 2000. Essentialist beliefs about social categories. *British Journal of Social Psychology* 39: 113–127.

Keller, J. 2005. In genes we trust: The biological component of psychological essentialism and its relationship to mechanisms of motivated social cognition. *Journal of Personality and Social Psychology* 88: 686–702.

Khalidi, M. 2010. Interactive kinds. *British Journal for the Philosophy of Science* 61: 335–360.

Lam, D., P. Salkovskis, and H. Warwick. 2005. An experimental investigation of the impact of biological versus psychological explanations of the cause of "mental illness." *Journal of Mental Health* 14: 453–464.

Meehl, P. 1977. Specific etiology and other forms of strong influence: Some quantitative meanings. *Journal of Medicine and Philosophy* 2: 33–53.

Meehl, P. 1992. Factors and taxa, traits and types, differences of degree and differences in kind. *Journal of Personality* 60: 117–174.

Meehl, P. 1995. Bootstraps taxometrics: Solving the classification problem in psychopathology. *American Psychologist* 50: 266–275.

Mehta, S., and A. Farina. 1997. Is being sick really better? Effect of the disease view of mental disorder on stigma. *Journal of Social and Clinical Psychology* 16: 405–419.

Phelan, J. 2005. Geneticization of deviant behavior and consequences for stigma: The case of mental illness. *Journal of Health and Social Behavior* 46: 307–322.

Racine, E., S. Waldman, J. Rosenberg, and J. Illes. 2010. Contemporary neuroscience in the media. *Social Science & Medicine* 71: 725–733.

Read, J., and N. Harré. 2001. The role of biological and genetic causal beliefs in the stigmatisation of 'mental patients'. *Journal of Mental Health* 10: 223–235.

Read, J., N. Haslam, L. Sayce, and E. Davies. 2006. Prejudice and schizophrenia: A review of the 'mental illness is an illness like any other' approach. *Acta Psychiatrica Scandinavica* 114: 303–318.

Ruscio, J., N. Haslam, and A. Ruscio, 2006. *Introduction to the Taxometric Method: A Practical Guide.* Erlbaum.

Williams, M., and J. Eberhardt. 2008. Biological conceptions of race and the motivation to cross racial boundaries. *Journal of Personality and Social Psychology* 94: 1033–1047.

Zachar, P. 2000. Psychiatric disorders are not natural kinds. *Philosophy, Psychiatry, & Psychology* 7: 167–182.

3 Deeply Rooted Sources of Error and Bias in Psychiatric Classification

Jeffrey Poland

DSM-III (American Psychiatric Association 1980) and its successors have dominated classification in mental-health practice for three decades. This classification scheme has played a role in the practices of the vast majority of mental-health clinicians and researchers, and is central to what I shall refer to as "conventional psychiatric practice" (CPP), a form of clinical and research practice geared to collecting clinical information sufficient for applying *DSM* diagnostic criteria for operationally defined mental disorders identified in the manual. In addition to its importance in mental-health research and clinical practice, the *DSM* has also played an important role in education about the nature of mental illness and its treatment: textbooks in psychiatry and abnormal psychology are typically organized in terms of *DSM* categories, clinicians are typically trained in terms of knowledge and techniques concerning specific *DSM* disorders, and the public is virtually always "educated" about mental-health matters in a vocabulary centered on *DSM* categories. Finally, a host of other institutions (government, courts, insurers, drug companies) organize policy and practice in terms of *DSM* categories. In sum, the *DSM* approach to classification of mental disorders is deeply entrenched in a broad array of institutions and practices concerning mental health and illness.

Defenders of the *DSM* claim that *DSM*-III was an important revolution in psychiatric classification and that the classification system is an invaluable tool in clinical practice and scientific research. Critics, on the other hand, argue that neither of these claims is defensible, that the *DSM* is profoundly flawed, and that *DSM*-III ushered in three decades of non-progressive research and misguided clinical practice. I agree with this critical position and will argue below that the *DSM* approach to classification is, indeed, profoundly flawed, as are the practices based on it. But more broadly, there is a crisis in contemporary mental-health practice: the deeply entrenched and very influential framework—*DSM*/CPP, consisting of the

DSM, the CPP practices, and a set of associated commitments—has profound problems that require reform, but in view of the deep entrenchment of this framework the prospects for reform are quite poor.

I will begin by clarifying the *DSM*/CPP framework and developing the argument for the existence of a crisis. Subsequently, to further clarify why this crisis exists, I will argue that the various components of the *DSM*/CPP framework exhibit a "lack of fit" with the domain of mental illness, and that this lack of fit breeds the problems characteristic of the crisis and stymies progress toward a more productive and defensible framework for mental-health practice. That is, I will argue that there are deeply rooted sources of error and bias within the *DSM*/CPP framework that play a significant role in explaining why the framework is problematic and why current reform efforts (e.g., the *DSM*-5 revision process, the National Institute of Mental Health's Research Domain Criteria project) are unlikely to be adequate. Finally, I will make some strategic suggestions for dealing with the crisis.

The *DSM*/CPP Framework

The *DSM*/CPP framework consists of an approach to classification (the *DSM*), a set of associated commitments (e.g., to medicalization), and a set of practices (e.g., clinical, research) based on the *DSM* and informed by the commitments.

The categorical scheme of *DSM*-IV (American Psychiatric Association 1994) comprises more than 300 categories of mental disorder, conceived of as harmful dysfunctions[1] that can be identified on the basis of atheoretical, polythetic diagnostic criteria framed in terms of clinically salient features or other characteristics (e.g., of history or context) that can be readily determined by the clinician. The idea that mental disorders can be identified in terms of "atheoretical" criteria (i.e., in terms not referring to either pathology or etiology) was a core assumption of the approach behind the *DSM*-III since its development during the 1970s and its publication in 1980 and continues to the present. The employment of criteria drawing on clinical phenomenology and other pre-theoretically conceived characteristics was insisted upon in the effort to make the criteria better operationalized and, hence, better suited for the purpose of increasing diagnostic reliability. The employment of "polythetic" criteria reflects the idea that mental disorders can manifest themselves in various ways across individuals with the same disorder. Finally, the specific disorders in the *DSM* presuppose a form of individualism requiring that such disorders are non-relational; thus, each disorder involves a putative (but unspecified) biological, psychological, or behavioral dysfunction of the individual, a dysfunction that manifests itself in terms of (among other things) the signs and symptoms specified by the diagnostic criteria (i.e., mental disorders are harmful dysfunctions).[2]

In addition to the *DSM* approach to classification of mental disorder, the *DSM*/CPP framework includes three other important commitments also stemming from the 1970s and persisting to the present:

(C1) that one system of classification can and should serve both research and clinical purposes, because such an arrangement will best serve the goal of translating scientific research into clinical practice,

(C2) that control over the process of developing and revising the *DSM* system of classification rests firmly in the hands of the American Psychiatric Association, even while the system is employed across a wide range of mental health contexts and forms of practice and is employed by a wide range of mental health professionals,

and

(C3) that mental health practices ought to be medicalized.

The medicalization of mental-health practice was codified by Klerman (1978) in what he dubbed the "Neo-Kraepelinean Credo," an admixture of claims concerning the disciplinary identity of psychiatry, the nature of the domain of mental illness, and the character of both clinical and research practice concerning mental illness. The following are typical expressions of the ways in which the medicalization of contemporary mental-health practice is currently understood:

Disciplinary identity Psychiatry is a branch of medicine and psychiatrists are physicians concerned with treating ill patients who suffer from mental illnesses; psychiatric practices should be based on biomedical, scientific evidence and knowledge.

Domain of mental illness Mental illnesses are brain diseases that involve a genetic, molecular, cellular, or biochemical pathology or abnormal neural connectivity (circuitry) and functioning; such "pathophysiology" develops as the result of genetic or other biological vulnerabilities interacting with environmental and experiential triggers (an "etiology"); mental illnesses are distinct from normal functioning and are neither myths nor moral failings nor problems in living experienced in the normal course of life; such brain diseases are universal over time and culture, although they may vary in their symptomatic expression with cultural context (sometimes necessitating adjustments in diagnostic criteria); the *DSM* is currently the best available classification scheme for conceptualizing the domain of mental illness and classifying the brain diseases in this domain.

Research practice As in other areas of medicine, research practices in psychiatry are based on modern scientific knowledge, technologies and methodologies (e.g., genomics, statistics, risk analysis, neuroimaging) and approach the study of brain diseases in ways comparable to research concerning cancer and cardiovascular disease; central research questions concern the pathophysiology and etiology of mental illnesses, the reliability and validity of diagnostic categories and associated criteria and dimensions, and biological and psychosocial treatments for these brain diseases.

Clinical practice As in other areas of medicine, psychiatric practice involves physicians diagnosing and treating patients for diseases in a context shaped by medical roles, identities, statuses, authority, and relationships; although there are no genetic or biological tests and the diagnostic criteria are atheoretical, psychiatrists know how to diagnose these diseases, using the diagnostic criteria found in the *DSM*; psychotropic drugs are typically the first line of treatment for these brain diseases since they treat biochemical dysregulations, restore functionality to neural circuitry, and reduce symptoms of disease; in many cases, such drugs must be taken continuously to prevent relapse and to prevent the disease from progressing; mental illness is like any other disease and in many cases bears strong similarities to diabetes and the necessity of insulin for proper disease management; as with other diseases, auxiliary behavioral, psychological, or social interventions can help to manage the disease; viewing mental illness as a brain disease (rather than a moral failing or a problem in living) reduces the social stigma associated with mental illness, provides understanding and a sense of relief for patients and their families, and makes individuals eligible for health care and financial resources; patients, their families, and the public should be taught that mental illness is a brain disease and that people suffering from such illnesses are sick; if patients resist such education they are said to lack insight into their illness.

In present-day psychiatry (CPP), both research and clinical practice are informed by the *DSM* approach to classification and the associated commitments (C1–C3). Research practice has routinely proceeded using *DSM* categories as independent or dependent variables and for purposes of sampling and subject grouping; typical investigations examine such diagnostically defined groups with respect to pathology, etiology, response to intervention, demographics, and so on. Intervention research within this framework typically involves randomized, placebo controlled, double-blind clinical trials that group subjects according to a *DSM* category and assess outcomes in terms of rating scales keyed to diagnostic criteria and other clinical signs and symptoms associated with a given diagnostic grouping.

Clinical practice typically proceeds via clinical interviews and diagnostic rating scales designed to collect information relevant to assessing the presence of the diagnostic criteria associated with *DSM* categories.[3] The planning of treatment is organized in terms of a *DSM* clinical diagnosis, and standards of care associated with a diagnosis are typically followed, which often means primarily prescribing a regimen of psychiatric drugs and monitoring for both symptom reduction and side effects. Ancillary interventions (psychological, social, rehabilitative, and so on) may be prescribed, but such interventions are usually not conceived of as primary or as directly targeting the diagnosed disorder as opposed to providing rehabilitative, palliative, or supportive care.

This package (the *DSM*/CPP framework), consisting of the *DSM* and the above described commitments and practices, has become widely prevalent in mental-health practice over the past three decades. Although there is some resistance to this framework and there are alternative forms of practice, there is little doubt that *DSM*/CPP has been a dominant force with respect to shaping both clinical practice and associated research agendas.

A Crisis Exists

It is the central claim of this chapter that there is a crisis in contemporary mental-health practice—a crisis constituted by two facts and their implications. First, the *DSM*/CPP framework has profound problems, and hence reform is needed. Second, the *DSM*/CPP framework is deeply entrenched, and hence the prospects for effective reform are poor.

Problems with the *DSM*

There are at least two serious problems with the *DSM* categories.[4] A problem of *validity* (i.e., measures of integrity and predictive power of a category, criterion, or other variable) is widely acknowledged in the literature (e.g., Kendell and Jablensky 2003; Andreassen 2007; Regier et al. 2009; Insel et al. 2010; Cuthbert and Insel 2010; Hyman 2010), although there is variation in how the validity of psychiatric categories is conceived and measured. Nonetheless, there is substantial agreement that many (perhaps most) of the *DSM* categories lack established construct validity and that such categories have limited predictive validity. Alternatively put, many (perhaps most) *DSM* categories have not been shown to be strongly associated with empirically validated syndromes, biological or psychological correlates, or other variables of interest (e.g., response to treatment, genes). To the extent that (weak) associations have been demonstrated, it is likely that the categories are essentially "free riders" contributing little or nothing to the association: i.e., specific symptoms and aggregations of small effects from independent sources are probably doing most of the work. To acknowledge that *DSM* categories lack demonstrated validity means that the categories are not suitable for research or clinical purposes that require well-defined constructs or that require categories that contribute information to clinical understanding and decision making.

The *DSM* categories are also widely acknowledged to exhibit substantial *heterogeneity* at all levels of analysis. (See, e.g., Regier et al. 2009; Hyman 2010.) Individuals who fall within a diagnostic category (schizophrenia, for example) typically vary with respect to the criterial features they exhibit, as well as in biological, psychological, behavioral, and social features and processes. The atheoretical, polythetic approach combined with the lack of demonstrated validity of the categories ensures that widely different individuals will all be subsumed under the same categorical description. Of special significance is the substantial "process heterogeneity" (i.e., heterogeneity of causal processes at all levels of analysis) that will be exhibited by groups of individuals subsumed under the same diagnostic label. Such heterogeneity of the categories means that their use in research will introduce uncontrolled sources of error and limit the interpretability of findings and that their use in clinical practice will mask variation in features and processes of clinical importance.

Problems with *DSM*-Based Practice

Each of the foregoing problems (validity, heterogeneity) with *DSM* categories contributes to problems with *DSM*-based practice in both research and the clinic. With respect to research, use of the *DSM* has failed to underwrite research programs concerning mental health and mental illness that are progressive. A progressive research program leads to productive questions and investigations that are well designed and controlled (e.g., free of uncontrolled sources of systematic and unsystematic error, employ well-defined variables) and that produce substantial results leading to the development of answers to the focal questions of the research (e.g., the validation of categories). *DSM* categories, however, have not been validated since they have fostered research programs typified by results that are negative, non-replicable, weak, inconsistent, non-specific, or uninterpretable. Even among defenders of the *DSM*/CPP framework (see, e.g., Kendell and Jablensky 2003; Andreassen 2007; Regier et al. 2009; Hyman 2007, 2010; NIMH 2011), it has been increasingly acknowledged that *DSM* categories have not been validated and that the non-progressive nature of *DSM*-based research over the past several decades leads to the conclusion that *DSM* categories are not useful for research purposes.[5]

DSM-based clinical practice is also compromised by the problems of validity and heterogeneity. Most clearly, a *DSM* diagnosis does not effectively contribute to serving important clinical functions and purposes because it leaves most of the important clinical assessment work undone. Clinical understanding and effective intervention planning and implementation require that a broad range of specific features and processes characteristic of individuals be identified and systematically understood before a clinician can effectively address clinical questions concerning what (if anything) is wrong and what (if anything) should be done.[6] But *DSM* diagnostic categories, along with the clinical information on which they are based, mask critical information and variation across individuals, and their lack of validity means that they do not effectively identify psychopathology or predict response to treatment, clinical course, and clinical outcome. As a consequence, *DSM*-based clinical practice does not lead to adequate clinical understanding, rational treatment planning, or the effective management of clinical uncertainty.[7, 8]

In view of the identified problems with the *DSM* and with CPP research and clinical practices, it is clear that serious changes are needed.[9] However, the deep entrenchment of the framework makes such changes difficult. Important dimensions of entrenchment mentioned earlier included various roles in clinical practice, research, education, and various social institutions. All such roles contribute to the shaping of professional and public consciousness concerning mental-health matters and constitute substantial inertial forces working against change concerning existing *DSM*/CPP practices.

The commitment to APA control over diagnostic classification (i.e., C2) represents another inertial force working against change. Since the American Psychiatric Association has vested guild and economic interests in perpetuating the *DSM*/CPP form of practice of its members, it has an inherent conflict of interest with respect to any proposed changes that would work against those interests. A related but different inertial force is the powerful influence of the drug companies who would perceive many changes as undercutting their commercial interests. Such interest groups potentially have a more or less direct effect on the sorts of changes that will even be entertained, let alone enacted.

Another factor that blunts the edge of criticism and undercuts the urgency of reform is the existence of apologies for *DSM*/CPP. These apologies include that the relevant science (e.g., genetics and neuroscience) is too immature, that the *DSM* is the best classification system available, that CPP is based on evidence, that a *DSM* diagnosis is useful for communication, that it is a good starting point for clinical practice, that drug therapies are helpful to many, that a *DSM* diagnosis serves an important clinical function by allowing clinicians and their patients to label a problem thereby providing reassurance and hope, and that such a diagnosis makes access to finances and clinical treatments possible. Such apologies, combined with the other factors mentioned above, effectively insulate the *DSM*/CPP framework from deep critical scrutiny. As a consequence, the prevalence and effect of alternative ideas, research agendas, and clinical practices have been diminished, thereby leading to a more impoverished background against which to understand the problems of current practices and to conceive of alternative possibilities. As a consequence, the prospects for reform are poor.

Why Does the Crisis Exist?

To argue for this pessimistic assessment, and to understand more fully and more deeply why the crisis exists, it is necessary to consider the *DSM*/CPP framework in relation to the domain of mental illness. I will argue below that at the root of the crisis is a substantial failure of the *DSM*/CPP framework to fit well with the domain of mental illness to which it has been applied. As a consequence of this lack of fit, *DSM* classification, the associated commitments, and the CPP practices all have tended to function as sources of error and bias that have, in various ways, led to the problems identified above, and have stymied and will continue to stymie efforts at reform (e.g., *DSM* revision processes, NIMH initiatives).

What is the domain of mental illness?
As I noted above, the domain of mental illness is conceptualized within the *DSM*/CPP framework as consisting of brain diseases that are mapped by the *DSM* classification system. However, in view of the limitations of the *DSM*, a conceptualization of the domain of mental illness should not be grounded in *DSM* categories or in any *a priori* commitments to brain

diseases,[10] but rather should be understood in terms of features that are largely agreed upon and that are related more closely to the sciences of human functioning.[11] From such a different starting point, relevant research programs aimed at more detailed understanding of the domain will probably be more productive than *DSM*-based research.

If we do not use *DSM* categories, how can we even begin to conceptualize the domain? To begin, we can usefully employ the term "mental illness" if it is understood as a colloquial term designed to pick out phenomena involving individual life problems, distress, disability, deviance, failures to perform social functions, and maladaptation, in which mental and behavioral capacities are centrally involved. This is not intended as a definition, but rather as an informal way to pick out a human domain of interest.[12] What follows is a brief overview of some of the features of this domain. (See table 3.1.) I view these features as relatively noncontroversial, as based on developments in the sciences of human functioning, and as representing a shared starting point for both a discussion of the problems with the *DSM*/CPP framework and a reconstitution of mental-health practices.[13]

The domain of mental illness exhibits *causal ambiguity* because features in the domain can be caused by many different causal processes. A paradigmatic example is speech that is labeled as "delusional," since such speech can be the product of a wide range of very different causal processes: e.g., an episodic central nervous system dysregulation, the manifestation of a social role performance, the manifestation of a strategy in the context of a power struggle, a "normal" psychological process. The significance of such ambiguity is to highlight the poverty of the *DSM* atheoretical approach to diagnostic classification and, more important, to highlight the difficulty and importance of rigorous assessment involving considerable background knowledge and technique. Unless such ambiguity is resolved, both research and clinical practice will be compromised.

The *hierarchical organization* of human biological systems concerns levels of complexity and organization that range from low-level molecular-cellular processes and functions to high-level socio-cultural processes; intermediate levels of organization include genetic, neural, biochemical, neuro-cognitive/computational, higher-level cognitive, behavioral, personal, interpersonal, and social. As with any hierarchical system, all levels are essential for understanding the system, its functioning, and the causal structures and processes of which it is composed and of which it is a part. Any clinical or research practice that is too partial to one level is vulnerable to the consequences of being blind to the others.

Table 3.1
Features of the domain of mental illness.

Causal ambiguity: Features in the domain can be caused by many different causal processes.

Hierarchical organization: Human biological systems consist of many levels of organization, ranging from low-level genetic, biochemical and neuroanatomical to high-level cognitive, behavioral and socio-cultural.

Multi-dimensionality: The state or condition of a person at a time consists of features and processes of many different sorts, within and across levels of organization.

Interactivity and context sensitivity: Features and processes are typically interactive with each other; hence, each is sensitive to the context in which it is embedded.

Dynamics: Features and processes evolve over time at various time scales, along varying trajectories, and can exhibit phase dependence and a variety of distinctive causal patterns.

Perspective and agency: Individuals suffering mental illness are persons who are agents and who have a first-person perspective on themselves, the world, their past, and their future.

Normativity: The identification of conditions as problematic, deviant, maladaptive, dysfunctional, distressing, or disabling presupposes background norms, values, or interests that may be theoretical, personal, social, or of some other sort.

Normal and abnormal conditions and processes: Although there may be conditions or processes that violate some specified norms, there are also conditions and processes that are normal by the same or different standards.

Relational and non-relational problems: The kinds of problems that people can suffer can be both non-relational (i.e., conditions of the individual) and relational (i.e., conditions involving relationships between an individual and other people or between an individual and some aspect of the non-personal environment).

Individual variability: Individuals suffering a mental illness vary widely and tend to exhibit relatively unique combinations of problems, functional profiles, embedding contexts, and causal processes.

The *multi-dimensionality* of conditions consists in their being constituted by features and processes of many different sorts, both within and across levels of organization. Such dimensions include the various cognitive capacities and states, affective capacities and states, social skills and other behavioral skills, aspects of physical and social environments, neural circuits and processes, biochemical states and processes, and genetics. Because such features and processes can have different sorts of research and clinical significance, a failure to take them into account may compromise research and clinical practice. Further, appreciating the fact and significance of multi-dimensionality makes it easy to appreciate the limitations of *DSM*-based psychiatric diagnostic classification: an assessment that relies exclusively on clinical phenomenology will fail to rigorously assess, understand, and manage the relations among features and processes of these various sorts.

The *interactivity* among features and processes at and across levels of organization means that each is *sensitive to the context* in which it is embedded and must be understood in that way. Examples include relations between cognition and mood and emotion, wherein self-attributions can directly affect self-directed emotion or mood, and vice versa (i.e., mood and emotion can affect cognition). More complex examples might concern relations among disruptive and compensatory or supportive processes in the context of exercising a capacity or displaying an impairment. Neuro-cognitive impairments might be masked by the employment of sophisticated compensatory social skills; or, in tact cognitive and behavioral capacities might be undermined by disruptive psychological or social processes—for example, a person who is constantly told that he has a chronic brain disease may find it difficult to muster the motivation, determination, and persistence required for acquiring skills that, in a different psychosocial context, he could acquire. In each of these examples, a certain feature or process has its character and unfolds in the way it does depending on what other features are present at the same or different level of analysis (i.e., depending on its context).

The *dynamical aspects* of the domain involve various types of causal structure, temporal course, phase dependence, and time scale. First, types of *causal structure* include linear cascades in which upstream processing activity influences downstream activity; in the case of pathogenic cascades, a pathological upstream event or process leads to downstream disruption or some other sort of pathology. A very different sort of structure is a cyclical one in which feedback relations modulate the functioning of component processes; negative feedback relations typically maintain a homeostatic balance of some sort, whereas positive feedback relations are often desta-bilizing. In extreme cases, positive feedback relations can lead to dramatic escalations in either downward or upward spirals. (Cf. Spaulding et al. 2003.) Second, the *time course* of a condition, a process, or an event involves important changes (or lack of change) with respect to variables at many levels of analysis that may be of research or clinical interest. For example, the phases of a psychotic episode include vulnerability, prodro-mal, acute, post-acute recovery, and residual. (Cf. Spaulding et al. 2003.) In each, the features that are most salient and the processes that are active vary, and hence careful measurement and discrimination is required to discern the stage of the process and the significance of certain features. Third, *phase dependence* concerns variation in functioning in different phases of a process, and discerning such variation can have considerable significance. For example, cognitive impairments in acute, post-acute, and residual phases can be indicative of disruptive interference of a cognitive process, a need for practice and tuning of a cognitive process, or an endur-ing deficit in a cognitive process that may or may not be remediable, respectively. (Cf. Spaulding and Poland 2001.) Finally, in complex systems involving features and processes at multiple levels of analysis, the time scales on which processing occurs and changes take place can vary widely and have various sorts of significance throughout the system. An example where different time scales of change can be important concerns the dif-ferential effects of interventions that target different processes but which may be introduced to effect a common change. Both drugs and cognitive-behavioral therapy are commonly introduced with the aim of ameliorating the symptoms of depression; since drugs directly target neurochemical processes, whereas cognitive-behavioral therapy targets cognitive or behav-ioral processes, the types of changes sought and the time scales on which they can be achieved and maintained are likely to be different. Being clear on relevant time scales and tracking change accordingly is of significance for both research and clinical practice.

The *first-person perspective and agency* of individuals constitutes another important feature of the domain of mental illness. Each individual suffer-ing a mental illness does so from a perspective characterized by subjectiv-ity, phenomenology, cognitive awareness, agency, and purpose. Such individuals, like all others, are at the center of their world and grasp from their point of view what is happening in them and in the world around them. Such individuals can have more or less "insight," can struggle for power with others, can have a set of goals and values that shape who they want to be and what kind of life they want to live, and can react to the activities of others (for example, to the activities of clinicians who choose to classify them in some way). As a consequence, the domains of human functioning generally, and of mental illness more specifically, are unlike most other natural domains in that, as Hacking (1999) has observed there are complicated "looping effects" in which individuals react to being classified and thereby change their behavior in light of being classified; and, this may ultimately lead to a change in the classifications themselves (that is, the nature of the condition changes). Further, in light of a person's unique perspective, there are certain perspectival and positional facts about an individual that are constitutive of their condition and their situation in the world (cf. Sen 1993), and to which the individual has a sort of privileged access. Finally, all of these features related to perspective mean that the domain is populated by persons who are moral agents, and again this is unlike most other natural domains. The significance of this for both research and clinical practice is of no small moment.

A further feature of the domain of mental illness is its inherent *normativity*. Whether one uses the language of "disease," "disorder," "problem," "pathology," or something else to evaluate a condition or behavior, such terms inevitably introduce norms by which the condition or behavior is being evaluated. Such norms can stem from interests, values, purposes, or theoretical standards of some sort, and they can be natural, personal, social, legal, clinical, or ethical/moral. Thus, there is a certain amount of normative pluralism in the domain of mental illness. The creation of various forms of practice focused on mental illness typically involves making choices about which norms are most appropriate; and, many of the controversies concerning mental illness may find their roots in disagreements over which norms should be employed.

The domain of mental illness includes both *normal and abnormal conditions and processes*. Given the variety of norms that are potentially applicable in the domain of mental illness, it is inevitable that an individual's functioning will be normal by some standards and abnormal by others (e.g., a biologically and psychologically normal person relative to some set of clinical norms may act in a socially deviant way). And, more importantly, given a specific standard, some processes or conditions may be normal while others are not. Of special importance are: the identification of normal brain processes that realize pathological cognitive states (e.g., delusions); normal processes that give rise to pain, distress, anxiety, fear, or other harmful and unwanted states (e.g., grief and other responses to loss); and the concurrent presence of normal and abnormal states, processes, and capacities such that normal processes may provide compensations for the abnormal processes or such that normal processes may be "strengths" that can provide a basis for recovery. Pathology-oriented clinical assessment and intervention practices are prone to misidentifying normal processes ("over-diagnosis") and to being blind to, or undermining, an individual's intact ("normal") functional capacities.

In the domain of mental illness, individuals can experience *problems that can be either non-relational or relational* in character. Non-relational problems (i.e., problems embodied in the individual) can be of many different sorts depending on the capacities, functions, or processes that may be impaired relative to some norm, or that may have consequences that affect conditions of interest or importance to the individual or others. Such problems can occur at any of the various levels of organization relevant to individual functioning (e.g., neurophysiological, genetic, cognitive, behavioral), and along any of the many dimensions of functioning at these various levels. Relational problems, on the other hand, can concern maladaption or some other lack of fit to some aspect of the physical or social environment, problematic inter-personal relationships, a lack of resources, or an oppressive social context. This distinction is especially important for an adequate assessment and understanding of the conditions, interests and needs of those who suffer mental illness.

The final feature of the domain is *individual variability*. Our earlier discussion of the heterogeneity exhibited by *DSM* categories points to the fact that individuals suffering mental illness will tend to vary in their functioning along multiple dimensions and in a range of dynamically evolving personal and social contexts. This means that such individuals will accumulate a variety of more or less independent problems and exhibit a substantial amount of individualized causal complexity in which relatively unique combinations of problems, functional capacities, and contexts lead to relatively unique processes involving multiple levels of analysis. (Cf. Spaulding et al. 2003.)

These ten features highlight the distinctive character of the domain of mental illness and they put considerable pressure on the construction of any approach to classification or form of practice concerned with that domain. Specifically, these features raise difficult questions about how to further conceptualize the domain (e.g., classification schemes, assessment tools), how to most effectively research the domain (e.g., research agendas, strategies, techniques), and how clinicians can most effectively engage it (e.g., epistemic and intervention practices). As will be argued in the next section, contemporary mental-health practices, as informed by the *DSM/ CPP* framework, are very poorly suited for responding to these pressures and answering these questions; that is, there is a lack of fit with this domain.

Why does the *DSM*/CPP framework fit poorly with the domain of mental illness?

The phrase "lack of fit" means different things depending on whether one is discussing the conceptualization of the domain, research practices, or clinical practices. The *DSM*/CPP framework exhibits a lack of fit with respect to all three.[14]

Conceptualization of the Domain

For there to be a "good fit" with the domain of mental illness with respect to conceptualization, the *DSM*/CPP framework (or any alternative) should satisfy the following conditions. First, whether an approach to classification is categorical or dimensional, such an approach should exhibit construct and predictive validity of the categories or dimensions involved. Second, the framework should have the resources for representing and managing important features, conditions, problems, processes, and groups in the domain. Third, the approach should not make any problematic assumptions about the domain.

The *DSM*/CPP framework fails to satisfy these conditions. We have already noted the *DSM*'s lack of validity, and the reasons for this are not difficult to spot. The *DSM* categories are atheoretically conceived and defined in terms of polythetic diagnostic criteria focusing on superficial and proto-scientifically conceived aspects of clinical phenomenology. When applied to a domain of phenomena with the characteristics listed in table 3.1, it is to be expected that diagnostic groupings will exhibit problems of validity: any given pattern of behavior and other clinically identified features will mask a wide range of distinct causal processes and a wide range of distinct features at all levels of analysis. Such heterogeneity combined with the dynamic interactivity and context sensitivity of such features make it highly likely that atheoretical and polythetic criteria focused on clinical phenomenology will lead to *DSM* categories that are artificial (i.e., lacking in validity).[15]

In addition to problems of validity of *DSM* categories, the *DSM*/CPP approach to clinical assessment, including clinical interviews, categorical diagnostic criteria, and supplementary axis 4 and 5 ratings,[16] simply lacks the descriptive resources and assessment tools for representing important features, conditions, problems, processes, and groupings in the domain of mental illness. For example, assessment of cognitive deficits, deficits in behavioral skills, social causes of problems, relationship problems, and the personal perspective and individual psychology of individuals is typically not rigorously pursued beyond a clinical interview. Assessment of the strengths and "normal" processes in an individual's life are typically neglected too. Thus, the focus on putative symptomatic manifestations of pathology with an eye toward a *DSM* diagnosis is effectively blind to such important problems, processes, and perspectives and, hence, screens off any deeper assessment and clinical understanding. As a consequence, a *DSM*/CPP clinical assessment doesn't produce an adequate representation of a person's relatively unique mix of problems, capacities, deficits, perspective, and psychosocial and biological context and hence is insufficient for managing variability, complexity, ambiguity, dynamic interactivity, context sensitivity, and resulting clinical uncertainty.

Finally, the *DSM*/CPP framework makes a number of problematic assumptions concerning the domain of mental illness. The assumption of individualism, explicitly made with respect to *DSM* categories, leaves out a number of relational problems (among them interpersonal relationship problems and social problems) that are partially constitutive of the domain of mental illness. Further, the alternative specifications of this individualism (viz., that mental illnesses consist of harmful dysfunctions or of brain diseases) haven't found much research support in the sense of discovering well-confirmed associated internal dysfunctions or brain diseases (e.g., a pathophysiology) for *DSM* categories.[17] The assumption that all mental illness is a harmful dysfunction or a brain disease is an unsubstantiated ideological projection onto the domain, and it is a projection that obscures many of the real problems from which people suffer.

Finally, the Neo-Kraepelinean assumption that mental illness is discontinuous from normal function, and that persons suffering mental illness are sick people who have something medically wrong with them (for example, they have diseased or disordered brains), is also an unsubstantiated ideological projection onto the domain of mental illness that obscures and misconstrues many of the real problems that people experience. Many such problems do not involve the operation of abnormal biological or psychological processes, but nonetheless they are of central importance to understanding what is wrong and what is likely to help (for example, a show of severe and persistent depressive symptoms consequent to a job loss is not a display of a brain disease in need of medical treatment so much as a personal employment problem calling for a new job). In addition, a focus on pathology tends to obscure the operation of normal processes and the availability of individual strengths and capacities. The importance of a broad functional profile in representing an individual who is experiencing problems is to identify the context of the problems and to identify resources available for response to those problems. A focus on pathology, such as is manifested in the *DSM*/CPP framework, will tend to misidentify the problems, their context, and the available pathways for their resolution. Finally, a focus on pathology tends to emphasize medical norms for evaluating a person's situation (viz., a statistical or theoretical norm concerning human biological functioning) at the expense of a range of other relevant norms, many of which are non-medical (e.g., social, personal, and moral norms), and hence yields a distorted understanding of the nature of an individual's problems.

Research Practice

With respect to research, a good fit with the domain of mental illness would consist in a research program that is based on a conceptualization that fits the domain of mental illness, that is structured by a research framework that makes no problematic assumptions about the domain or the methods appropriate for studying it, and that is "well ordered." The research program rooted in the commitments of the *DSM*/CPP framework doesn't satisfy these conditions.

For the purposes of criticism, and drawing on our previous characterization of the *DSM*/CPP framework, the *DSM*/CPP research program can readily be represented as follows[18]:

Domain specification The domain is mapped by the *DSM* system of classification on the basis of clinical signs and symptoms (e.g., expressions of distress, disability, deficits, maladaption, deviance) viewed as manifestations of distinct mental disorders.
Substantive assumptions (S1) Mental disorders are individualistic (i.e., non-relational). (S2) Mental disorders are distinct from normal functioning. (S3) mental disorders are brain diseases having a characteristic etiology and pathophysiology.
Methodological assumptions (M1) Research ought to proceed by targeting *DSM* disorders and addressing questions concerning their etiology, pathophysiology, demographics, treatment, etc. (M2) The *DSM* approach to classification of mental disorders is adequate for serving both clinical and research purposes and it is the best means for translating basic research for use in the clinic.

The discussion in the preceding section suffices to show that the *DSM*/CPP research program is not based on a conceptualization that fits the domain of mental illness. In addition, that discussion suffices to make the domain specifying assumptions of the *DSM*/CPP research program implausible, and casts serious doubt on the substantive assumptions S1–S3.

Similarly, the lack of success of *DSM*-based research (e.g., the failure to validate the categories) raises serious questions about the utility of the methodological assumptions M1 and M2. Indeed, as will be discussed below, the NIMH is now pursuing an initiative to dissociate the *DSM* classification system from research bearing on mental illness, explicitly because the *DSM* has not proven useful for research purposes.

In addition to embodying a faulty conceptualization of the domain and problematic domain specifying, substantive, and methodological assumptions, the *DSM*/CPP research program fails the criteria for goodness of fit with respect to being "well ordered." As I understand this term,[19] a well-ordered research program is *productive* in that it yields robust findings that address the important research questions of the program, is *relevant* in that it yields findings that address the interests and needs of those who have a stake in the research (e.g., those who will use or otherwise be affected by the research), and is *balanced* in that it yields relevant research findings that address the full range of interests and needs of those who have a stake in the research.[20]

The *DSM*/CPP research program, designed to validate the *DSM* categories, has not been productive. A cardinal feature of the current crisis is that, for the most part, the *DSM*-based research agenda has not delivered the long sought for validation of the categories and it has not provided well confirmed and well developed models concerning the etiology or pathology of the putative mental disorders identified in the *DSM*. Nor has it, for the most part, produced a body of findings to substantiate the predictive validity of the categories concerning response to treatment, course and outcome. These results are also readily understood in terms of the poor conceptual fit between the categories and the domain: the *DSM* categories and associated criteria are simply ineffective in representing important features, conditions, processes, problems, and groups, and, hence, in managing uncertainty related to causal ambiguity, multi-dimensional complexity, and other features of the domain. As a consequence, they cannot support a progressive research program concerning mental illness because they are ill-suited for representing significant variables, for managing systematic and unsystematic sources of error, or for grouping subjects with similar features and processes. Rather, they are superficial and artificial categories that create heterogeneous groupings that will very probably compromise the research.[21]

Is *DSM*/CPP-based research relevant and balanced? Again, arguably not. A large percentage of available but limited resources has been and continues to be committed to research programs focused on the *DSM* categories, especially with respect to genetic and neuroscientific levels of analysis (e.g., to identify the etiology and pathophysiology of *DSM* mental disorders), and to research programs focused on interventions aimed at symptom reduction, especially drug and other physical means of intervention targeting criterial symptoms of *DSM* disorders.

The problems here are twofold. First, since the *DSM* categories have, for the most part, not been validated, and since the *DSM*-based research program makes problematic assumptions about the domain and is poorly tuned to the features of that domain, it has not produced the sorts of results relevant to serving the interests and needs of those who will use or otherwise be affected by the research (i.e., it is focused on unvalidated *DSM* categories of mental disorder, and it has failed to be productive). To continue deploying resources to *DSM*-based research is to pursue research that is probably wasteful and irrelevant to the aims of research concerning mental illness, the demands of the clinic, and the interests and needs of those seeking help. Second, the research agenda is *not properly balanced* in the light of the interests and needs of those who have a stake in the research findings. Because it is heavily focused on pathology, low levels of analysis, and physical means of intervention, it is skewed away from research on normal processes, higher levels of analysis, and non-physical means of intervention. Alternatively put, the *DSM*/CPP research agenda is skewed away from other research questions and goals that are likely to be more relevant to the interests of scientists, clinicians, and the public—for example, (1) research involving the deployment of all the relevant basic sciences[22] for the purpose of understanding the domain of mental illness more rigorously and in a more nuanced way than is characteristic of *DSM*/CPP research, (2) research addressing higher levels of analysis (e.g., social, behavioral, psychological) bearing on many of the problems people experience,[23] and (3) research concerning alternative approaches to intervention that target a wide range of problems in the domain (i.e., alternatives to stock psychiatric interventions such as drugs, electroconvulsive therapy, surgery, and stimulation).

Thus, in addition to resting on a faulty conception of the domain and making a variety of problematic assumptions, the *DSM*/CPP research program fails to be well ordered (that is, productive, relevant, balanced), and hence it does not fit well with the domain of mental illness.

Clinical Practice

With respect to clinical practice there are several dimensions that contribute to a good fit with the domain of mental illness. Given a set of appropriate clinical interests, values, and purposes,[24] a good fit consists in: a conceptual framework that fits the domain of mental illness; effective epistemic practices of assessment, classification, inference, explanation, and understanding concerning the domain; appropriate and effective intervention practices; and appropriate and effective psychosocial milieu. The *DSM*/CPP has not successfully informed clinical practice with respect to these dimensions and hence does not fit well with the domain of mental illness.

We have already seen that there is a lack of fit with respect to conceptualization of the domain. I have argued elsewhere (Poland 2003) that, in light of this conceptual lack of fit, the *DSM* categories (as exemplified by schizophrenia) are harmful clinical stereotypes that bias *DSM*/CPP clinical practice with respect to epistemic practices, intervention practices, and psychosocial milieu.

The *DSM* categories and associated epistemic practices related to information processing, inferential practice, explanatory practice, and clinical understanding, are ineffective and harmfully biased because, given their atheoretical focus on clinical phenomenology, they do not effectively identify and represent important features, problems, contexts, and processes (e.g., cognitive functioning, behavioral skills, relationships, psychosocial processes, personal perspectives) and they do not effectively identify and represent variation in such features, problems, contexts, and processes across individuals and across time in the same individual. As a consequence, typical *DSM*/CPP epistemic practices do not collect and process an adequate body of information that enables the management of ambiguity, heterogeneity, hierarchical complexity, dynamic interactivity, context sensitivity, and the perspectival and normative dimensions of mental illness, or that effectively manages the resulting clinical uncertainty (i.e., they do not underwrite sound clinical inferences and judgments concerning what is wrong and what is likely to be helpful).

Intervention practices within the *DSM*/CPP framework, with its medicalized focus on treating putative brain diseases and their symptoms, tend to be biased toward reducing symptoms with medications and away from identifying and responding to a wide range of problems from which people suffer (for example, cognitive deficits, skills deficits, relationship problems, employment problems). As a consequence, there is a bias away from alternative forms of intervention that are likely to be more responsive to this wider range of problems thereby making the *DSM*/CPP approach to intervention poorly suited for the promotion of clinical goals for individuals with relatively unique problem sets, functional profiles, embedding contexts, causal processes, and personal outlooks. The results of such shortcomings are simplified clinical practices guided by harmful clinical stereotypes that lead to overdiagnosis, overmedication, and non-responsiveness to the needs of people seeking help for mental illness.

With respect to the clinical psychosocial milieu, the *DSM*/CPP framework projects a medicalized psychosocial infrastructure onto clinical practice that shapes identities, roles, relationships, and patterns of interaction (for example, doctor and patient roles, identities, and relationships). Within such an infrastructure there are strong tendencies to pathologize people and their problems, to medicalize difference, deviance, disruption, and eccentricity, and to employ medicalized concepts (e.g., brain disease) and educational approaches[25] that can have a stigmatizing effect on first-person and third-person identity. Since there are substantial grounds for thinking that the psychosocial milieu of clinical practice is a potent variable in influencing outcome and that the milieu shaped by the *DSM*/CPP framework is toxic in important respects, such forms of practice are neither appropriate nor effective for promoting the purposes of clinical practice in the domain of mental illness.

In view of the above-described defects of the *DSM*/CPP conceptualization of the domain, and the research program and clinical practices based on it, the various problems characteristic of the current crisis in mental-health practice (e.g., problems of heterogeneity, validity, unproductive research, misguided clinical practice) are relatively straightforward consequences of them.

Why are current efforts at reform not likely to succeed?

To this point, I have argued that the *DSM*/CPP framework, consisting of an approach to classification, a set of practices, and a host of associated assumptions, fits poorly with the domain of mental illness, in view of the general features of that domain. As a consequence of this lack of fit, the dominant approach for conceptualizing that domain is defective, the research program based on that framework makes problematic assumptions and is not well ordered, and clinical practice employing that framework is structured by harmful clinical stereotypes that compromise clinical epistemic and intervention practices as well as the clinical psychosocial milieu. But this doesn't exhaust a full understanding of why we are in the crisis we are in: past and ongoing efforts at improving the classification scheme and the practices based on it are proving to have been, and to be, ineffective. This is because many of the assumptions and commitments of the *DSM*/CPP framework drive and direct the reform efforts. More specifically, neither of the two current efforts (viz., the *DSM* revision process and the NIMH RDoC initiative) holds out much hope for substantial reform.

The *DSM*-5 Revision Process

The process of development of the *DSM* system of classification is controlled by the American Psychiatric Association and guided substantially by considerations and constraints that promote the guild interests of psychiatrists. Specifically, the essentially conservative guidelines for change (cf. Kendler et al. 2009; American Psychiatric Association 2013) have centered on (1) requiring a high threshold for change based on research evidence, (2) the utility of the diagnostic system in routine clinical practice of psychiatrists, (3) continuity with previous editions to avoid disruption of clinical and research practice, and (4) no *a priori* constraints on the degree of change between DSM-IV and DSM-5. In addition, it has been documented that members of the task force and work groups associated with both the *DSM*-IV and the *DSM*-5 revision process have substantial levels of financial conflict of interest due to associations with the drug industry (Cosgrove et al. 2006, 2009). There are, however, other shortcomings of the *DSM* revision process beyond the existence of these guild and financial sources of bias.

Especially significant is the fact that categories that had no demonstrated validity when they were introduced in 1980 have been continuously "grandfathered through" on the grounds that there is no substantial evidence to justify their removal, and that their removal would be too disruptive of ongoing clinical and research practice. This line of reasoning has been advanced in both the *DSM*-IV and the *DSM*-5 process as an instance of how science is being appealed to in the development of the system. As a consequence, essentially the same categories as were introduced in *DSM*-III are retained and augmented by more of the same, despite there being no solid evidence for the construct and predictive validity of the categories, the acknowledgment that they have questionable value in research, and there being no serious evidence for their clinical utility. This "grandfathering" of unvalidated clinical categories is the result of a process that is highly constrained by its task specification (to review and revise the existing *DSM*), the questions posed (which typically concern whether to add, retain, revise, or delete categories or criteria), the problematic knowledge base relative to which these questions are addressed (viz., *DSM*-based research findings), the stringent standards on any revision, the aforementioned guild and financial biases, and, in sum, the importance of keeping the *DSM* highly tuned to preserving clinical practice as it currently exists. This constellation of factors effectively keeps more fundamental questions regarding the domain and the central assumptions of the *DSM*/CPP framework off the table. Hence, the revision process is largely restricted to tinker-ing with diagnostic categories, and has yielded a *DSM*-5 that is in important respects little changed from *DSM*-IV and that retains categories exhibiting the same problems of heterogeneity and lack of demonstrated validity.

The work groups of the *DSM*-5 process did consider other sorts of revi-sions, and some of them have been implemented.

First, there is the idea of adding genetics-based and neuroscience-based diagnostic criteria, thereby challenging the assumption of atheoreticity that has prevailed for the past 30 years. (Cf. Hyman 2007.) However, it is widely agreed that this cannot be done at present, because the research doesn't support it; none of the categories, after all, have been sufficiently validated in these ways. Indeed, the idea of eventually adding such cri-teria to existing categories appears to be based on a much too optimistic hope that eventually the *DSM* categories will be vindicated by *DSM*-based research. This is something that is increasingly drawn into question, for reasons discussed above. Short of introducing genetic or neuroscientific diagnostic criteria, information concerning genetic and neuroscientific findings related to various *DSM* categories have been introduced in a superficial way into the text for some categories (e.g., schizophrenia), although in view of the problems with the *DSM* categories and the *DSM*-based research program it isn't clear how meaningful or useful such dis-cussions are.

Second, there has been a provisional addition of dimensional assessment tools in Section III ("Emerging Measures and Models") of DSM-5. At present these tools provide clinicians and researchers with some assessment options designed to aid the diagnostic process, thereby broadening diagnostic assessment beyond the assignment of individuals to a categorical diagnostic grouping. Such tools are rating scales to be completed by either the patient or the clinician and they are aimed at quantifying the severity of various symptoms and impairments, and thus, the severity of diagnoses. These scales, however, are highly constrained by the requirement that they be usable by clinicians in routine clinical psychiatric settings; hence, they are tuned to the *DSM*-based training of clinicians and the pragmatics of con-ventional psychiatric practice more than they are tuned to the features of the domain of mental illness and the epistemic demands of the clinic (both of which require a more nuanced and powerful dimensional approach). The limits of the training of clinicians and the context of clinical use make more serious dimensional assessment approaches impracticable: the pro-posed dimensional tools are simple, superficial, and atheoretically con-ceived rating scales of clinical phenomenology, and hence they are likely to contribute little to the formidable assessment tasks posed by the features of the domain of mental illness. Among other limitations, they may lack important psychometric properties (cf. Frances 2010), they focus on too narrow a range of features, and they are not theoretically related to underlying processes.

Third, prior to the publication of DSM-5, there was discussion of introducing a new organizational structure for *DSM* categories by identifying groups of categories that share similarities concerning such factors as neural substrates, family traits, genetic risk factors, specific environmental risk factors, biomarkers, temperamental antecedents, abnormalities of emotional or cognitive processing, symptom similarity, course of illness, high comorbidity, and treatment response (American Psychiatric Association 2013; Andrews et al. 2009; Bernstein 2011). The idea was to assemble existing categories of disorder into clusters based on these factors and to encourage research within and across them. Under initial consideration were five clusters:

neurocognitive (based on neural substrate abnormalities),
neurodevelopmental (based on early and continuing cognitive deficits),
psychosis (based on clinical features and biomarkers for information processing deficits),
emotional (based on temperamental antecedents of negative emotionality),

and

externalizing: based on temperamental antecedents of disinhibition.

Subsequently, on the basis of the clinical utility of developmental and lifespan considerations and empirical support for the value of the distinction between internalizing and externalizing factors, the final organizational structure of the DSM-5 involves an ordering of groupings as follows: neurodevelopmental disorders, internalizing disorders, externalizing disorders, neurocognitive disorders, and other disorders. The stated purposes of this structure (American Psychiatric Association 2013, pp. 12–13) include "to enable future researchers to enhance understanding of disease origins and pathophysiological commonalities between disorders," to thereby provide a base for assessing validity, to develop new diagnostic approaches, and to provide a basis for explaining heterogeneity and comorbidity of current categories.

Although the spirit of this change is of interest, and the identification of significant features and processes such as those listed above is on the right track with respect to research concerning the domain of mental illness, the idea of proceeding by creating super-groups of *DSM* categories is problematic in view of the lack of validity and the heterogeneity of *DSM* categories—the super-groups probably will exhibit the same problems. What is needed is an approach to research, free of *DSM* categories and commitments, that focuses more directly on significant features and processes.

In any event, the proposed sorts of revision (revising categories and criteria, adding dimensional scales, adding genetic/neuroscientific information, identifying a metastructure of the categorical system[26]) do not seriously address the deeper shortcoming of the *DSM*/CPP framework: its lack of fit with the domain of mental illness.

The NIMH RDoC Project

Another current effort at reform is the initiative at the NIMH to develop a novel conceptual framework for pursuing research concerning mental illness: the Research Domain Criteria (RDoC) project (NIMH 2011). This project is explicitly premised on an acknowledgment of the shortcomings of *DSM* categories for the purposes of scientific research, and its immediate aim is to encourage and fund research proposals that do not rely on the *DSM*. More specifically, it calls for proposals that are focused on studying genetics and neural circuitry in specific research domains (for example, functional domains such as executive function, memory, and fear) without necessarily employing *DSM* categories. The ultimate aim is to build a research base that will underwrite a new classification system based on genetics and neural circuitry and that will promote new approaches to treatment (especially, but not exclusively, drugs, surgery, and stimulation technologies).

This project is admirable insofar as it represents an effort to improve on the current highly problematic research program structured by *DSM* categories and to abandon both the atheoretical approach and the assumption (C1) that one classificatory framework can serve both research and clinical purposes. This project, which is promising in that it draws on basic science for understanding the phenomena in the domain of mental illness, may lead to findings of scientific and clinical significance such as: improved assessment techniques, causal models of various normal and abnormal capacities, functions, and processes, an improved understanding of and management of the characteristics of mental illness identified in table 3.1, and the possibility of improved intervention strategies and techniques. Thus, the initiative promises the sorts of knowledge and techniques that are necessary to serve the interests and needs of researchers as well as of those of people with mental illness and those trying to help them.

Although promising (and, certainly long overdue), there are reasons to be skeptical. For while the RDoC project has turned its back on the *DSM* categories, it is being pursued squarely within the *DSM*/CPP framework and, as a consequence, exhibits numerous biases and limitations that compromise its otherwise lofty aims and promises.

Consider, for example, how Thomas Insel (director of the NIMH) and colleagues characterize the three assumptions of the RDoC project (Insel et al. 2010):

A1 Mental illnesses are brain disorders, i.e., disorders of brain circuits.

A2 The dysfunction in neural circuits can be identified with the tools of clinical neuroscience, including electrophysiology, functional neural imaging, and new methods of quantifying connections *in vivo*.

A3 Data from genetics and clinical neuroscience will yield biosignatures that will augment clinical symptoms and signs for clinical management.

Such assumptions imply that, although the RDoC project rejects the methodological assumptions of the *DSM*/CPP research program, it affirms many of the other assumptions and commitments of the *DSM*/CPP framework. This raises serious questions about how well it is suited for responding to the current crisis in mental-health practice.

The project explicitly rejects M1 (the methodological assumption that research should target *DSM* categories) and M2 (the methodological assumption that *DSM* classification can serve both clinical and research purposes and that it is the best means for translating basic research to the clinic). In their place, the revised methodological assumptions might be framed as follows:

(M1′) Research ought to target functional domains and aim to identify a) genetic and other etiological factors and b) dysfunctional neural circuitry associated with mental illnesses.

(M2′) Even if the *DSM* is clinically useful, the best means for translating basic research to the clinic is to pursue a research agenda that is informed by genetics and clinical neuroscience in accordance with M1′.

However, A1–A3 make it clear that the RDoC project affirms the substantive assumptions of the *DSM*/CPP research program, S1–S3 (individualism, abnormality, brain disease). In addition, they implicitly affirm C3, the *DSM*/CPP commitment to medicalization of the domain of mental illness. As a consequence, we shall now see that the RDoC research framework exhibits many of the same problems as the *DSM*/CPP research framework: it makes problematic substantive and methodological assumptions, it will probably lead to a flawed conceptualization of the domain of mental illness, and it is not well ordered.

First, as discussed above, it is implausible that all mental illness is brain disorder (disease).[27] Indeed some mental-health problems are psychological or behavioral problems involving a pathology of some sort or severe pain and suffering, but this is consistent with there being no pathology of the brain conceived of in terms of genetics, neural circuitry, or other lower levels of analysis. Such things might best be conceived of as problems in living not appropriately treated on a medical model. In this way, for example, behavioral skills deficits, severe depression or anxiety, deficient social cognitive capacities, and even delusions and hallucinations all might involve violations of some sort of norm of high-level functioning without implying a brain pathology is present.[28] Further, some mental-health problems are best conceived of as relational or social problems, again without any implication that a brain disease is present. And finally, not all problems in the domain of mental illness are biologically or medically abnormal in any way, even if they involve pain, suffering, and diminished functional capacities (e.g., grief). As a consequence, the RDoC research framework makes several problematic substantive assumptions (S1–S3) about the domain of mental illness.

Second, the methodological assumptions, M1′ and M2′, prescribe a strong research bias toward low levels of analysis (genetics and neuroscience) that threatens a neglect of research focused on higher levels of analysis (psychological, computational, behavioral, social). Such higher levels are essential for understanding the domain of mental illness, and they are not important only to the extent that they bear on putative brain diseases (e.g., causal factors, modulators of course and outcome). Rather, they contribute to the independent analysis of higher-level causal processes, of personal perspectives, of a wide range of problems from which people can suffer, and of the contexts in which they suffer them. As a consequence, the biased research of RDoC will probably fail to provide a thorough analysis of the domain of mental illness in terms of all relevant levels of analysis and hence will probably fail to produce the knowledge required for comprehending and managing the various features of that domain. Thus, RDoC is at risk for providing a flawed conceptualization of the domain because, in addition to making problematic assumptions, it will probably fail to produce sufficient resources for representing important problems, features, conditions, processes, and groups in the domain.

The methodological assumptions M1′ and M2′ suggest a further research bias toward the development of pharmaceutical (and other physical) forms of medical intervention that can influence genetic, neural, and biochemical targets and their symptomatic expressions. This threatens to neglect research on interventions that target other types of problems and processes (i.e., not brain diseases). So long as the focus is on brain diseases, these other forms of intervention will probably be studied only to the extent that they are thought to affect such putative diseases and their manifestations. But such a restricted focus will be too narrow since psychological, behavioral, and social interventions are not necessarily tethered to amelioration of such brain pathologies and symptoms; for example, they might be directly responsive to a deficit in behavioral skills, or to a problem of psychological attribution, or to a difficulty with social relationships, in none of which is brain disease a likely cause or a target of intervention. Just as there are other types of problems unrelated to brain diseases, there are other types of intervention (psychological, behavioral, social) that target these problems, even if they do not target a brain disease.

Finally, the RDoC project is clearly committed to the *DSM*/CPP medicalization of clinical practice with associated commitments to clinical understanding (e.g., a pathologizing focus, a view of mental illness as brain disease, a view of people as sick), clinical epistemic and intervention practices (e.g., diagnosis and treatment of disease with medical techniques of assessment and intervention), and medicalized psychosocial infrastructure (e.g., doctor-patient relationships, roles, identities). There is no indication in the RDoC initiative (e.g., as expressed by M1′ and M2′) that research concerning the psychosocial infrastructure of clinical practice is on the agenda, despite the fact that psychosocial infrastructure is a potent factor in clinical change and that some psychosocial forms are more effective than others. (See Spaulding et al. 2003.)

Thus, the stated aims and assumptions of the RDoC project appear to open it up to the charges of making false domain specifying and substantive assumptions about the domain of mental illness and of being biased in a way that will lead to a research agenda that neglects important research issues (i.e., it is heavily focused on pathology, low levels of analysis, and physical means of intervention at the expense of research on normal processes, higher levels of analysis, and non-physical means of intervention). This limits how effectively it will contribute to an adequate re-conceptualization of the domain of mental illness and to the development of sound research and clinical practices that are appropriate to the features of that domain and are responsive to the needs and interests of researchers, clinicians, and individuals seeking help. These biases and their likely consequences suggest that M1′ and M2′ are flawed prescriptions for how best to proceed with research concerning the domain of mental illness.

I conclude that the RDoC project is poorly tuned to the domain of mental illness and that it is not a form of well-ordered research: it is unbalanced, and it is likely to produce research that isn't relevant to many of the interests and needs of stakeholders.[29] As a consequence, the NIMH RDoC project isn't likely to be an effective response to the current crisis.

What Should Be Done?

The current crisis exists largely because the dominant *DSM*/CPP framework fits poorly with the domain of mental illness; as a consequence, the *DSM* classification system and the associated practices, assumptions, and commitments function as deeply rooted sources of error and bias that compromise all aspects of mental-health practice directed upon the domain of mental illness. Specifically, these sources of error and bias lead to a defective conceptualization of the domain, to non-progressive and non-well-ordered research programs, and to misguided and sometimes toxic clinical practices and infrastructures. Further, reform efforts (e.g., the *DSM* development process, the NIMH RDoC project) are so compromised by these sources of error and bias that, as they currently stand, they hold out little promise for responding effectively to many of the significant features of the crisis; indeed, these reform efforts will probably increase the entrenchment of many components of the *DSM*/CPP framework. And insofar as this framework and associated practices are pervasively and deeply entrenched, the crisis can now be understood more fully, both with respect to what it consists in and why it exists and is likely to persist.

Unfortunately, there are no quick fixes. The crisis must be addressed cautiously and carefully, proceeding in various stages that will effectively lead to divestment of problematic commitments, assumptions, and practices, to reconceptualization of the domain of mental illness, and to reconstitution of research, clinical, and educational practices. Before such a process can begin, a few things will have to happen. First, there should be widespread and balanced education regarding the crisis so that a full and accurate appreciation becomes shared. Second, meaningful reform regarding conflict of interest should be pursued aggressively. Third, control over the development of any "official" system of classification should be removed from the hands of psychiatry and located in a more guild-neutral institutional setting.[30] Fourth, the NIMH should be brought more in line with the demands of well-ordered research, by divesting commitments to the *DSM*/CPP framework and drawing on the full range of relevant basic sciences. These four steps will set the stage for a reconceptualization of the domain of mental illness based on a more balanced research agenda rooted in basic science and responsive to the various features of that domain. Such a reconceptualization will, in turn, set the stage for a reconstitution of research and clinical practices designed to better fit the domain and to be responsive to the needs and interests of stakeholders. The process of effectively making a transition from current forms of training and practice to their reconstituted forms will be quite protracted, given the deep entrenchment of current practices. However, such a transition is required, although it should be pursued with as little collateral damage as possible.

Acknowledgments

Thanks to George Graham, Jennifer Radden, Harold Kincaid, and Steve Sloman for comments on earlier drafts. Special thanks to Barbara Von Eckardt for close reading and comments on several drafts. Thanks to Will Spaulding and Mary Sullivan for enduring influences on my thinking about these issues.

Notes

1. There is substantial confusion and disagreement about how to conceive the categories in the *DSM*. Consistent with the conceptualization of the original authors of *DSM*-III, the concept of mental disorder presented in the introduction to the volume, and much of contemporary discourse about mental disorder in conventional psychiatric practice, many conceive of the categories as picking out conditions that involve an underlying pathology (the dysfunction) that is the cause of the harmful signs and symptoms specified in the diagnostic criteria. Others have thought that it is best to think of the categories as picking out syndromes or clinical prototypes, without any implications regarding pathology or etiology. In what follows, I shall assume the first of these views, although the former approach doesn't fare any better.

2. In this limited sense, the categories in the *DSM* are theoretical: each is conceived of as a "syndrome with unity" in which a constellation of signs and symptoms is viewed as caused by an underlying dysfunction. (See Poland et al. 1994.) For a

discussion of the concept of mental disorders as harmful dysfunctions, see Wakefield 1992.

3. Of course, other information is sometimes gathered, but not in the systematic way that clinicians search for signs and symptoms of disorder. Whether, what, and how much additional information is collected will depend on idiosyncrasies of resources, context, clinician training, clinician bias, and so on.

4. Although the reliability (i.e., a measure of inter-rater agreement) of the categories is considered by many to be established, it appears that, although many categories exhibit tolerable reliabilities in controlled conditions with trained raters, the reliability of the categories "in the field" is not so certain. Indeed, owing to the subjective, normative, and atheoretical character of the diagnostic criteria and the substantial complexity of many clinical presentations and the relatively uncontrolled character of clinical contexts, the reliability of many categories is suspect.

5. This does not mean that all research focused on *DSM* categories is of no value. For example, some such research has produced findings that contribute to clarifying aspects of specific symptoms that are associated with a given category. This, however, is not a validation of the category itself, and a focus on the category leads to distortions in sampling and subject grouping that tend to mask meaningful results.

6. For an example of how this can be done in the context of severe mental illness, see Spaulding et al. 2003.

7. For further development of this line of criticism, see Poland et al. 1994.

8. Three further markers for the shortcomings of *DSM*-based clinical practice are the substantial increase in psychiatric diagnosis over the past two decades, the substantial increase in the use of psychotropic drugs over the past two decades, and the reactions of the public to a perceived lack of responsiveness by CPP to the needs of those seeking help and related concerns about the overuse of drugs as a surrogate for more appropriate interventions. Such markers have been widely discussed and provide *prima facie* grounds for suspecting that something is seriously awry with contemporary mental-health clinical practices. Concerns about over-diagnosis, over-medication, and non-responsiveness to the needs of people seeking help are arguably expressions of deeper concerns about a perceived over-medicalization of mental-health practices and an inappropriate level of influence exerted by the pharmaceutical industry on clinical practice.

9. There are also problems with the associated commitments of the *DSM*/CPP framework. These will be discussed below.

10. There may well turn out to be identifiable brain diseases involved in the psychological, behavioral, and social problems from which some people suffer, but it is far from obvious that all (or even many) such problems are best conceptualized in this way, especially in view of the very limited track record of such disease hypotheses and the profound lack of clarity that accompanies the term "disease."

11. Conceptualization of the domain of mental illness must also, of course, draw on various normative considerations that bear on the harmful, problematic, or otherwise distressing components of human suffering.

12. The term "illness" should not be understood in this context as implying that a disease is present; rather, it is a colloquial term picking out conditions that involve life problems, distress, disability, etc., as described in the text.

13. The following discussion draws on Spaulding et al. 2003.

14. The idea of a "lack of fit" also applies to the associated commitments of the framework as well, and below we shall see that these also fall short.

15. For elaboration of this argument, see Poland et al. 1994.

16. In DSM-IV, Axis 4 ratings concern identification of recent psychosocial and environmental problems, and Axis 5 ratings consist of a single number between 0 and 100 on a Global Assessment of Functioning scale.

17. Mechanisms and processes associated with specific symptoms or other traits (e.g., cognitive deficits) are being studied with some success, but this is not the same as identifying a dysfunction or a disease associated with the diagnostic categories.

18. Research programs can be usefully viewed as being typically structured by three sets of assumptions: domain-specifying assumptions that pick out the domain to be investigated, substantive assumptions (hypothesized working assumptions about some feature of the domain), and methodological assumptions (proposed methods and strategies for studying the domain). For more on this way of characterizing a research program, see Von Eckardt 1993.

19. This notion of a research program being well ordered draws on but departs from Kitcher's (2001) discussion of the notion of well-ordered science.

20. Those who have a stake in the research include not only clinicians and people who suffer mental illness, but also social institutions, the general public, and researchers who have an interest in understanding the domain.

21. For elaboration of this argument, see Poland et al. 1994.

22. In view of the features of the domain, the relevant basic sciences include biological, psychological, and social sciences, with no one category having special privilege, as appears to be the case in the DSM/CPP framework where genetics and the neurosciences are accorded a special status because of the commitment to mental illnesses as brain diseases.

23. Insofar as the domain comprises persons with problems defined from their perspective and concerned with a wide range of physical, psychological, behavioral, personal, and social phenomena, a research agenda focused on genetics, neural circuitry, and interventions at these levels will be too narrow and will produce too limited a set of results (even if successful) to be responsive to that broader array of problems.

24. Although limitations of space preclude discussion, setting these interests, values, and purposes is a substantial social issue that bears on the issues discussed in this chapter.

25. With respect to "patient education," the problems include the introduction of attributions with potentially toxic psychological and social consequences. With respect to "public education" designed to reduce the stigma of mental illness, the problems include the apparent likelihood that such "education" might serve to increase stigma. (Cf. Corrigan and Watson 2004.)

26. There has been discussion (see, e.g., American Psychiatric Association 2013, p. 13) of the idea of making *DSM*-5 a "living document" (that is, one that can be updated on much shorter time scales than previous *DSM* revisions). This, however, seems to be a move in the wrong direction, since what is needed is to slow the process down and reconceive it rather than to speed it up.

27. The terms "disease" and "disorder" are often used uncritically and with the understanding that they play an important role in health care even if they cannot be successfully analyzed: they allow for access to health-care resources for those who need them, and they can be useful in reassuring individuals about their problems (e.g., "it isn't your fault"). Neither of these sorts of functions provides a sound scientific basis for conceptualizing the domain of mental illness, however, and these terms suggest a level of precision and understanding that is often lacking. In particular, their usage clearly presupposes a conception of normality and abnormality that goes largely unexplicated.

28. Two responses, neither of which is compelling, are (1) that any norm violation with respect to functioning of a high-level capacity ipso facto is a norm violation of brain functioning because higher-level functions are functions of the brain and (2) that a pathology at some high level of brain functioning (e.g., behavioral capacity, cognitive process) must mean that something is wrong with the biological realization of that function or process or capacity. The first of these responses misses the point of identifying all mental illnesses as brain disorders, since that claim is intended to direct attention to low-level brain processes and pathologies conceived of at those low levels of analysis. The second is simply a non-sequitur, since high-level pathologies (e.g., misspelled words, defective computer programs) do not imply low-level pathologies (e.g., defective ink, damaged computers).

29. This problem is compounded by the fact that a substantial portion of the NIMH research funding is directed toward *DSM*-based research, thereby exhibiting a continuing bias toward an unproductive, irrelevant, and unbalanced research agenda.

30. The idea that traditional psychiatric diagnostic practices and categories (as embodied by the *DSM*) are appropriate or adequate for all mental-health contexts is blatantly implausible. Nonetheless, such diagnostic practices and categories are viewed within the *DSM*/CPP framework as if they were appropriate across settings and forms of practice. As a consequence, many forms of practice are held hostage to the *DSM* and the putative legitimacy of a psychiatric diagnosis. Breaking the grip of the APA on classification schemes that will be recognized by various entities (e.g., regulators, insurers) is an important step in undoing the entrenchment of the *DSM*/CPP framework.

References

American Psychiatric Association. 1980. *Diagnostic and Statistical Manual of Mental Disorders*, third edition.

American Psychiatric Association. 1994. *Diagnostic and Statistical Manual of Mental Disorders*, fourth edition.

American Psychiatric Association. 2013. *Diagnostic and Statistical Manual of Mental Disorders*, fifth edition.

Andreassen, N. 2007. The *DSM* and the death of phenomenology in America. *Schizophrenia Bulletin* 33 (1): 108–112.

Andrews, G., D. Goldberg, R. Krueger, W. Carpenter, S. Hyman, P. Sachdev, and D. Pine. 2009. Exploring the feasibility of a metastructure for *DSM*-V and ICD-11: Could it improve utility and validity? *Psychological Medicine* 39 (12): 1993–2000.

Bernstein, C. 2011. Metastructure in *DSM*-5 process. *Psychiatric News* 46 (5): 7.

Corrigan, P., and A. Watson. 2004. At ISSUE: Stop the stigma: Call mental illness a brain disease. *Schizophrenia Bulletin* 30 (3): 477–478.

Cosgrove, L., S. Krimsky, M. Vijayaraghavan, and L. Schneider. 2006. Financial ties between *DSM*-IV panel members and the pharmaceutical industry. *Psychotherapy and Psychosomatics* 75: 154–160.

Cosgrove, L., H. Burstzajn, and S. Krimsky. 2009. Developing unbiased diagnostic treatment guidelines in psychiatry. *New England Journal of Medicine* 360 (19): 2035–2036.

Cuthbert, B., and T. Insel. 2010. Classification issues in women's mental health: Clinical utility and etiological mechanisms. *Archives of Women's Mental Health* 13: 57–59.

Frances, A. 2010. Rating scales: *DSM*5 bites off far more than it can chew. *Psychiatric Times*, May 7.

Hacking, I. 1999. *The Social Construction of What?* Harvard University Press.

Hyman, S. 2007. Can neuroscience be integrated into the *DSM*-V? *Nature Reviews. Neuroscience* 8: 725–732.

Hyman, S. 2010. The diagnosis of mental disorders: The problem of reification. *Annual Review of Clinical Psychology* 6: 155–179.

Insel, T., B. Cuthbert, M. Garvey, R. Heinssen, D. S. Pine, K. Quinn, C. Sanislow, and P. Wang. 2010. Research Domain Criteria (RDoC): Toward a new classification framework for research on mental disorders. *American Journal of Psychiatry* 167 (7): 748–751.

Kendell, R., and A. Jablensky. 2003. Distinguishing between the validity and utility of psychiatric diagnoses. *American Journal of Psychiatry* 160 (1): 4–12.

Kendler, K., D. Kupfer, W. Narrow, K. Phillips, and J. Fawcett. 2009. Posting on *DSM*-5 development website (http://www.dsm5.org/ProgressReports/Documents/Guidelines-for-Making-Changes-to-DSM_1.pdf).

Kitcher, P. 2001. *Science, Truth, and Democracy*. Oxford University Press.

Klerman, G. 1978. The evolution of a scientific nosology. In *Schizophrenia: Research and Practice*, ed. J. Shershow. Harvard University Press.

NIMH. 2011. NIMH Research Domain Criteria (RDoC). Posted at http://www.nimh.nih.gov.

Poland, J. 2003. Bias and schizophrenia. In *Bias in Psychiatric Diagnosis*, ed. P. Caplan and L. Cosgrove. Jason Aronson.

Poland, J., B. Von Eckardt, and W. Spaulding. 1994. Problems with the *DSM* approach to classifying psychopathology. In *Philosophical Psychopathology*, ed. G. Graham and G. L. Stephens. MIT Press.

Regier, D., W. Narrow, E. Kuhl, and D. Kupfer. 2009. The conceptual development of *DSM*-V. *American Journal of Psychiatry* 166 (6): 645–650.

Sen, A. 1993. Positional objectivity. *Philosophy & Public Affairs* 22 (2): 126–145.

Spaulding, W., and J. Poland. 2001. Cognitive rehabilitation for schizophrenia: enhancing social cognition by strengthening neurocognitive functioning. In *Social Cognition and Schizophrenia*, ed. P. Corrigan and D. Penn. American Psychological Association.

Spaulding, W., M. Sullivan, and J. Poland. 2003. *Treatment and Rehabilitation of Severe Mental Illness*. Guilford.

Von Eckardt, B. 1993. *What Is Cognitive Science?* MIT Press.

Wakefield, J. 1992. The concept of mental disorder: On the boundary between biological facts and social values. *American Psychologist* 47 (3): 373–388.

4 Psychopharmacology and Natural Kinds: A Conceptual Framework

Dan J. Stein

Although *Homo sapiens* probably has used psychotropic compounds for thousands of years, it is only recently that basic and clinical psychopharmacology have developed as productive scientific fields. The availability of a broad range of psychotropic medications has in turn led to a range of conceptual and ethical questions (Stein 2008). I begin by noting that many psychopharmacologists have assumed that mental disorders are natural kinds, but that empirical data tend not to support such a view. I then propose a naturalistic framework for addressing relevant questions at the intersection of psychopharmacology and philosophy.

Psychopharmacology and Natural Kinds

A broad range of psychotropic medications have been developed. On the basis of considerations such as molecular structure, receptor binding, and behavioral studies (in animals and humans), such psychotropics have been classified into different classes. Early work in psychopharmacology emphasized the anti-psychotic, anxiolytic, anti-depressant, and mood-stabilizer classes and provided paradigmatic exemplars of each, including phenothiazenes (which were useful for psychotic disorders such as schizophrenia), benzodiazepines (which were useful for symptoms of anxiety), tricyclic anti-depressants and monoamine oxidase inhibitors (which were useful for depression), and lithium (which was useful for bipolar disorder).

An early approach also emphasized the possibility of psychopharmacological dissection (Klein 1964). Donald Klein suggested that benzodiazepines and tricyclic anti-depressants had different effects in different kinds of psychiatric disorder. Thus benzodiazepines were useful for non-specific anxiety, while tricyclics were useful for panic disorder. The idea that different psychiatric disorders were specific entities (or natural kinds), with characteristic neurobiological foundations, responsive to particular medications, provided an important foundation for psychiatric nosology and research in the second half of the twentieth century (Klein 1978).

However, with the introduction of increasing numbers of psychotropic medications, and clinical trials of many of these agents across a variety of psychiatric disorders, the empirical data seem increasingly at odds with such a view. Thus, anti-psychotic agents turn out to be efficacious in the treatment not only of psychotic disorders but also in the management of symptoms of anxiety disorders, major depression, and bipolar disorder (Ipser et al. 2006; Komossa et al. 2010). Although anti-depressants may be less promiscuous in their effects, they may be useful for mood symptoms in a broad range of conditions, and they are also useful in the anxiety disorders (Bandelow et al. 2002).

Although differentiation of various psychiatric disorders remains an issue in psychiatry, perhaps an equally important issue is the differentiation of mental disorder from normality. Psychopharmacology has offered an important potential solution to this issue. Thus, patients with schizophrenia require fairly large doses of anti-psychotic medication for the relief of symptoms. In contrast, an individual with no psychotic symptoms may experience enormous sedation on exposure to such high doses of anti-psychotics. Further, it might be hypothesized that individuals with genetic vulnerability to psychosis (say, family members of individuals with schizophrenia who have schizoptypal personality disorder) respond to low doses of anti-psychotics. Schizotypal personality disorder may then be considered an intermediate phenotype, or endophenotype, which is genetically transmitted, and which is associated with vulnerability to schizophrenia (Gottesman and Gould 2003).

Empirical data do provide some support for such an approach to the differentiation of psychiatric disorder from endophenotypic vulnerability from normality, perhaps particularly with the anti-psychotics (Siever and Davis 1991). On the other hand, there are few data from the mood and anxiety disorders to support such a view. It turns out that anti-depressants are particularly easy to differentiate from placebo in studies of severe depression and anxiety. However, in patients with mild depression, placebo responses are higher, and it becomes quite difficult to differentiate the effects of anti-depressants and placebo (Stein and Mayberg 2005). It is not necessarily the case that anti-depressants differentiate between severe and mild depression (as both kinds of depression respond to anti-depressants); rather, it seems that placebo response differentiates these conditions (severe depression responds to anti-depressants but not to placebo, while mild depression responds to both anti-depressants and to placebo).

Arguably, like pain and fever, depression and anxiety are often non-specific responses that emerge in response to multiple different problems, that are governed by multiple underlying mechanisms, and that respond to a range of interventions (including the non-specific intervention of placebo). Such factors are likely to frustrate attempts to find specific bio-markers, including selective response to particular pharmacotherapies, for these conditions. Each patient requires a comprehensive assessment, and a range of facts and values are weighed in deciding on a treatment plan (see below). However, this situation is perhaps not dissimilar from the rest of medicine, where medical syndromes are often characterized by blurry boundaries, non-specific biomarkers, and multiple causes (Nesse and Stein 2012).

Conceptual Approaches

The observation that psychopharmacology has been less successful at dis-secting nature at her joints (Rowe 1986) than many would have hoped is consistent with a range of other arguments that psychiatric disorders (or most psychiatric disorders) are not natural kinds (Zachar 2000), or that they exist at the weak end of the spectrum of natural kinds (Phillips et al. 2012), characterized not so much by single biological essences, but rather by multiple cross-level mechanisms (Kendler 2011). In this section I argue that the expectation of psychopharmacology to delineate natural mental kinds reflects a number of more general issues in our understanding of the category of psychiatric disorders. The argument that it is heuristically useful to differentiate classical, critical, and integrative approaches to understanding categories such as mental disorders has been made else-where (Stein 1991, 1998), and will be drawn on again here.

A classical perspective on science, medicine, and psychiatry takes the view that scientific categories, including psychiatric disorders, are natural kinds that can be defined in necessary and sufficient terms. A square, for example, can be defined as a figure of equal sides with right angles. In medicine, particular disorders can be operationalized in terms of their characteristic signs and symptoms. Similarly, in psychiatry, specific psychi-atric disorder can be operationalized in terms of their defining diagnostic criteria. Such an approach to psychiatric diagnosis is sympathetic to the view that particular psychiatric conditions are natural kinds that would respond differently to different psychiatric medications.

A critical perspective on science, medicine, and psychiatry emphasizes that scientific categories, including psychiatric disorders, are defined differently at different times and in different places. The definition of a weed, for example, varies from time to time and from place to place. Whereas some authors who take a critical stance hold that medical categories have an objective basis, a critical perspective emphasizes that what counts as a psychiatric diagnosis varies from time to time, and from place to place, and necessarily entails a range of values. The critical view sometimes vigorously opposes the use of psychotropic agents, arguing that such use is based on a faulty analogy between physical and mental disorder. Others who take a critical stance have, however, argued for the value of psychotropic agents (including substances of abuse) in enhancing or expanding experience.

An integrative perspective on science, medicine, and psychiatry argues that scientific categories have both transitive and intransitive aspects; they are necessarily defined by human communities, but they also are characterized by specific underlying mechanisms which are open to scientific investigation (Bhaskar 1978). The category of birds, for example, includes the more typical robin (which can fly, and which is quickly recognized as a bird) as well as the more atypical ostrich (which cannot fly, and which may not be recognized as a bird in all cultures). However, a detailed understanding of the biology of avian species shows that both robins and ostriches are clearly members of the category. Similarly, typical medical and psychiatric conditions are readily recognized as medical disorders across time and place, but atypical medical conditions (e.g., gynecomastia) and atypical psychiatric conditions (e.g., substance dependence) are not universally recognized as such.

From an integrative perspective, pharmacological dissection is possible to the extent that any particular psychiatric disorder is characterized by universal underlying mechanisms that can be uniquely targeted by a particular psychotropic agent. However, an integrative perspective recognizes that any particular psychiatric disorder may be characterized by a broad range of different underlying mechanisms, and that such mechanisms may lie on dimensions that can't always easily be differentiated into "normal" and "pathological." Thus, it is not surprising that psychopharmacological dissection often fails. Even were it possible to provide sensitive and specific biomarkers of aberrant brain-mind mechanisms (and currently it is not), the diagnosis of psychiatric disorder necessarily entails a range of value judgments. Such judgments can, however, be reasonably debated; there are pros and cons, for example, to deciding that substance dependence is a psychiatric disorder, and that it deserves treatment with psychotropic agents (see below).

A Naturalistic Approach

There are different ways to defend the framework of scientific, medical, and psychiatric categories proposed here. In this section I briefly outline a naturalistic defense, drawing on empirical data from the cognitive-affective neurosciences (among them cognitive psychology, neuroscience, and anthropology). A more detailed naturalistic defense, drawing on a broader array of the cognitive-affective neurosciences, is provided elsewhere (Stein 2008).

Cognitive psychology teaches us that some categories are typical and others are atypical. Thus, empirical studies of the way in which people categorize birds is readily able to indicate that robins are typical birds and that ostriches are atypical (Rosch 1978). Similarly, empirical study of the way in which people categorize mental phenomena would show that there is universal agreement that certain kinds of mental phenomena are indicative of disorder and that there is much more controversy about others (Sorsdahl, Flisher, Wilson, and Stein 2010).

Neuroscience teaches us that categories often have a real basis in universal human experience. Thus, although color categorization varies quite widely from one culture to another, agreement across cultures on particular colors is possible because of the physiology of vision. Furthermore, disorders such as color blindness occur across cultures; in such instances, owing to specific alterations in the physiology of vision, there is a predictably altered experience of color. Similarly, particular psychiatric disorders may well be characterized by quite specific underlying aberrant processes, which result in pathognomonic changes in thoughts, feelings, or behaviors.

Anthropology teaches us that categories are widely influenced by social constructions. It is clear that color categorizations vary across cultures, ranging from very simple (e.g., cultures which divide colors into "light" and "dark") to very complex (e.g., cultures that have a wide range of commonly used colors). Many cultures differentiate disease, crime, and sin (Parsons 1951). In cases of typical diseases, crimes, and sins, such differentiation is relatively easy; however, there may be significant debate as to whether an atypical mental phenomenon is a disease, a crime, or a sin.

When psychopharmacological treatment of a psychiatric disorder is being considered, the metaphors used for typical disease support the use of such interventions. Thus, if the category of disease is viewed using the metaphor of an "imbalance" it would not be surprising if a clinician were to recommend a psychotropic agent to restore "balance." In cases of atypical entities, however, more moral kinds of metaphors may be used. For example, if substance abuse is viewed as a personal failing, it will not be surprising if social interventions focus on personal responsibility rather than on psychotropic agents. In the next section, I will consider more fully the question of whether atypical conditions should be treated with psychopharmacological interventions.

Psychopharmacology: A Good Thing?

I have argued in this chapter that the evidence from psychopharmacology refutes the idea that mental disorders are natural kinds. Furthermore, I have suggested that data from the cognitive-affective neurosciences support an approach in which psychiatric disorders, like other scientific categories, have both transitive and intransitive aspects; they are both constructed by human practices in particular contexts, and they are underpinned by underlying universal mechanisms.

To the extent that a particular psychiatric condition is characterized by universal underlying aberrant mechanisms, and is spoken of in terms of typical medical metaphors, it will seem natural for the sick role to be provided by society, and for a pharmacological intervention to be used by a clinician. Indeed, there is overwhelming evidence that the use of psychotropic agents for severe psychiatric disorders, such as schizophrenia and bipolar disorder, has relieved much individual suffering and lowered the societal costs of these illnesses. On the other hand, to the extent that a behavioral phenomenon is not clearly linked to underlying aberrant mechanisms, and is spoken of in moral metaphors, it will seem natural for society to refuse the sick role, and for non-medical kinds of societal intervention to be employed. Indeed, it seems entirely appropriate for psychopharmacological interventions for particular kinds of deviant behavior (e.g., sexual deviancy) to remain matters of controversy and debate.

Some thinkers are more inclined than others to use medical or moral metaphors in relation to deviant human behavior. Pharmacological "Calvinists," for example, are likely to emphasize that humans must take responsibility for how they behave, and to argue that the use of psychotropic agents discourages patients from taking such responsibility. Pharmacological utopians, on the other hand, are likely to argue that, in view of the complexity of the brain-mind, medical metaphors are often appropriate for thinking about individual variations in behaving, thinking, and feeling, and that many individuals may well benefit from targeted psychopharmacological interventions that enable enhanced function. In any particular clinical case, it is important to weight the relevant facts and values in order to determine a judicious course of action.

Substance-use disorders are atypical exemplars of medical or psychiatric disorders insofar as the individual bears responsibility for having taken the first drink or dose. (A patient with pneumonia doesn't typically bear responsibility for having an infection.) At the same time, there is increasing evidence that substance use is characterized by genetic vulnerability, and that, once a substance has been consumed, aberrant neurobiological processes make it difficult to discontinue its use voluntarily. Therefore, it would seem quite reasonable, when scientific evidence exists for the efficacy and cost-effectiveness of a particular pharmacological intervention for substance dependence (e.g., methadone for opioid dependence), for a clinician to prescribe such an intervention. Furthermore, a judicious clinician may well prescribe an evidence-based psychopharmacological treatment to a particular patient with a substance-use disorder and, at the same time, insist that the individual take personal responsibility for adhering to the prescription.

In the case of sub-threshold conditions (for example, excessive shyness), there is a paucity of data as to whether pharmacological treatments are efficacious and cost effective. Arguably, the more evidence there was that shyness responded well to a particular agent, and that such an agent provided more benefits than costs, the more reasonable it would seem to employ a medical metaphor to describe excessive shyness and to prescribe a pharmacological intervention. In the absence of sufficient data, it may be prudent to be cautious about over-prescribing, and to advise a person with this set of traits to learn a range of social skills in order to function more successfully, thereby increasing the person's self-efficacy and adhering to the injunction of *primum non nocere*. A judicious clinician may, however, be swayed by a range of factors—for example, a family history of severe depression may encourage the use of a psychotropic, whereas if the patient has a strong explanatory model involving the need for social skills training a cognitive-behavioral approach may seem appropriate. There is a clear need for more data that would allow clinicians and patients to make more informed choices.

Conclusion

This chapter has noted that an important hypothesis in psychopharmacology proposes that specific psychotropics work for specific psychiatric disorders—so called "psychopharmacological dissection." A variant of this hypothesis suggests that response of a particular set of behavioral symptoms to a psychotropic distinguishes such symptoms from "normal" phenomena. There is increasing evidence that the first hypothesis is not always correct, but there is relatively little work on the psychopharmacology of sub-threshold symptomatology.

This chapter has put forward a naturalistic conceptual framework for addressing issues in psychiatric diagnosis. This begins by contrasting classical and critical concepts of categories, and then puts forward an integrative position that is based on findings in cognitive-affective neuroscience. This position can in turn be used to consider the debate between pharmacological Calvinism (which may adopt a moral metaphor of disorder) and psychotropic utopianism (which may emphasize a medical metaphor of disorder).

It seems reasonable to argue that psychiatric treatment of serious psychiatric disorders is justified, and that psychotropics are an acceptable kind of intervention. Even in the case of atypical disorders, such as substance dependence, there are good arguments for using medical interventions, including psychotropic agents. The use of psychotropics for sub-threshold phenomena, however, requires a judicious weighing of the relevant facts (which are often sparse) and values.

References

Bandelow, B., J. Zohar, E. Hollander, S. Kasper, H. Moller, and the WFSBP Task Force on Treatment Guidelines for Anxiety. 2002. World Federation of Societies of Biological Psychiatry (WFSBP) guidelines for the pharmacological treatment of anxiety, obsessive-compulsive and posttraumatic stress disorders. *World Journal of Biological Psychiatry* 3: 171–199.

Bhaskar, R. 1978. *A Realist Theory of Science*, second edition. Harvester.

Gottesman, I., and T. Gould. 2003. The endophenotype concept in psychiatry: Etymology and strategic intentions. *American Journal of Psychiatry* 160 (4): 636–645.

Ipser, J., P. Carey, Y. Dhansay, N. Fakier, S. Seedat, and D. Stein. 2006. Pharmacotherapy augmentation strategies in treatment-resistant anxiety disorders. *Cochrane Database of Systematic Reviews* 4, CD005473.

Kendler, K. 2011. Levels of explanation in psychiatric and substance use disorders: Implications for the development of an etiologically based nosology. *Molecular Psychiatry* 17: 11–21.

Klein, D. 1964. Delineation of two drug responsive anxiety syndromes. *Psychopharmacology* 5 (6): 397–408.

Klein, D. 1978. A proposed definition of mental illness. In *Critical Issues in Psychiatric Diagnosis*, ed. E. Spitzer and D. Klein. Raven.

Komossa, K., A. Depping, A. Gaudchau, W. Kissling, and S. Leucht. 2010. Second-generation antipsychotics for major depressive disorder and dysthymia. *Cochrane Database of Systematic Reviews* 12, CD008121.

Nesse, R., and D. Stein. 2012. Towards a genuinely medical model for psychiatric nosology. *BMC Medicine* 10: 5.

Parsons, T. 1951. *The Social System*. Free Press.

Phillips, J., A. Frances, M. Cerullo, J. Chardavoyne, H. Decker, M. First, et al. 2012. The six most essential questions in psychiatric diagnosis: A pluralogue. Part 4: General conclusion. Philosophy, ethics, and humanities in medicine. *Philosophy, Ethics, and Humanities in Medicine* 7: 14.

Rosch, E. 1978. Principles of categorization. In *Cognition and Categorization*, ed. E. Rosch and B. Lloyd. Erlbaum.

Rowe, C. 1986. *Plato: Phaedrus, with Translation and Commentary*. Aris and Philips.

Siever, J., and L. Davis. 1991. A psychobiological perspective on the personality disorders. *American Journal of Psychiatry* 148 (12): 1647–1658.

Sorsdahl, K., A. Flisher, Z. Wilson, and D. Stein. 2010. Explanatory models of mental disorders and treatment practices among traditional healers in Mpumulanga, South Africa. *African Journal of Psychiatry* 13 (4): 284–290.

Stein, D. 1991. Philosophy and the *DSM*-III. *Comprehensive Psychiatry* 32 (5): 404–415.

Stein, D. 1998. Philosophy of pharmacotherapy. *Perspectives in Biology and Medicine* 41: 200–211.

Stein, D. 2008. *Philosophy of Psychopharmacology*. Cambridge University Press.

Stein, D., and H. Mayberg. 2005. Placebo: The best pill of all. *CNS Spectrums* 10 (6): 440–442.

Zachar, P. 2000. Psychiatric disorders are not natural kinds. *Philosophy, Psychiatry, & Psychology* 7 (3): 167–182.

5   Beyond Natural Kinds: Toward a "Relevant" "Scientific" Taxonomy in Psychiatry

Peter Zachar

I began writing about natural kinds and psychiatric disorders in 1997. Just before submitting my first work on the subject for publication, I asked a former philosophy professor to read what I had written and tell me whether he found it adequately philosophical. He responded: "It's very philosophical, too much so. In using specialized concepts like 'natural kind,' people in psychiatry and psychology won't know or care what you are talking about."

The situation certainly has changed. Talk about natural kinds has become common in both psychiatry and psychology (Barrett 2006; Gelman 2003; Haslam 1998; Hyman 2010; Kramer 2009; Livesley 2012; Machery 2005). Why such an interest in natural kinds? One reason is that the concept of natural kind is relevant for establishing scientific validity. If something were a legitimate natural kind, then it would be a valid scientific kind, and psychiatrists and psychologists are very keen on establishing the validity of their disciplines.

Among psychiatrists and psychologists, validity questions are typically operationalized within one of two paradigms: the medical model and the psychometric model. Each paradigm offers a menu of "validators." The validators of the medical model include confirmed etiology, consistent time course, and treatment response. The validators of the psychometric model include internal consistency, predictive validity, and factorial validity. With these validation strategies in hand, tests of validity can be formulated as empirical questions. Two empirical questions that are asked are "Does the disorder have identifying biological markers?" and "Is the construct better modeled as a latent category or a latent dimension?" Often these empirically testable questions are considered promissory notes for an all-purpose answer to the validity question. It is doubtful, however, that an abstract concept such as validity can be reduced to one of these precise definitions. What talk about natural kinds does is make validity into a big question again, specifically by connecting the problem of diagnostic validity in psychiatry with related issues in the natural and biological sciences.

Natural Kinds, Biological Psychiatry, and Philosophy

How the concept of natural kind elevates the validity question into something deep and significant can be readily illustrated by examining some theoretical claims of biological psychiatry. Early in the twentieth century, chemists discovered that the number of protons in the nucleus (called the atomic number) can be used to identify elements. The distinctive properties of any element are lawful consequences of its atomic number. According to the biological psychiatrists, discovering the biological pathologies underlying mental disorders would do for the science of psychiatry what atomic numbers did for chemistry. The goal is to have a natural (rather than an arbitrary) classification that can be said to "carve nature at the joints."

The confidence that psychiatrists expressed in the promise of the biological psychiatry revolution of the 1980s was partly inspired by a concrete example: general paresis of the insane. At the beginning of the twentieth century, general paresis accounted for 25 percent of admissions to psychiatric hospitals. After scientists proved that paresis was the result of untreated syphilis and developed a successful treatment for syphilis, the disorder was eradicated.

In their push for a revolutionary shift from a psychoanalytic to a biomedical paradigm, biological psychiatrists also critically examined the psychological explanations of disorders such as Parkinson's Disease, correctly observing that those explanations were confabulations. For example, Jean-Martin Charcot claimed that Parkinson's Disease was an emotional reaction to ongoing political unrest (Roth and Kroll 1986). In fact, Parkinson's Disease results from the degeneration of dopamine pathways in the basal ganglia. The biological psychiatrists stated that psychological explanations for schizophrenia and depression would also be shown to be confabulations (Andreasen 1984; Winokur 1981). The most radical of these psychiatrists favored merging psychiatry and neurology into a single discipline. Consider this passage:

The lesson of psychiatry is that progress is inevitable and irrevocable from psychology to neurology, from mind to brain, never the other way around. Every medical advance leads to the list of diseases which may cause mental derangement. (MacAlpine and Hunter 1974, cited on p. 39 of Hill, Murray, and Thorely 1986)

It has probably not been lost on readers that the biological psychiatrists' argument about psychological explanation parallels that of the eliminative materialists (Zachar 2000c). Paul Churchland argues that pain and sensations are identical with brains states, but beliefs and desires are not. He states that because beliefs and desires cannot be accounted for in terms of brain states, they will have no place in a successful scientific psychology. They will have the same fate as phlogiston and epicycles—concepts that were once used in scientific explanations but came to be seen as referring to nothing real (that is, they are not natural kinds). Here is Churchland on psychiatry:

Imipramine controls depression, *lithium* controls mania, and *chlorpromazine* controls schizophrenia. Imperfectly, it must be said, but the qualified success of these drugs lends strong support to the view that the victims of mental illness are the victims primarily of sheer chemical circumstances, whose origins are more metabolic and biological, than they are social or psychological. (1984, p. 145)

According to the eliminativists, no version of psychiatry that formulates disorder constructs using folk-psychological terms can discover legitimate natural kinds.

In this chapter I will examine different viewpoints on the possibility of establishing the validity of psychiatric disorders through discovering natural kinds. Before proceeding further, let me summarize my perspective on natural kinds and psychiatric disorders—a perspective that will be articulated further in what follows. *Although it may be empirically possible to calibrate a disorder construct so that it meets all the criteria that have been used to demarcate "natural kinds," it is not necessary to do so in order to establish validity and is not the only option for making scientific progress.*

I will begin by expanding on a previously published analysis of the concept of natural kind (Zachar 2008). I will then survey three general approaches to natural kinds in psychiatry, specifically the essentialist perspective of Jerome Wakefield, two non-essentialist perspectives (those of Rachel Cooper and Richard Boyd), and three approaches that are suspicious of the tradition of natural kinds (those of Nelson Goodman, Ian Hacking, and Peter Zachar). Next, I will examine the relevance of the features associated with natural kinds to a psychiatric taxonomy.

Natural Kind as a Cluster Concept

Rachel Cooper (2007) notes that when philosophers adopt different definitions of natural kind, they often talk past one another. Her point is an excellent one. Insofar as "natural kind" is what statisticians call a cluster concept, disagreement is almost inevitable. By "cluster concept" I mean that the concept of natural kind encompasses a cluster of features, and philosophers emphasize or minimize different features as they see fit.

The features commonly associated with the concept of natural kind are occurring naturally, operating according to rules (lawfulness), supporting induction, and being discrete. Natural kinds are also conceptualized within an essentialist framework. Features of natural kinds associated with the essentialist framework include the possession of causally important underlying properties that are also necessary and sufficient criteria for identification. The judgment that the kind "carves nature at the joints" is also typically paired with essentialism. Finally, and quite importantly for the validity issue, natural kinds are considered to be things about which scientists can speak with authority.

In the following subsections, I elaborate on these criteria and briefly review problematic aspects of each feature in question.

Features directly associated with natural kind

Occurring naturally is the feature that non-philosophers are most likely to emphasize. What most psychiatrists or clinical psychologists mean by agreeing that bipolar disorder and autism are natural kinds is that they occur naturally. Being labeled autistic, they would claim, is more like being diagnosed with smallpox (a natural category) than like being classified as living below the poverty line (a social construction).

What is problematic about naturally occurring kinds is that the concept of "natural" is vague, meaning that it has borderline cases (Van Deemter 2010). Although heroin and pure sugar are more natural than polyester, they are both products of technology. Chemical elements such as gold are paradigmatic natural kinds, but all elements with a proton number greater than 94 exist only when made in a lab. They are even called synthetic elements. We have a tendency to consider cooking and clothing to be technological products, but they predate modern human evolution by hundreds of thousands of years (via *Homo erectus*) and therefore form part of the natural *Homo sapiens* environment.

Throughout the twentieth century, the most problematic aspect of naturalness—that it is not value free—was a subject of intense political debates about naturalness (e.g., debates about the roles of men and women, sexual orientation, and family structure). Uncovering the value assumptions behind assertions of naturalness is one of the services provided by social constructionists.

The second feature—operating according to rules—states that natural kinds possess regularity. The most important rules are scientific laws that go beyond mere regularity and into necessity. To say that copper conducts electricity as a matter of scientific law is to say that anything that is copper must conduct electricity. In this view, legitimate natural kinds are governed by laws.

In recent decades, there has been ongoing philosophical debate about the usefulness of modeling scientific knowledge on the construct of law (Cartwright 1983, 1999; Giere 1999). Even if positing "laws of nature" is informative for thinking about physics, it is not clear that it is helpful elsewhere. For example, scientific laws are supposed to be universal—true at all times and all places ("spatiotemporally unrestricted"). As Ghiselin (1974) and Hull (1976) argued, biological species are typically adapted to specific environments, and environments change. As environments change, new species appear and old species go extinct. Insofar as species are therefore "spatiotemporally restricted," there can be no scientific laws proper about species. The same might be said about many objects of the "special sciences," including the sciences of psychology and psychiatry.

If lawfulness is a necessary feature of a natural kind, then there may be no natural kinds proper in biology, psychology, or psychiatry. Another possibility is that the concept of natural kind doesn't require explaining kinds with respect to universal scientific laws. This leads us to a discussion of the third feature.

Supporting induction is a feature of natural kinds that most philosophers emphasize. We lose information about individuals when we classify them into groups; we also gain information about individuals by classifying them as the same kind of thing. We learn more about "schizophrenia" by studying commonalities between particular cases. Understanding shared features allows us to make inferences about the kind in general. The important inferences about kinds that we want to make are inferences about how they come to be (causal explanation), what members of the kind are like now (description), and what to expect of them in the future (prediction).

In psychiatry, one strategy for defining good kinds is to require that members of the kind be highly homogeneous. Copper is a good kind because different samples of copper do not vary with respect to physical properties. Species are less good kinds. As Hull (1988) notes, organisms that belong to a clearly demarcated lineage may vary considerably. Likewise, one of the difficulties with making inferences about psychological and psychiatric kinds is that they are sensitive to environmental variability, and as a result psychological kinds tend to be heterogeneous. Copper wire behaves precisely the same in the United States as in China; schizophrenia and depression do not. There is some evidence that cases of schizophrenia tend to have better outcomes in developing countries than in industrialized countries (Vahia and Vahia 2008).

If natural kinds are defined with respect to inductive potential, however, the list of potential natural kinds becomes extremely long and the concept of natural kind loses some of its special status. One can make fairly valid inferences about many kinds of things. Electrons, steel, bronze, mitosis, the Krebs cycle, market economies, Libertarians, Scientologists, and female psychiatrists could all be considered natural kinds.

The fourth defining feature of natural kinds is discreteness. Kendell and Jablensky (2003) emphasize discreteness in their definition of valid psychiatric disorders. They argue that valid disorders should be separated from other disorders and from normality by a zone of rarity (a gap between the groups where no cases occur). If no zone of rarity exists, there should at least be a qualitative difference between members of the kind and others (such as plaques and tangles in Alzheimer's Disease, but not in other kinds of dementia).

The psychologist and philosopher Paul Meehl (1995) also demarcated natural kinds by the presence of objective boundaries between members and non-members—what some would call a real class. Examples of such categories include even numbers and U.S. senators. One either is or is not a member of these categories; there are no interforms.

One of Meehl's favorite examples of natural kinds was species. There are gophers and there are chipmunks, he said, but there are no gophmunks. However, as long-standing interest in missing links demonstrates, species are the kind of thing where interforms do occur (Zachar 2008). There are tigers and there are lions, but there are also the interforms ligers and tigons. In addition, there are wholphins, zorses, plumcots, and tangelos. The problem with discreteness is that it is an optional feature at best. Having fuzzy rather than discrete boundaries does not disqualify something's potentially being a natural kind.

Features of natural kind associated with essentialism

Essentialism is a more multi-factorial and abstract cluster than "natural kind." The psychologist Nick Haslam (2000) has developed a model that lists seven features of essentialist thinking. The more of these features one attributes to a particular category, the more essentialist one's thinking about that category. In the twentieth century, very few philosophers of science were willing to advocate essentialism; that seems to be changing a bit, at least in the physical sciences (Bird 2007; Ellis 2001).

In philosophy, essences played important roles in both classical and medieval versions of the Aristotelian tradition. These essences had both causal and classificatory (sortal) roles. The causal role referred to the presence of underlying properties that determined and sustained visible properties (for example, what makes an acorn grow into an oak and not an elm). Because these underlying properties were supposed to be unchanging, they were identified with the nature of a kind—that which makes it be what it is.

After Scholasticism was superseded by natural philosophy in the seventeenth century, the essential hidden properties (which Locke called "real essences") came to be identified with underlying structural properties. Candidate properties include the number of protons in the nucleus for chemical elements, the genotype for species, and the underlying biopathology for diseases. One's ability to make inferences about members of a natural kind is explained with reference to their shared underlying properties. For example, Michael Devitt (2010) claims that *dog* is a natural kind. Being a dog "explains" why Fido has the features he does, and that explanation is to be found in studying the intrinsic underlying properties Fido shares with other dogs. The same explanatory significance, says Devitt, is not associated with being a cousin.

With respect to the classificatory role, if one can identify the essence (or nature) of a thing, one can (in theory) correctly determine its place in the order of the world. According to essentialism, if you want to know whether any putative chemical substance, organism, or disease is a true member of a valid natural kind, you should check whether the causally important underlying properties are present; such properties are necessary and sufficient conditions for kindhood.

One important philosophical implication of essentialism (and natural kinds) is that, because things supposedly have stable inner natures, there is a correct classification (the list of true natural kinds) out there waiting to be discovered. In poetic terms, nature can be "carved at the joints." Such a viewpoint is particularly evident among those biological psychiatrists who adopt disease realism. According to them, all valid psychiatric disorders are diseases of the brain; once psychiatrists discover the underlying pathology, they will be able to diagnose disorders with a high degree of reliability and will know where to target their interventions.

Let me mention two problems with using the criteria of essentialism to define natural kinds. First, rarely is a single underlying property a necessary and sufficient determinant of a kind, and even different combinations of causally important properties do not determine outcomes without many additional factors being involved. Consider the genetics of psychiatric disorders: any single gene increases the chances that a disorder will develop only slightly (Kendler 2005). Rather than being a causally important internal property, DNA is more like a collection of ingredients for organizing recipes that get applied in development. Second, what counts as the most important internal property often depends on an earlier decision about what to classify; it is not only a matter of discovery. For example, in nuclear physics it is important to distinguish between hydrogen and deuterium; the number of protons is not the crucial internal property (both have one proton in their nucleus). The number of neutrons in the nucleus is more important (zero in hydrogen atoms, one in deuterium atoms). The meaning of essence can readily be downgraded to refer to most important distinguishing feature, but one has to wonder how much of metaphysical essentialism remains.

Natural kinds and the authority of science

Being subject to scientific authority is a feature of natural kinds that is rarely discussed in the literature, although it was an important aspect of Saul Kripke's (1972) and Hilary Putnam's (1975) revival of the natural-kind concept in the 1970s. The re-introduction of natural kinds into philosophy came upon the heels of Kuhnian skepticism about the stability of scientific knowledge. The concept of natural kinds provided a framework for thinking about stability across generations of scientists. For Kripke and Putnam, scientific discoveries about shared underlying properties "govern" our understanding of kinds.

Scientific discoveries can sometimes require slight modifications of our classification; for example, early-onset Alzheimer's Disease and what used to be called senile dementia are associated with the same underlying pathology—they are now both called "Alzheimer's." Scientific discoveries can also be quite revolutionary for our classifications; for example, discoveries about the nature of memory and the powers of suggestibility led to suspicions about the validity of multiple-personality disorder, and the ability to make it go away by using different interview strategies led to its deletion/reformulation (McHugh 2008). I will return to the issue of scientific authority at the end of the chapter.

Three Perspectives on Natural kinds in the Philosophy of Psychiatry

Wakefield's black-box essentialism

Arguably, the most important philosophical theory about the nature of psychiatric disorders is Jerome Wakefield's (1992, 1999a,b) harmful-dysfunction (HD) model, which acknowledges the Szaszian claims about the evaluative nature of psychiatric diagnosis without abandoning scientific realism about psychiatric disorders as Thomas Szasz (1961) did in calling mental illness a myth.

Adopting an evolutionary-historical understanding of natural function, Wakefield claims that the presence or absence of a dysfunction is a factual matter. How so? Natural functions, Wakefield says, were selected for during evolution because of their contribution to the survival of the organism. The reasons why such functions exist are matters of historical fact. Therefore, evaluative statements about functions, such as "the pancreas should secrete insulin to regulate blood sugar," can be translated into objective, factual statements about evolutionary history. The pancreas secretes insulin because of the selection pressures that were in play during its long evolution. If natural functions are objective, so are dysfunctions. According to Wakefield, however, the presence of an objective dysfunction is not sufficient for the attribution of "disorder" status. In addition to expressing an objective dysfunction, for something to be a disorder there must also be evidence that the condition in question is harmful to its bearer. Evidence of harm includes suffering (e.g., the emotional pain of depression) and impairment (e.g., inability perform one's job as a consequence of psychomotor retardation).

The HD analysis is, therefore, a type of conceptual essentialism. The presence of an objective dysfunction combined with harm constitutes an Aristotelian conceptual essence—a clear and intuitively plausible articulation of the concept of a disorder. Wakefield's conceptual analysis has been so informative that the architects of the *DSM-IV* definition of mental disorder, especially Robert Spitzer and Michael First, are among its most committed advocates (Spitzer and Wakefield 1999; Wakefield and First 2003; Wakefield, Schmitz, First, and Horwitz 2009).

Wakefield's (2004) black-box essentialism follows the scenario proposed by Putnam and Kripke. At some point in history there occurs a "baptismal" event in which a disorder is clinically observed and named. "This is psychopathy," said Hervey Cleckley (1941). "This is autism," said Leo Kanner (1935). If the original disorder concept can be developed into a proper scientific construct (one based on an objective dysfunction), the clinician's original concept can be said to have indirectly referred to the objective dysfunction all along. Until those discoveries are made, the essence is in a black box.

With respect to the natural-kind cluster, Wakefield is essentialist in focusing on shared underling properties of disorders, but the feature of essentialism to which he has the strongest commitment is carving nature at the joints (or, to put it another way, distinguishing valid psychiatric disorders from normal problems in living). The original purpose of the HD analysis was to help resolve the problem of false-positive diagnoses. A false positive occurs when a disorder is diagnosed but is not actually present. One famous example is Samuel Cartwright's claim that slaves who had a compulsion to escape from their condition of servitude had a disorder termed drapetomania (Caplan, McCartney, and Sisti 2004). The HD analysis was introduced to help mental-health professionals think clearly about what disorders really are so that such errors can be avoided.

There is also a disciplinary or guild aspect to Wakefield's commitments that philosophers may miss. Wakefield is a trained social worker. One of the important insights of the profession of social work is that many distresses and life problems are understandable responses to one's psychosocial environment. Consider a 27-year-old depressed woman who is raising five children, all under the age of seven years, has no meaningful activity outside the home, lacks social support, and is under financial stress. Rather than locating the problem inside her (a mental illness) and proscribing Prozac to help her adapt to this situation, a more elegant solution would be to improve her living conditions.

In contrast, the work of psychologists and psychiatrists tends to be office-based. One of the things that psychologists in training have to learn is that they cannot hope that a client's boyfriend will stop hitting her or that her father will criticize her less often. Thinking "if only these external things could change, the problem will go away" is paralyzing to therapy. In office-based work, one has to focus on what it is that the client contributes to the problem and intervene there (e.g., exploring assumptions and feelings about relationships between men and women).

Both of these approaches are valuable, and neither offers a "magic-bullet" solution. They also influence professional beliefs about where the "joint" between problems inside the person and negative living conditions may lie. None of us should be in the business of telling people they should accept their station in life, nor can people always change the world to suit their own needs—and it is important to find healthy ways to adapt.

Interestingly, Wakefield's model is more subject to the traditional empiricist critique of essentialism than are many essentialist models. The traditional critique was offered by Locke, who stated that the real essences of things are underlying microstructural properties but such properties are not observable. It is fair to say that Locke underestimated what kinds of observations advancing technology would allow us to make. But natural psychological functions pose a problem that electrons and DNA do not. As some critics of evolutionary psychology have pointed out, there is almost no empirical evidence in biology and paleontology about the evolution of the human brain, and even less about the selection pressures responsible for the development of specific psychological capacities (Richardson 2007). According to this updated empiricist critique, what were once factual historical events are undiscoverable, and therefore natural psychological functions in the evolutionary sense are not observable facts at all.

Kinds-in-science arguments I: Natural kinds

"Kinds-in-science" is a term used by Cooper (2005, 2007) to describe a group of non-essentialist approaches that emphasize the ability of scientific kinds to support generalizations. The two approaches explored here attempt to explain why scientific kinds support induction.

Cooper's extensional account

One of the arguments that Cooper (2007) uses to demarcate natural kinds is an extensional argument. According to this argument, chemical elements and biological species are natural kinds (i.e., are part of the extension of the term "natural kind"), so whatever it means for them to be a kind is what a natural kind is. A similar argument is offered by Paul Griffiths (1997).

What does it mean to be a natural kind according to Cooper? To be a natural kind is for the members of the group to possess objective similarities that systematically influence other properties associated with the kind. Cooper has a very liberal notion of similarity—the theoretically important properties do not have to be identical, nor do the outcomes. For example, the standard taxonomic approaches in biology would not consider higher biological taxa such as mammals to be natural kinds, but on Cooper's account mammals do form a natural kind. Because of similarities among mammals, we can make generalizations about them (e.g., that mammals give birth to live young), and the taxon can be used in scientific explanations (e.g., that mammals are emotional creatures because of their extended dependency on caretakers for survival).

Cooper asks whether psychiatric disorders should be considered natural kinds along the lines of species and elements. In view of her broad definition of natural kind, it is not surprising that she answers in the positive. As she notes, there would be no reason to diagnose someone with depression or schizophrenia if the diagnosis was not informative.

An equally broad view of kinds is quite explicit in psychiatric diagnosis. For example, one of the founding fathers of contemporary biological psychiatry, Samuel Guze, states that "the value of clinical experience is based on the assumption that the current clinical problem shares crucial attributes with past clinical problems[,] so that it may be helpful to approach the current problem with concepts similar to those that seemed helpful in the past," and that "if similar phenomena differing in time or place have no dependable, valid, shared crucial attributes that we can describe, it is hard to see what we might mean by the value of experience" (Guze 1992, p. 38).

Boyd's Homeostatic Property Clusters

The most important recent account of natural kinds is Richard Boyd's (1989, 1991) notion of homeostatic property clusters (HPCs). Boyd's goal was to advocate for scientific realism. To do that, he adopted the "abductive" or inference-to-the-best-explanation strategy for defending scientific realism. How are we to account for the success of scientific theories? The abductive answer to this question is that successful theories must be at least approximately true. Furthermore, the kinds to which theories refer can be considered to be approximately valid.

The primary application of the HPC model has been to species. The reality of the species category has been a vexing question ever since Darwin expressed his doubts that "species" was a real category in nature. Over the years, taxonomists have proposed a variety of species models. They include the biological species model of the systematists (Mayr 1988), the phylogenetic species model of the cladists (Ridley 1986), and the phenetic species model of the numerical taxonomists (Sneath and Sokal 1973). Each of these models carves the species domain in slightly different ways, and no single model accounts for all the things that scientists call species.

One implication of the species problem, echoing Darwin, is that the overall species category (the category that includes all species models) is not a natural kind. Tiger, lions, and bears may be natural kinds but not the category of species itself. A similar argument, contra Wakefield, can be made for the global category of psychiatric disorder. Psychiatric disorder is a disjunctive category or collection of very distinct conditions. Bipolar I disorder, conduct disorder, and anorexia may be natural kinds, but the general category of psychiatric disorder itself is not a natural kind (Flanagan and Blashfield 2000).

Another implication of the species problem, according to Darwin's theory, is that there are no such things as natural groups of organisms united by an underlying essential nature. Boyd's insight was that a species such as tiger is a cluster of co-occurring properties that supports induction. Those features, however, need not be explained with reference to a shared inherent essence. A variety of homeostatic mechanisms can result in the properties associated with any cluster hanging together.

In psychiatry, mechanisms can include underlying properties (for example, alterations in hippocampal volumes correlated with exposure to trauma), systematic connections between properties at the same level (e.g., high anxiety leads to dissociation and confusion, the associated lack of control results in panic attacks, ongoing panic attacks increase background levels of anxiety), and external conditions (aftershocks following an earthquake maintain traumatic states). All the mechanisms need not be operative for every member of the cluster; therefore, there will be variation within the cluster, and no property or fixed set of properties will be necessary and sufficient. As a result, membership in the cluster can itself be indeterminate, and some individuals will be closer to the fuzzy boundary of the cluster. What is important is that the various properties of the kind hang together over time, and *they do so because they are the outcomes of shared causal processes.*

Boyd's notion of natural kind was also intended to be consistent with Wittgenstein's non-essentialist family resemblance model, a goal that has important implications for the validity of psychiatric classification. Beginning with *DSM*-III in 1987, psychiatrists borrowed the term "polythetic category" from the numerical taxonomists to describe their classifications. In polythetic as opposed to monothetic classification, in order for an individual to be a member of a cluster, a certain number of criteria have to be met, but not all the criteria. If there are nine criteria for a disorder and five of them have to be met for a diagnosis, any combination of five criteria will do. Polythetic diagnostic categories can therefore be considered to refer to a family of related states.

The polythetic system has led psychiatrists and psychologists to criticize the *DSM* for its heterogeneity, pointing out, for example, that there are hundreds ways to meet criteria for borderline personality disorder (Krueger and Eaton 2010; Trull and Durrett 2005; Widiger and Sanderson 1995). From the HPC standpoint, if BPD supports induction and the best current evidence suggests that this cluster might result from shared causal processes, then it is potentially a legitimate natural kind. The same could be true for the shared causal processes that lead to depression and generalized anxiety disorder (Kendler, Neale, Kessler, and Heath 1992), and for those that lead to schizophrenia and bipolar disorder (Lichtenstein et al. 2009).

An even stronger argument for tolerating heterogeneous categories can be found in Boyd's HPC model. The argument is that the "real kinds" are not always the most homogeneous kinds. How so? Boyd (1989) asserts that the causal processes that produce species also produce varieties, incipient species, hybrids, and so on. Any taxonomy that makes species more homogeneous by ignoring inconvenient outcomes of the causal processes is not a natural classification. In some cases, the same may be true for psychiatric disorders.

Kinds-in-Science Arguments II: Beyond Natural Kinds

The three approaches reviewed here do not contend that science requires a concept of natural kind, or, to be more exact, they state that what counts as a good scientific kind is not well explained by the theory of natural kinds.

Goodman's relevant kinds

Unlike Cooper or Boyd, the nominalist philosopher Nelson Goodman (1978) does not advocate for natural kinds or scientific realism, but he does offer a theory of relevant kinds. According to Goodman, the many things of the world are similar to one another in a multitude of ways. We classify by lumping things together, or by splitting extant categories apart. We weight properties in terms of importance, order properties relative to one another, simplify properties for ease of use, and ignore or distort properties. Observed similarities between things are actual, not fictional, but there is some selection involved in what is emphasized. As a result, the class of relevant kinds is rather large. Furthermore, there is no *a priori*, pre-determined list of relevant kinds out there waiting to be discovered. We inherit lists, systems, and theoretical conceptualizations of kinds that have been used in the past, and we continue to use them in the present.

What counts as a scientifically relevant kind? Goodman is a minimalist in this respect. Good scientific kinds "support induction"; as Goodman (1983) puts it, they have properties that are "projectible."

"Projectible" means that if we observe certain properties in a subset of the kind (for example, anhedonia and loss of appetite in 100 cases of major depressive disorder) we can infer that these properties will occur in other instances of that kind. A projectible property can also be used to confirm the generalizations we make about a kind (given appropriate background theories about the relationship between evidence and hypotheses for the kind in question). For example, Hamlet's consideration of suicide would be taken as confirming evidence for a generalization about suicidal ideation among depressives (a projectible feature), but no one would say that Hamlet's skepticism about his father's ghost counts as evidence for a generalization about beliefs in the supernatural among depressives (not a projectible feature). What counts as a relevant scientific kind (with projectible properties) depends on the framework.

Hacking's good scientific kinds

Ian Hacking (1990, 1991, 2002) advocates for a Goodman-style approach from a Foucauldian perspective. His perspective is best exemplified by his interest in styles of scientific reasoning. According to Hacking, styles of reasoning are historical developments. A new style is like a tool that makes new kinds of knowledge possible. The style of reasoning to which the concept of natural kind belongs is called *ordering diversity by taxonomy*.

Ordering diversity by taxonomy is the style of scientific reasoning that received the least amount of attention from A. C. Crombie (1994), the inspiration for Hacking's own list. It involves finding systematic rules that can be used to group things together. These rules are almost always conceived as lying hidden behind observations. Once a menu of kinds is accepted, there is a tendency to see things in terms of that menu, and to take those "seeings" to be confirmatory.

What is fascinating, as Crombie's work shows, is that many of the problems and viewpoints expressed in the contemporary debates about classification and natural kinds are immediately evident in Locke, Leibniz, Linnaeus, and Buffon. Our philosophical frameworks continually evolve and change, but within these frameworks many of the ideas that we debate have long histories.

In the seventeenth and eighteenth centuries, the existence of a natural order was assumed. The natural order was also considered to be hierarchically organized, from simple organisms at the bottom up to God at the top—a concept termed "the scale of nature." The important taxonomic question was whether the natural order is like a preconfigured boxology the rules of which are waiting to be discovered or whether we impose a boxology on the natural order—which is more accurately seen as collection of individuals that overlap in a variety of ways. Here, speaking for the latter view, is one of the great scientific writers of his day, Georges Leclerc (comte de Buffon):

[G]oing deeper into this idea, one sees clearly that it is impossible to give a general system, a perfect method, not only for natural history as a whole, but even for a single one of its branches; for . . . it is necessary to divide. . . . But nature progresses by unknown gradations, and consequently she cannot lend herself wholly to those divisions . . . ; so that there will be a large number of intermediate species and bipartite objects which one does not know how to place, and which necessarily upset the plan for a general system. (quoted on p. 1282 of Crombie 1994)

In a similar manner, Hacking rejects "natural kind" as a legitimate term for all of nature's inherent boxes. According to Hacking, natural-kind accounts of minerals, plants, animal species, and diseases are distinct theories that share a family resemblance, but they do not form a unitary coherent concept. Hacking (2007) suggests that the tradition of natural kinds, like Humpty Dumpty, has fallen off the wall and cannot be put back together.

Practical kinds

Also in the tradition of Goodman and Hacking is the *practical-kinds* model of psychiatric classification (Zachar 2000a,b, 2002; Zachar and Kendler 2007), which conforms to the kinds-in-science view by saying that kinds are useful to the extent that they support induction (to a greater or a lesser degree).

The practical-kinds model also emphasizes that discovery of fact contributes greatly to progress in classification, but discovery alone cannot tell us how to classify. For example, discovering that a mild form of cognitive disorganization (schizotypy) is common in families of people with schizophrenia was an important finding that highlighted an objective feature of the world. Should schizotypy, therefore, be classified as mild manifestation of a unitary schizophrenic spectrum (a genetic grouping)? Another possibility is that should it be classified as a premorbid personality style that represents a vulnerability to the mental illness of schizophrenia. In which box should it be placed?

If the goal is to develop genetically based classifications, nosologists may decide that schizotypy and schizophrenia should be classified as being of the same kind (because they result from the same "genetic" causes). If the goal is to identify serious mental illnesses, schizophrenia may be classified as a distinct kind that appears only after a severity threshold has been crossed. Apart from goals for classification and theoretical frameworks, neither of these demarcations is privileged in and of itself.

From the practical-kinds perspective, classification is not just a matter of finding the proper method that can be mechanistically applied to discover the real categories; rather, classifications are developed through a process in which competing or even contradictory goals (e.g., treatment goals, research priorities, and disciplinary standards of validity) are balanced against one another in a search of a satisfactory adjustment that works in practice.

Are Psychiatric Disorders Natural Kinds?

Now that we have an adequate grasp of the different perspectives on the role that natural kinds should play in a psychiatric taxonomy, let us return to the features of the natural-kind cluster and see how they might be employed in psychiatry. In this section I will not consider occurring naturally, subject to scientific laws, or discreteness. The first feature is vague and contentious; the second is less relevant for biology, psychology, and psychiatry; and discreteness is not a requirement for the cluster approach to kinds that I am advocating.

Supporting induction

The minimal criterion of kindhood is *supporting induction*. We immediately get into trouble with respect to psychiatric disorders because most categories of psychiatric disorder are heterogeneous—what Goodman called "imperfect communities." Even for those disorders that are considered serious mental illnesses, such as schizophrenia, bipolar disorder, and major depressive disorder, generalizations about how they come to be and what to expect of them in the future are tenuous. Causality is multi-factorial, and the outcomes can be quite variable (Gottesman 1991; Kendler, Gardner, and Prescott 2002, 2006; Tohen et al. 2009).

Currently, the properties that define psychiatric kinds are symptoms. For major depressive disorder, symptoms include depressed mood, loss of interest in pleasure, and difficulty concentrating. Even with heterogeneous polythetic symptom categories, however, induction is still possible. Some examples of useful generalizations about depression are that women are twice as likely to get depressed as men, that every new episode of depression increases the risk that another episode will occur in the future, and that the presence of stress in the past six months often precipitates a depressive episode.

Suppose we accept the minimalist feature of supporting induction as adequate for natural-kind status. The issue that then bedevils psychiatric taxonomy is the problem of selecting broad versus narrow classifications. For example, it has been argued that the narrow category of depression and generalized anxiety disorder (GAD) are over-specified (Hyman 2010).

The problem is that some people fit into the depression box, some fit into the GAD box, and many fit wholly or partially into both. One currently popular option is to lump major depressive disorder and generalized anxiety disorder together as the "internalizing" spectrum. There is empirical evidence favoring such a broad classification (Achenbach 1995; Krueger 1999; Watson 2005). Furthermore, broad kinds are more reliably diagnosed (Williams et al. 1992). Psychiatrists would agree that a patient is on the internalizing spectrum more easily than they would agree that a patient is depressed or anxious. (This lumping is potentially a conceptual improvement as well because the high level of negative emotionality common to the internalizing disorders is what Quine (1969) called a theoretically relevant property for defining kinds.)

Broad categories such as internalizing spectrum typically license correspondingly broad inferences. One inference is that selective serotonin-reuptake inhibitors (SSRIs) and other drugs that reduce high levels of negative emotionality should be effective throughout the spectrum. These drugs are, therefore, not "anti-depressants," but attenuators of negative emotionality (fear, anger, sadness, and so on). This is a pretty useful inference. However, the narrower categories of depressed, anxious, obsessive, traumatized, and phobic remain inductively useful. For example, the treatment called "exposure with response prevention" works for obsessive-compulsive disorder but not for depression (Rowa, Antony, and Swinson 2007). It might also be most practical to adopt a mid-level generalization and say that exposure via psychotherapy works with most fear-based disorders (obsessive-compulsive disorder, phobias, trauma), whereas medication is less useful.

In biological taxonomies the issue of the broad versus the narrow is called the problem of ranking. For example, it is difficult to decisively sort the hundreds of kinds of salamanders into ranks—varieties, incipient species, species, and so on. It is even more difficult to choose among the large number of overlapping possibilities for higher-level classifications. Take the categories predator and mammal. Each of these higher-order categories has the potential to be inductively useful, but they sort species differently—for example, the category predator contains wolves, bats, and eagles, whereas the category mammal contains wolves and bats but not eagles.

The ranking problem is equally complicated in psychiatry. Consider the classification of personality disorders. Researchers have discovered that patients diagnosed with one personality disorder can usually be diagnosed with two or three others, but one cannot thereby conclude that such patients have four distinct personality disorders (Widiger et al. 1991).

The fact that categories of personality disorder do not seem to be distinct "species" has led to the development of an alternative approach to classifying personality pathology: the *dimensional model* (Clark, Watson, and Reynolds 1995; Livesley 2003; Widiger and Sanderson 1995). Proponents of this model use statistical techniques such as factor analysis to discover latent structures that underlie the various symptoms of personality disorders. In this way a large number of symptoms can be accounted for by a smaller number of statistically independent dimensions. The goal of factor analysis is to use these non-overlapping dimensions to model the symptom space of personality disorders comprehensively.

In a model introduced by Livesley (2003), once the pathological dimensions have been identified, patients meeting criteria for a broad category called "personality disorder" are distinguished from one another by their position on the dimensions. Candidate dimensions include narcissism, impulsivity, anxiousness, social detachment, and hostility (Clark and Livesley 1994; Widiger, Livesley, and Clark 2009).

It might seem that the dimensional model would eliminate the proliferation of categories or boxes that plagues any emphasis on "inductive potential," but it might make the problem even worse. A big unknown in psychiatric taxonomy is how mental-health professionals would make inferences from multi-dimensional profiles. One thing is certain: Humans are terrible at knowing how to weight and combine different types of information (Garb 1998; Meehl 1972). Asking them to integrate information from multi-dimensional profiles is an invitation to wild diagnosis. If the history of personality testing can be considered a reliable guide, multi-dimensional profiles will be used to construct types that can be individually researched—for example, "high on narcissism and impulsivity, low on anxiousness" versus "high on social detachment and anxiousness, low on hostility."

Depending on the number of dimensions in the profile (and what counts as high and low), the number of potential types of personality disorder about which inferences can be made may be too large to classify succinctly. No doubt sets of personality types can also be grouped into inductively useful higher-order clusters.

Causally important internal properties

So the various categories of psychiatric disorder are imperfect communities. Does that mean that the ground should be ceded to the nominalists and pragmatists? The answer is No—at least, not automatically. One of the shortcomings of a practical-kinds approach is that it is descriptive rather than prescriptive. As Kendler, Zachar, and Craver (2011) argue, the practical-kinds approach calls attention to the adjustments and compromises that actually occur in classification, but says little about how to make progress. In this light, they advocate a more ambitious program for developing causally based classifications. It is important (and practical) to understand "why" we can make inferences about members of a kind, and to use that information in developing scientific classifications.

Causal classifications in medicine typically emphasize discovering underlying pathological processes. Does such a program re-introduce an essentialist framework? Not necessarily, but it does leave the door to an essentialist framework open. Almost everyone would agree that it would be convenient to have a list of all valid psychiatric disorders, to discover their causal essences, and to cure them. Unfortunately, these discoveries have not occurred. One reasons is that biological and psychological kinds tend to be outcomes of the interaction (over time) of a large number of internal and external causes (Kendler 2005; Kendler et al. 1992).

Rather than waiting for the discovery of the inherent essences that seem to be always just around the next corner, Boyd's property-cluster approach is probably more appropriate for conceptualizing (most) psychiatric disorders. If there are no essences but there are mechanisms that produce and sustain disorders, information about those mechanisms will suggest new classification strategies and new treatment possibilities.

The elephant in the room: Carving nature at the joints

The philosophical question that is most often asked when natural kinds are put on the table is whether such kinds exist independent of human activities and interests. But what, exactly, does "independent of human interests" mean? According to Boyd, the crucial question is whether the kind is individuated by objective causal processes. The outcome of those processes should determine what we take to be real kinds in nature.

Many philosophers believe that the important causal processes can be modeled as mechanisms. It is important, then, to understand how mechanisms are demarcated as distinct kinds. Boyd's model of natural kinds assumes that individuating causal processes is not problematic, but others have expressed doubts. Carl Craver (2009), for example, argues that identifying kinds of mechanisms requires appealing to practical considerations in addition to the objective, mechanistic structure of the world.

Let's look more closely at how Carver's analysis might apply to psychiatry. Disorders such as depression and schizophrenia are the products of causal processes operating at multiple levels of analysis—genetic, anatomical, physiological, cognitive-affective, social-psychological, and cultural. Which mechanisms count? An explanation that contained all mechanisms and all their interactions would be unwieldy, so some weighting, ignoring, and distorting in Goodman's senses of those words are required.

Background assumptions can occasionally play a role in how the causal structure of the world is divided up. A mechanism may be given more weight by conceptual fiat. For example, an implicit materialist ontology might make someone weight genes higher than cognitions, and, therefore, be more prone to carve the world up in one way rather than another. Such implicit ontologies might well be influenced by training as a psychiatrist, a psychologist, or a social worker, insofar as psychiatrists, psychologists, and social workers make slightly different generalizations to help them achieve their respective professional goals.

Craver makes the important point that the problem of broad versus narrow classifications (or the ranking problem) goes all the way down to the task of discovering underlying mechanisms. Consider strokes. One could model the mechanisms underlying a stroke at a high level of abstraction (loss of oxygen leads to slowing of the Na^+K^+ pump, accumulation of ions on both side of the membrane, alteration of resting potential, dumping of stored glutamate, overstimulation, and widespread cell death) or at increasingly detailed levels of abstraction (e.g., the mechanisms involved in the glutamate dump). What objective factors lead us to say that the causal processes that produce the glutamate dump are part of a larger mechanism regulating responses to a stroke, are a discrete mechanism, or are a combination of multiple underlying mechanisms? How we draw the boundaries around mechanisms will depend on what we want to (and can) do with the resulting model, and not simply on the causal structure of the world.

Mechanisms also have to be mechanisms of something. It is conceivable that the set of mechanisms relevant for explaining the cases of depression that can be treated with interpersonal therapy would be demarcated differently from the mechanisms that help us explain those cases that can be treated with an SSRI. Taking the HPC model literally, these might be considered two kinds of depression. Such kinds are individuated, in part, relative to the scientific priorities of therapists versus those of pharmacologists. One could even tentatively suggest that mechanistic property clusters are practical kinds that emphasize the importance of causal explanation. (Here the reader should not think "only practical kinds" or "merely practical kinds." Goodman emphasized that discovering robustly relevant kinds is hard work, and the same is true of practical kinds.)

To summarize: A natural kind is supposed to be "out there," independent of human interests, goals, and purposes. The causal structure of the world is arguably objective in that sense. According to Boyd, a property cluster is a natural kind if it is the product of some objective causal mechanism. But, as Craver shows, what we take to be "the" causal mechanism is not demarcated independent of interests, goals, and purposes, and neither, therefore, are the property clusters that interests, goals, and purposes produce and sustain. Kinds can be demarcated on the basis of causal processes, but it is a simplification to say that causal processes uniquely fix which demarcations are relevant for different practical purposes.

The world has many "joints," but carving occurs with respect to goals and purposes. To push the metaphor a bit: How we carve a chicken will depend on whether we are making chicken soup, fried chicken, or curry chicken with white meat (Zachar 2006). White meat is an objective property in the world, but to "find it" we have to slice through some bones. It is present in the world independent of our interests, but it is not demarcated by the world alone. The same is true of kinds of psychiatric disorders.

Kinds and the Authority of Science

To what extent should the scientific community be considered to speak with authority about psychiatric disorders? If the questions are about genetic influences, pathogenesis, treatment efficacy, and so on, then in the long run we should look to the scientific community for answers. The trouble is that being a valid scientific kind does not, in itself, justify the attribution of disorder status. This situation is most clearly described in Wakefield's harmful-dysfunction model, where being a valid scientific kind is necessary but not sufficient for being a valid psychiatric disorder.

Whether something is a psychiatric disorder requires considerations in addition to whether or not it is a scientific kind. Let us assume for the sake of argument that anorexia nervosa is a valid scientific kind. According to the Pro-Ana movement, however, anorexia is a lifestyle choice and not a psychiatric disorder (Udovitch 2002). This belief does not require Pro-Ana advocates to deny that anorexia is a valid scientific kind, since being a scientific kind need not entail disorder. In making decisions about "disorder" status, therefore, additional normative considerations are unavoidable.

One way to deal with such quandaries is to use a prototype-matching strategy. Doing so involves identifying features associated with uncontroversial disorders (where adopting the sick role is readily accepted) and gauging the extent to which problematic cases are associated with proto-typical features of the sick role. Examples of such features are decline in functioning (Zachar and Kendler 2010), involuntariness or unresponsive-ness to reason (Graham 2010), increased mortality (Gert and Culver 2004), risk of developing an additional noncontroversial disorder (Zachar and Potter 2010), and even a self-diagnosis that something is wrong (Harré 2004). Quite probably, the only normative feature the Pro-Ana movement can dispute is "self-diagnosis," and even in doing that members of the movement represent a minority among people with anorexia.

There are also genuinely complicated cases on the fuzzy boundary between normal and abnormal where consensus on norms is difficult to achieve. Attention-deficit disorder in young children, oppositional defiant disorder, and grief-triggered depression are current examples. When hard-call cases such as these present themselves, it is important to minimize both false-positive and false-negative diagnoses, but we must also recog-nize that there may be no unambiguous joints of nature to discover.

Consider bereavement and grief. Let us imagine two cases. Each involves a decline in functioning from a previous level of adaptation, and six months later each of the individuals has sufficient reasons to be positive but remains anhedonic. Is this enough to make a call in favor of a depres-sive disorder as opposed to normal grief ? Perhaps not. The first individual is not eating or exercising; the second is. Is this enough to make the call? Some might claim that once enough features of the sick role are present, the demarcation has been made by objective facts in the world, and we merely recognize it. In this case, we would say the first person has a depres-sive disorder, the second does not.

In the case of depression versus normal grief, I am skeptical that carving the domain is so straightforward. For instance, the depression versus grief demarcation is also made against a background theory about the proper role of suffering in processing a loss. Various religious and philosophical traditions point to the value of suffering, despite its unpleasantness. Assume that the first individual claims that he still wants to feel bad and to mourn and the second individual begins to believe that there is some-thing wrong with him. Is this relevant? What weights should we assign to a patient's attachment style, history of depression, the nature of the lost relationship, and the quality of the patient's social support in demarcating melancholia from mourning? Because there are many layers of concepts that orient us to *this* objectivity rather than *that* objectivity, one cannot not say that the "best" classification is a matter of discovery, not of deci-sion. It is both.

Conclusion

What are we to make of the psychiatrists and philosophers who claim that it is necessary to discover natural kinds of psychiatric disorder, particularly kinds with biological essences, in order to transform psychiatry into a valid medical science, or to justify its merger with neurology?

To some extent, the current expectations of many biological psychiatrists mirror the expectations of social scientists in the 1940s that poverty could be studied, understood, and then eliminated. It turned out that the causes of poverty were not as simple, or as controllable, as those social scientists thought, and in retrospect they appear to have been overly optimistic. Likewise, the humanitarian goals of the biological psychiatrists are admirable, and they should be our goals too, but their expected time line for progress and plans for solutions have so far failed. Their paradigm for studying psychiatric disorders has been overly optimistic.

My initial foray into the topic of natural kinds, which I described at the beginning of this chapter, was described in an article titled "Psychiatric disorders are not natural kinds" (Zachar 2000b). The claim of that article would be more accurately summarized as "Psychiatric disorders do not have to be natural kinds (as traditionally understood) in order to be scientifically and professionally relevant categories." The problem is that not everyone feels obligated to limit the term "natural kind" to its traditional, essentialist formulation. It can also be defined broadly.

Viewed from a pragmatist perspective, "natural kind" is a philosophical distinction that was introduced in the nineteenth century and again in the twentieth to serve a variety of purposes. The question is: For what purposes is it being used? I am disinclined to forbid the use of any term, or to get dogmatic about either broad or narrow definitions being privileged, but many of the things people want to say when they talk about natural kinds can be communicated more clearly if they talk about one or more of the component features—for example, supporting induction or underlying causal properties.

Unlike Hacking, I'm not sure that the tradition of natural kinds, like Humpty Dumpty, has fallen off the wall, or that, if it has fallen, many people have not noticed its plight. I do suspect that the concept of natural kind is a bit of a rotten egg, but I also find that the term has its uses. In a classroom, for example, it works well to frame the dramatic rise and fall of multiple-personality disorder by telling students that autism is a natural kind but multiple-personality disorder is not. Something akin to autism would be out there whether or not psychiatrists noticed it, but multiple-personality disorder was created by the application of interview techniques that encouraged the patients to enact the symptomatic behaviors. But philosophical frameworks and scientific research paradigms are another matter. The essentialist baggage associated with natural kinds, such as "preconfigured list of categories waiting to be discovered," can potentially interfere with the recognition of the variety, and the overlapping and conflicting regularities, that are empirically there.

Acknowledgments

Thanks to Melvin Woody, Andrea Solomon, George Graham, and Harold Kincaid for helpful comments on an earlier version.

References

Achenbach, T. 1995. Empirically based assessment and taxonomy: Applications to clinical research. *Psychological Assessment* 7 (3): 261–274.

Andreasen, N. 1984. *The Broken Brain: The Biological Revolution in Psychiatry*. Harper & Row.

Barrett, L. 2006. Are emotions natural kinds? *Perspectives on Psychological Science* 1 (1): 28–58.

Bird, A. 2007. *Nature's Metaphysics: Laws and Properties*. Oxford University Press.

Boyd, R. 1989. What realism implies and what it does not. *Dialectica* 43: 5–29.

Boyd, R. 1991. Realism, anti-foundationalism and the enthusiasm for natural kinds. *Philosophical Studies* 61: 127–148.

Caplan, A., J. McCartney, and D. Sisti. 2004. *Health, Disease, and Illness: Concepts in Medicine*. Georgetown University Press.

Cartwright, N. 1983. *How the Laws of Physics Lie*. Oxford University Press.

Cartwright, N. 1999. *The Dappled World: A Study of the Boundaries of Science*. Cambridge University Press.

Churchland, P. M. 1984. *Matter and Consciousness*. MIT Press.

Clark, L., and W. Livesley. 1994. Two approaches to identifying the dimensions of personality disorder: Convergence on the five-factor model. In *Personality Disorders and the Five-Factor Model of Personality*, ed. P. Costa Jr. and T. Widiger. American Psychological Association.

Clark, L., D. Watson, and S. Reynolds. 1995. Diagnosis and classification of psychopathology: Challenges to the current system and future directions. *Annual Review of Psychology* 46: 121–153.

Cleckley, H. 1941. *The Mask of Sanity: An Attempt to Reinterpret the So-Called Psychopathic Personality*. Mosby.

Cooper, R. 2005. *Classifying Madness: A Philosophical Examination of the Diagnostic and Statistical Manual of Mental Disorders*. Springer.

Cooper, R. 2007. *Psychiatry and Philosophy of Science*. McGill–Queen's University Press.

Craver, C. 2009. Mechanisms and natural kinds. *Philosophical Psychology* 22 (5): 575–594.

Crombie, A. 1994. *Styles of Scientific Thinking in the European Tradition*, volume III. Duckworth.

Devitt, M. 2010. *Putting Metaphysics First: Essays on Metaphysics and Epistemology*. Oxford University Press.

Ellis, B. 2001. *Scientific Essentialism*. Cambridge University Press.

Flanagan, E., and R. Blashfield. 2000. Essentialism and a folk-taxonomic approach to the classification of psychopathology. *Philosophy, Psychiatry, & Psychology* 7 (3): 183–189.

Garb, H. 1998. *Studying the Clinician: Judgment Research and Psychological Assessment*. American Psychological Association.

Gelman, S. 2003. *The Essential Child*. Oxford University Press.

Gert, B., and C. Culver. 2004. Defining mental disorder. In *The Philosophy of Psychiatry: A Companion*, ed. J. Radden. Oxford University Press.

Ghiselin, M. 1974. A radical solution to species problem. *Systematic Zoology* 23: 536–544.

Giere, R. 1999. *Science without Laws*. University of Chicago Press.

Goodman, N. 1978. *Ways of Worldmaking*. Hackett.

Goodman, N. 1983. *Fact, Fiction, and Forecast*, fourth edition. Harvard University Press.

Gottesman, I. 1991. *Schizophrenia Genesis: The Origins of Madness*. Freeman.

Graham, G. 2010. *The Disordered Mind*. Routledge.

Griffiths, P. 1997. *What Emotions Really Are*. University of Chicago Press.

Guze, S. 1992. *Why Psychiatry Is a Branch of Medicine*. Oxford University Press.

Hacking, I. 1990. *The Taming of Chance*. Cambridge University Press.

Hacking, I. 1991. A tradition of natural kinds. *Philosophical Studies* 61: 109–126.

Hacking, I. 2002. Historical Ontology. Harvard University Press.

Hacking, I. 2007. Natural kinds: Rosy dawn, scholastic twilight. *Royal Institute of Philosophy* 82 (Supplement): 203–239.

Harré, R. 2004. Setting benchmarks for psychiatric concepts. In *The Philosophy of Psychiatry: A Companion*, ed. J. Radden. Oxford University Press.

Haslam, N. 1998. Natural kinds, human kinds, and essentialism. *Social Research* 65 (2): 291–314.

Haslam, N. 2000. Psychiatric categories as natural kinds: Essentialist thinking about mental disorder. *Social Research* 67: 1032–1058.

Hill, P., Murray, R., and Thorely, A. 1986. *Essentials of Postgraduate Psychiatry*, second edition. Grune & Stratton.

Hull, D. 1976. Are species really individuals? *Systematic Zoology* 25: 174–191.

Hull, D. 1988. *Science as a Process: An Evolutionary Account of the Social and Conceptual Development of Science*. University of Chicago Press.

Hyman, S. 2010. The diagnosis of mental disorders: The problem of reification. *Annual Review of Clinical Psychology* 6: 155–179.

Kanner, L. 1935. Autistic disturbances of affective contact. *Nervous Child* 2: 217–250.

Kendell, R., and A. Jablensky. 2003. Distinguishing between the validity and utility of psychiatric diagnoses. *American Journal of Psychiatry* 160 (1): 4.

Kendler, K. 2005. "A Gene for": The nature of gene action in psychiatric disorders. *American Journal of Psychiatry* 162 (7): 1243–1252.

Kendler, K., C. Gardner, and C. Prescott. 2002. Toward a comprehensive developmental model for major depression in women. *American Journal of Psychiatry* 159 (7): 1133–1145.

Kendler, K., C. Gardner, and C. Prescott. 2006. Toward a comprehensive developmental model for major depression in men. *American Journal of Psychiatry* 163 (1): 115–124.

Kendler, K., M. Neale, R. Kessler, and A. Heath. 1992. Major depression and generalized anxiety disorder: Same genes, (partly) different environments? *Archives of General Psychiatry* 49 (9): 716–722.

Kendler, K., P. Zachar, and C. Craver. 2011. What kinds of things are psychiatric disorders. *Psychological Medicine* 41: 1143–1150.

Kramer, P. 2009. Secrecy and made-up illnesses: The latest fight over psychiatric diagnosis. *Slate*. Retrieved from http://www.doublex.com.

Kripke, S. 1972. *Naming and Necessity*. Reidel.

Krueger, R. 1999. The structure of common mental disorders. *Archives of General Psychiatry* 56 (10): 921–926.

Krueger, R., and N. Eaton. 2010. Personality traits and the classification of mental disorders: Toward a more complete integration in *DSM-5* and an empirical model of psychopathology. *Personality Disorders: Theory, Research, and Treatment* 1 (2): 97–118.

Lichtenstein, P., B. Yip, C. Björk, Y. Pawitan, T. Cannon, P. Sullivan, et al. 2009. Common genetic determinants of schizophrenia and bipolar disorder in Swedish families: A population-based study. *Lancet* 373 (9659): 234–239.

Livesley, J. 2012. Tradition versus empiricism in the current *DSM-5* proposal for revising the classification of personality disorders. *Criminal Behaviour and Mental Health* 22: 81–91.

Livesley, W. 2003. Diagnostic dilemmas in classifying personality disorder. In *Advancing DSM: Dilemmas in Psychiatric Diagnosis*, ed. K. Phillips, M. First, and H. Pincus. American Psychiatric Association.

MacAlpine, I., and R. Hunter. 1974. The pathology of the past. *Times Literary Supplement*, March 15: 256–257.

Machery, E. 2005. Concepts are not a natural kind. *Philosophy of Science* 72 (3): 444–467.

Mayr, E. 1988. *Toward a New Philosophy of Biology: Observations of an Evolutionist.* Belknap.

McHugh, P. 2008. *Try to Remember: Psychiatry's Clash over Meaning, Memory, and Mind.* Dana.

Meehl, P. 1972. Why I do not attend case conferences. In *Psychodiagnosis: Selected Papers.* University of Minnesota Press.

Meehl, P. 1995. Bootstraps taxometrics: Solving the classification problem in psychopathology. *American Psychologist* 50 (4): 266–275.

Putnam, H. 1975. *Mind, Language and Reality: Philosophical Papers*, volume 2. Cambridge University Press.

Quine, W. 1969. *Ontological Relativity and Other Essays.* Columbia University Press.

Richardson, R. 2007. *Evolutionary Psychology as Maladapted Psychology.* MIT Press.

Ridley, M. 1986. *Evolution and Classification: The Reformation of Cladism.* Longman.

Roth, M., and J. Kroll. 1986. *The Reality of Mental Illness.* Cambridge University Press.

Rowa, K., M. Antony, and R. Swinson. 2007. Exposure and response prevention. In *Psychological Treatment of Obsessive-Compulsive Disorder: Fundamentals and Beyond*, ed. M. Antony, L. Summerfeldt, and C. Purdon. American Psychological Association.

Sneath, P., and R. Sokal. 1973. *Numerical Taxonomy: The Principles and Practice of Numerical Classification*. Freeman.

Spitzer, R., and J. Wakefield. 1999. *DSM*-IV diagnostic criterion for clinical significance: Does it help solve the false positives problem? *American Journal of Psychiatry* 156 (12): 1856–1864.

Szasz, T. 1961. *The Myth of Mental Illness*. Harper & Row.

Tohen, M., E. Frank, C. Bowden, F. Colom, S. Ghaemi, L. Yatham, et al. 2009. The International Society for Bipolar Disorders (ISBD) task force report on the nomenclature of course and outcome in bipolar disorders. *Bipolar Disorders* 11 (5): 453–473.

Trull, T., and C. Durrett. 2005. Categorical and dimensional models of personality disorder. *Annual Review of Clinical Psychology* 1 (1): 355–380.

Udovitch, M. 2002. The way we live now: 9-08-02: Phenomenon; A secret society of the starving. *New York Times*. Retrieved from www.nytimes.com.

Vahia, V., and I. Vahia. 2008. Schizophrenia in developing countries. In *Clinical Handbook of Schizophrenia*, ed. K. Mueser and D. Jeste. Guilford.

Van Deemter, K. 2010. *Not Exactly: In Praise of Vagueness*. Oxford University Press.

Wakefield, J. 1992. Disorder as harmful dysfunction: A conceptual critique of *DSM*-III-R's definition of mental disorder. *Psychological Review* 99 (2): 232–247.

Wakefield, J. 1999a. Disorder as a black box essentialist concept. *Journal of Abnormal Psychology* 108: 465–471.

Wakefield, J. 1999b. Evolutionary versus prototype analyses of the concept of disorder. *Journal of Abnormal Psychology* 108 (3): 374–399.

Wakefield, J. 2004. The myth of open concepts: Meehl's analysis of construct meaning versus black box essentialism. *Applied & Preventive Psychology* 11: 77–82.

Wakefield, J., and M. First. 2003. Clarifying the distinction between disorder and nondisorder: Confronting the overdiagnosis (False-positives) problem in *DSM*-V. In *Advancing DSM: Dilemmas in Psychiatric Diagnosis*, ed. K. Phillips, M. First, and H. Pincus. American Psychiatric Association.

Wakefield, J., M. Schmitz, M. First, B., and A. Horwitz. 2009. The importance of the main effect even within an interaction model: Elimination vs. expansion of the bereavement exclusion in the diagnostic criteria for depression. *American Journal of Psychiatry* 166 (4): 491–492.

Watson, D. 2005. Rethinking the mood and anxiety disorders: A quantitative hierarchical model for *DSM*-V. *Journal of Abnormal Psychology* 114 (4): 522–536.

Widiger, T., A. Frances, M. Harris, L. Jacobsberg, M. Fyer, and D. Manning. 1991. Comorbidity among Axis II disorders. In *Personality Disorders: New Perspectives on Diagnostic Validity*, ed. J. Oldham. American Psychiatric Association.

Widiger, T., W. Livesley, and L. Clark. 2009. An integrative dimensional classification of personality disorder. *Psychological Assessment* 21 (3): 243–255.

Widiger, T., and C. Sanderson. 1995. Toward a dimensional model of personality disorders. In *The DSM-IV Personality Disorders*, ed. W. Livesley. Guilford.

Williams, J., M. Gibbon, M. First, R. Spitzer, M. Davies, J. Borus, et al. 1992. The Structured Clinical Interview for *DSM-III-R* (SCID) II: Multisite test-tetest reliability. *Archives of General Psychiatry* 49 (8): 630–636.

Winokur, G. 1981. *Depression: The Facts*. Oxford University Press.

Zachar, P. 2000a. Folk taxonomies should not have essences either: A response to the commentary. *Philosophy, Psychiatry, & Psychology* 7 (3): 191–194.

Zachar, P. 2000b. Psychiatric disorders are not natural kinds. *Philosophy, Psychiatry, & Psychology* 7 (3): 167–182.

Zachar, P. 2000c. *Psychological Concepts and Biological Psychiatry: A Philosophical Analysis*. John Benjamins.

Zachar, P. 2002. The practical kinds model as a pragmatist theory of classification. *Philosophy, Psychiatry, & Psychology* 9 (3): 219–227.

Zachar, P. 2006. The classification of emotion and scientific realism. *Journal of Theoretical and Philosophical Psychology* 26 (1–2): 120–138.

Zachar, P. 2008. Real kinds but no true taxonomy: An essay in psychiatric systematics. In *Philosophical Issues in Psychiatry: Explanation, Phenomenology, and Nosology*, ed. K. Kendler and J. Parnas. Johns Hopkins University Press.

Zachar, P., and K. Kendler. 2007. Psychiatric disorders: A conceptual taxonomy. *American Journal of Psychiatry* 164 (4): 557–565.

Zachar, P., and K. Kendler. 2010. Philosophical issues in the classification of psychopathology. In *Contemporary Directions in Psychopathology*, ed. T. Millon, R. Krueger, and E. Simonsen. Guilford.

Zachar, P., and N. Potter. 2010. Valid moral appraisals and valid personality disorders. *Philosophy, Psychiatry, & Psychology* 17 (2): 131–142.

6   Natural Kinds in Folk Psychology and in Psychiatry

Dominic Murphy

In this chapter, using delusions as my chief example, I will argue that our attribution of mental illness relies on a conception of psychiatric kinds as fundamentally psychological categories with distinctive if unknown causal signatures—characteristic ways of producing similar effects across different people. This aligns psychiatric thought, as well as the folk psychology of psychiatry, with well-established practices of scientific discovery and explanation that assume that mental illnesses are natural kinds. I shall follow other recent writers in assuming that the relevant conception of natural kind for psychiatry is Richard Boyd's. However, the ways in which folk psychology groups patients together may not match the ways in which nature does it. Our folk thought may be a poor guide to natural kinds in psychiatry.

Natural Kinds

Let me begin by sketching an account of the representation and explanation of psychiatric conditions. Psychiatric diagnoses should be seen as referring to idealizations: exemplars (Murphy 2006) or ideal types (Ghaemi 2003). These are representations of disorders that abstract from the details of their realization in patients. We may think of exemplars as representing the ideal, textbook patient with a particular condition, even though such an ideal patient may never in fact enter the clinic. We group symptoms together according to their tendency to occur together in nature and unfold in particular ways, and we assume that causal connections exist both synchronically between symptoms in the group and diachronically between the cluster of symptoms itself and some earlier processes, genetic and developmental, that cause the symptoms to appear. The causal connections between components of the exemplar can sometimes be formulated with great precision, investigated experimentally and tested with great rigor. But often they cannot, since we are in the dark about the nature of the causal connections. When they are applied to individual cases, however, much of the precision is lost, since the disorder afflicts different people in different ways. Perhaps not all symptoms are present, or not in their typical form. Patients may also suffer from other conditions at the same time, and those other conditions may interfere with the predicted expression of the diagnosis. It does not follow that the diagnosis is incorrect. The expression of the condition might vary greatly, but that might depend on regularities in the failure of normal function within a human being in a given social or natural environment.

A diagnosis then, is useful insofar as it captures a genuine phenomenon and at the same time directs our attention to cases that can be further specified. Armed with an exemplar, we go on to construct a model to inform our understanding of an individual's condition: in that sense, explanation in psychiatry, as in medicine more generally, is indirect. We first try to understand the explanatory relations that hold among parts of an idealization, for no one is exactly like the exemplar. The bet is that real patients will be similar to the exemplar in enough respects so that the explanation of the exemplar carries over to the patient. We assume that within the individual there are phenomena and causal relations that are relevantly similar to those worked out for the exemplar, but we cannot expect very precise predictions.

The exemplar is thus a partial representation of the class of people who receive the diagnosis. It is silent about most of their properties, including most of those that are in the provinces of medicine, psychology, and neuroscience. What it represents is a disorder that is shared by a population of subjects; their possession of the disorder explains a number of things about them.

One way to express this idea is to argue that a mental disorder is a natural kind. Because we assume that membership in a natural kind depends on a common basis that holds the kind together, we have a ready solution to the problem of why patients who meet the diagnosis share a set of symptoms, viz. that they are all undergoing the same processes and the symptoms are effects of those processes. Betting on a shared causal process in this way also gives us a basis for inquiry; we can attempt to tie the manifestations of the disorder to underlying mechanisms. What we are looking for in these cases is what I will call a causal signature—telltale manifestations of the disorder that suggest that in every case we are dealing with the same causal processes, or perhaps a small family of related processes.

The existing *DSM* nosology does not list natural kinds and is not designed to. It comprises what Kendler et al. (2010) call "practical kinds," which aim at grouping patients into useful classes that serve professional scientific goals such as predicting future behavior, assessing genetic risk, or selecting a treatment. However, it has been a longstanding hope of psychiatry to uncover what Emil Kraepelin called "natural disease units." Kraepelin hoped that in the long run pathology, etiology, and clinical manifestations would converge on a natural classification—ideally, the one true natural classification—that would tie psychiatric conditions to a broader understanding of human psychology and physiology. One obvious interpretation of the Kraepelin project is that it treats mental disorders as natural kinds, at least putatively. In this chapter, I discuss one way to understand the Krapelinian project and one epistemic issue that it raises.

A widespread view holds that members of a natural kind share an essence—an underlying physical constitution that necessitates the properties that define the kind. Several recent treatments complain that this account of natural kinds is far too metaphysically demanding. Beebee and Sabbarton-Leary (2010), Kendler et al. (2010), and Samuels (2009) all argue that the appropriate concept of natural kindhood for psychiatry is Boyd's (1990, 1991) concept of property clusters. On this view, a kind is defined by the co-occurrence of a set of properties that vary somewhat from individual to individual. Not all properties in the set are shared by all members of the kind. The clustering of properties is due to causal mechanisms that ensure that the properties more or less get instantiated together. So a set of causal mechanisms brings about the clustering of a set of properties. When inductive reasoning works, Boyd thinks, it works because our theories have latched onto these underlying causal mechanisms. They populate the world with kinds that obey non-accidental generalizations, such as "all metals expand when heated," rather than accidental generalizations such as "all objects over 2 meters tall are made of wood" (Samuels 2009). It may, in our experience, be the case that all objects more than 2 meters tall are wooden, just as it is the case that all metals expand when heated. But the claim about wood will not stand up to further investigation and license new ampliative inferences, whereas the claim about metals will. That difference is due to the causal mechanisms that are responsible for the nature of metal and the fact that our thoughts about metal can track those mechanisms. In the successful cases, we detect a genuine causal signature that leads us to the mechanisms responsible for the characteristics of the kind.

Lots of accounts of natural kinds would reach similar conclusions about metal, since they would hold that metals have essences. The crucial difference that makes Boyd's account so appealing to so many is its much more relaxed view of the underlying nature of a kind. Boyd's homeostatic property clusters lack essences in the traditional sense. A traditional essentialist view rules out counting species as natural kinds because there is no genetic constitution that all and only the members of a biological species share. But members of a species do share an evolutionary history that has bequeathed to them more or less uniform causal mechanisms and processes that permit inductive inferences across species and other taxa, so that if we find an enzyme in one raptor we may bet that it will show up in closely related species. On a Boydian account, species can be natural kinds. The causal mechanisms that individuate the kinds are similar across instances of the kind, but not always the same, and they are correspondingly associated with some variety in the properties of the kind. The causal structure of the kind explains the nature of the properties associated with it and why they tend to occur together.

Diseases are an obvious kind of phenomenon to explain with this account. Many diseases have characteristic symptoms that permit diagnosis but are not always present uniformly, and those symptoms may occur alongside less usual symptoms. Smallpox, for example, begins with a mix of symptoms, including head and back pain, chills, fever, and convulsions; then the characteristic rash usually starts on the face before spreading to the lower body. Smallpox is consistent enough across cases to allow clinicians to it tell it apart from similar conditions, such as measles. The two conditions were first distinguished in the ninth century by Rhazes (Muhammad ibn Zakaria al-Razi). Smallpox has a distinctive signature, notwithstanding its different manifestations; some patients have dreadful nightmares in the early stages, some suffer from internal hemorrhaging (in which case they do not have a typical rash), and the rashes vary in severity, localization, and appearance (Hopkins 2002). Such a cluster of properties is exactly what Boyd's account seems to capture. Physicians learned to identify the condition on the basis of its characteristic symptoms, and to make predictions about the typical course and outcome. There were atypical cases, and not every prediction was correct, but in general we learned enough about smallpox to make sound inductive inferences that eventually led us to the causal mechanisms (chiefly, the *variola major* virus and its ways of multiplying in the body).

Disease kinds do indeed seem a natural home to Boydian thoughts, so it is understandable that theorists who are sympathetic to the medical model in psychiatry should be drawn to the idea of homeostatic property clusters. However, the utility of the HPC view in the biomedical sciences, including psychiatry, can be defended without a commitment to a stronger view that Boyd's account is the one true definition of what a natural kind is. Asking whether the essentialist conception, or the property-cluster conception, or some other conception is the single correct account of natural kindhood strikes me as unlikely to be fruitful. It is certainly the case that Boyd's concept of homeostatic property clusters fits a good deal of scientific practice. But perhaps other conceptions of natural kindhood score higher on other dimensions of our thought about taxonomy—in some contexts our understanding of natural kinds might demand a more restrictive account of essence, for example, and Boyd's theory would not fit those contexts.

I will continue to use the language of natural kinds, but what interests me is the idea of property clusters as an answer to the question of what a mental illness is. As the scholars I cited earlier note, Boyd's view has some great attractions for psychiatry. First, because the HPC account dispenses with essences in the traditional sense, it makes room for a great variety of causal mechanisms. Everyone recognizes a tremendous diversity in the causes of mental illness. Second, the account recognizes that members of a kind can vary among themselves, depending on the actually occurring cluster in particular cases.

On the first point: The causes and properties of mental illness operate at what are, intuitively, many different levels. Some may be straightforwardly psychological—for instance, Bentall (2003, pp. 412–413) notes that there are often connections between different psychotic symptoms and other underlying psychological phenomena. He cites as examples the mutual feedback relations between delusions and hallucinations, and argues for similar connections between paranoia and incoherent speech, mediated by working-memory problems. These phenomena reinforce each other so as to produce stable patterns of symptoms. But of course the symptoms are not uniform across all patients. Boyd's theory seemed tailor-made for mental illness, since it doesn't bother with invariant essences but bets that science can identify and explain kinds that share just a set of complicated causal mechanisms.

The second point is also worth reiterating. Mental disorders appear to be affected by socio-cultural variables and other environmental inputs, and vary in their manifestations both within and across cultures. The cross-cultural case is interesting, since any depiction of mental disorders as natural kinds will be weakened if we cannot argue that mental disorders span cultural boundaries. If depression, say, is a natural kind, we should expect it to afflict lots of people around the world. If it strikes only Westerners, it looks more like a cultural inheritance than like a natural kind. The case for a common core underlying cultural variation in the symptoms of major depression was made by Arthur Kleinman, who argued that "depression experienced entirely as low back pain and depression experienced entirely as guilt-ridden existential despair are such substantially different forms of illness behavior with different symptoms, patterns of help-seeking, course and treatment responses that though the disease in each instance may be the same, the illness rather than the disease is the determinant factor" (1987, p. 450).

Boyd's picture might not seem to fit here if the symptoms of depression are completely different in the East than in the West, as Kleinman's remarks suggest. But in fact there may be more overlap than Kleinman allows. Ryder et al. (2008) argue that Chinese depressives tend to report more somatic symptoms, whereas Western depressives tend to understand their depression in largely psychological terms. (Ryder et al. think that this, not somaticization, may be the culturally specific response.) Nonetheless, depressives of European descent did show somatic symptoms, and psychological suffering was not uncommon in Chinese depressives.

As Horwitz and Wakefield (2007, p. 199) suggest, one can "agree with Kleinman's distinction between disease as a universal underlying dysfunction and illness as the culturally shaped expression of a given dysfunction" without thinking, as Kleinman sometimes seems to, that different cultures experience depression in entirely different ways. There may remain some commonality across cases from different cultures—at least enough to let us recognize depression—and, as Horwitz and Wakefield go on to say, "if there are indeed underlying common dysfunctions, then treatment presumably depends in large part on the science of identifying and intervening in such dysfunctions irrespective of their cultural presentation." That is, we can identify and explain depression across cultures on the assumption of shared, albeit diverse, causal stories. That is just the Boydian picture. Of course, it makes the empirical assumption that the structure of the mind is not entirely relative to cultural contexts. But Boyd thinks that natural kinds are found out *a posteriori*. The point is that the theory gives us the resources to generalize diagnoses without insisting that there must be a universal shared essence to them, as there probably is not.

To sum up this section: Mental disorders seem to causally depend on diverse phenomena and to differ in their manifestations across patients (and within patients over times) and across cultures. Both of these properties are consistent with features of the homeostatic-property-cluster account. Thus, that account that has obvious merit as the metaphysical basis for a theory of psychiatric classification.

However, in the rest of this chapter I will wonder if in some cases the apparently Boydian nature of some mental disorders is just an artifact of folk psychology. I will suggest that in the case of delusions we should take seriously the idea that we are not dealing with a natural kind at all, even though the evidence suggests that we are confronting a homeostatic property cluster. The idea I will explore is that the apparent unity of the condition reflects the workings of the folk-psychological systems that underpin our detection of mental illness, and not any natural category.

Folk Psychology and the Detection of Mental Illness

Human beings share expectations about normal cognitive function. Although some of these are culturally local, many seem to be the same all over the world. For example, there seems to be a very widespread idea that memory is a store into which items are deposited for later retrieval. Boyer (2010) argues that our *intuitive detection* of mental disorder involves judging that a particular type of behavior is so different from what the culture expects that it is evidence that some mental systems are dysfunctional. On his account, people notice that some behavior is deviant or unusual, and this often drives them to look for an explanation, especially if the behavior tends to recur. The detection of unexpected behavior will often trigger an explanatory causal model for the behavior. Such a model is a set of mental representations that form part of our folk psychology. Models may often vary culturally, in which case they will tend to be more explicit and use culturally inherited categories (e.g., demonic possession or the Oedipus complex). Other models are unconscious and much more widespread.

There are two ideas here: intuitive expectations about normal behavior and underlying models. The models may be explicit and consciously accessible explanatory beliefs about the world that are accepted in a culture— someone's behavior may be seen as evidence of demonic possession or some sort of scientifically explicable brain disorder. On the other hand, the intuitive expectations that we harbor about one another may be very hard to state explicitly—some people strike us as behaving oddly, but in a particular way that seems to indicate underlying dysfunction rather than just harmless deviance, temporary drunkenness, or eccentricity.

This intuitive, defeasible recognition of mental disorder depends on the principles that organize our understanding of other people's behavior—in other words, our "theory of mind" or "folk psychology." We can understand this very broadly. Many philosophers have seen these expectations about the minds of other people as organized around a body of principles, or even laws (akin to those of a scientific theory) that define beliefs and desires in terms of their relations to each other and to behavior. It is obvious, however, that our beliefs or expectations about the minds of others cover more ground than the folk psychology of philosophers. Every culture has a body of lore about emotion, moods, traits of character, memory, and dreams, for instance. Mental illness, too, belongs in this broad purview of folk psychology. Paul Churchland raised the question of these further aspects of folk psychology in a 1981 paper arguing that folk psychology is indeed a theory, but a really terrible one whose posits should be abandoned by a serious science. Churchland did not deny that there are intuitive expectations about aspects of the mind that go beyond the belief-desire core that he treated as a theory. But he argued that they could not be theoretically regimented as propositional attitudes could be.

We can admit that there is little prospect of taking the principles that govern our thinking on these matters and regimenting them in some traditional theory-like way. Boyer suggests that our thoughts on these wider mental phenomena may be seen as a family of models. Every culture has tacit expectations about what normal behavior and thought should be in many areas of mental life that go beyond belief-desire psychology.

Boyer contends that theory-of-mind assumptions provide clear intuitions that certain specific kinds of behavior signal underlying disorder and also constrain possible explanations of disorder. Theory of mind depends on a neurocognitive system that is, to a large degree, cross-culturally invariant. The deeper principles of intuitive psychology—for example, the idea that memory is a store—are generally beyond conscious access and independent of cultural variations.

Thus, the claim before us is that our intuitive detection of mental disorder relies on the failure of our default expectations about human behavior to be met. That failure directs our attention to some inner process that explains the outer failure. We cast about for an explanation of why someone is acting in that strange manner, and our explanation will often appeal to our theory of mind models of the structures underlying behavior. The models may be combined with facts or guesses about less proximate causes—for example, you may think that your brother-in-law's comportment is evidence of his being drunk again, but that depends on your assumptions about how alcohol interacts with human psychology, and perhaps on some specific knowledge about your brother-in-law.

Boyer's theory has a lot going for it as an explanation of why we attribute mental illness in the ways and circumstances that we do. It is not a theory of mental illness, but a theory about our attribution of it. Some behaviors violate our expectations of intuitive psychology and bring about an explanatory need: What accounts for the behavior, if not the underlying psychological structures that our models say should be there in normal agents? We can meet this explanatory need by filling in the causal story with a model of dysfunction (combined with environmental data) that is licensed by our culture.

In the next section I explore some consequences of thinking like this. Roughly, I take this idea of mental illness as a defeater of folk psychology and assess it as a heuristic. Is it a good tool to use in uncovering natural psychiatric kinds? As a case study, I will consider delusion.

Delusion

Psychiatry currently employs a concept of delusion that is, broadly, as set forth in a recent textbook (Sadock and Sadock 2007, p. 505): "A false belief, not ordinarily accepted by members of the person's culture, based on incorrect inferences about external reality. They are firmly sustained despite what almost everyone else believes and despite what constitutes incontrovertible and obvious proof of evidence to the contrary."

The *Diagnostic and Statistical Manual of Mental Disorders* says that a delusion is a "false belief based on incorrect inference about external reality that is firmly sustained despite what almost everyone else believes and despite what constitutes incontrovertible or obvious proof to the contrary. The belief is not one ordinarily accepted by other members of a person's culture or subculture (e.g., it is not an article of religious faith)." (American Psychiatric Association 2000, p. 819)

First, the belief has to be false; second, it has to be based on an incorrect inference about ordinary reality. These two requirements suggest a purely epistemic understanding of delusion, in which an experience is taken as evidence for something false. This epistemic reading is enhanced by the subsequent demand that the delusion be firmly sustained in the face of both conventional wisdom and obvious proof that the delusional belief is false. The problem, apparently, is one of a relation to the evidence.

However, the definition then takes this epistemic understanding of delusions, and qualifies it by adding the rider that what might otherwise seem to be a delusion is in fact not a delusion if we see it as culturally appropriate. There is something odd about this parenthetical acknowledgment that religious beliefs, or some other culturally sanctioned beliefs, are not delusional. Why should a false, incorrectly inferred belief suddenly come to be non-delusional just because the surrounding culture goes along with it? (Even if you think your religious beliefs are true, presumably you don't think that about everyone else's. At most one set of religious beliefs are true.)

I think the clause about cultural aptness captures something important about the working of our concept of delusion. However, its significance is obscured if we carry on thinking of delusions as primarily an epistemic problem. They are not, at least not in the narrowly philosophical sense of "epistemic" that is concerned only with justification. The cultural appropriateness clause directs our attention away from justification and truth and toward the beliefs people have and the mechanisms that form those beliefs. Roughly, the clause about cultural acceptance means something like this: Religious or other culturally apt beliefs, no matter how strange they may appear, are not delusional, because we think it is normal for adult humans to accept or profess the religious beliefs of their culture, or at least some shared religious belief, and the same goes for other beliefs that we expect people to pick up from those around them. Our expectations about normal human belief formation include expectations about the kinds of beliefs people are likely to acquire in the course of normal human development. Since religion is ubiquitous, we can see how people might come to be religious via straightforward cultural learning. Even if you are a hardcore rationalist, it is hard to argue that religion is not natural to human beings. Samuels (2009, pp. 69–70) argues that the cultural relativity of delusions shows "the insensitivity of delusions to an important source of epistemic warrant and epistemic defeat: *testimony*" and suggests that we disqualify normal religious beliefs from being delusions precisely because they rely on widespread testimony and hence are justified (even if they are not true). There is clearly something right about this position, but thinking in terms of testimony makes the treatment of delusions too narrowly epistemic.

Recent philosophical discussions of delusion have tended to assume that the term "delusion" denotes a psychological kind whose basic structure can be worked out via attention to paradigmatic cases such as the Capgras Delusion. This furthers an explanatory project that characterizes delusions as brought about by failures of normal relations among components of our cognitive architecture, or at least those parts of it that have to do with the fixation of belief. It is the philosopher's job to provide an abstract specification of the sorts of processes that are awry in cases of delusion, drawing on a general picture of the sorts of things that we think go on when people normally form warranted beliefs. These are subpersonal processes, but the explanatory project should not be seen as an attempt to uncover specific subpersonal systems; it just attempts to say what processes take place, not how they are realized. In consequence, analyses of delusion look like inversions of the attempts made by analytic epistemologists to define knowledge. I suggest that the error in most existing theories of delusion is a focus on the end product of belief acquisition—the weird beliefs of deluded people and their roles in the patients' lives. Although its role in a patient's life is often what calls attention to a delusion and focuses clinical efforts, it does not follow that such effects are the right way to think about delusions.

A better way to think about delusions comes from thinking more broadly about reasoning. The psychiatric definition takes accuracy of the end product of reasoning—namely, the belief(s) one acquires—as conceptually primary. But I will argue that what is conceptually basic about delusions is the process by which they are formed, not the end product of that process. What is conceptually basic about delusion is the perversion of normal mechanisms of belief acquisition and revision, not just the weird beliefs that one ends up with through that perverted changing of one's mind. "Normal" here does not mean "according to our best scientific theory." It means that folk psychology, broadly construed, endorses some avenues of belief formation and rejects others. Delusional people are people who are hooked up to the world in ways that folk psychology or (as I shall say) folk epistemology says are weird, in the sense of falling outside normal human expectations about other people's psychology. The weirdness of the ensuing belief is (defeasible) evidence for the abnormality of their reasoning mechanisms, but the weirdness itself is not the conceptually crucial element. I claim that the picture I come up with makes sense of a number of features of current psychiatric practice as well as the folk-psychological grounds for distinguishing the delusional and the non-delusional.

In sum: I am betting that the psychiatric concept of a delusion grows out of a widespread human tendency, which Boyer tries to explain via cognitive science, to see psychopathology in cases where someone's behavior fails to accord with folk-psychological assumptions about how the mind works. I conjecture that a delusion is a belief that is acquired through a process that does not fit folk theories of belief acquisition. I see folk epistemology as only loosely related to epistemology in the philosopher's sense: as a subcomponent of our everyday thinking about human nature that incorporates assumptions about normal belief fixation. In part, then, it is a normative theory, but it involves departures from what an episte- mologist would see as a theory of justification, and it includes assumptions about psychological functioning that belong in a naturalistic psychology of reasoning.

If I am correct about the folk-psychological attribution of delusion, we should conclude that a delusion is a belief that is caused in a special and abnormal way. There could be many such ways, and this suggests the futil- ity of a general neuropsychological account based on a theory of the cause of delusions. But a good naturalistic theory of the subpersonal basis of belief acquisition might preserve enough of the concept of delusion to make it scientifically useful. There might be a psychological causal signa- ture that we can track. Or it may be that the underlying causal explanations are too various for "delusion" to earn its keep as anything but a heuristic. I will sketch some reasons for thinking this later in the chapter.

Folk Epistemology

Let us consider, in the light of Boyer's theory, the existing concept of delu- sion. Suppose we assume that our expectations about normal human belief psychology include expectations about the kinds of beliefs people are likely to acquire in the course of normal human development. These expecta- tions depend on folk models of human psychology that include assump- tions about cognitive development that explain why children and adults believe some of the things they do. They may also include other models that explain belief in terms of synchronic processes. As I noted above, religion is ubiquitous, and we all find it easy to explain why people might be religious. Even if you are a hard-core rationalist, it is hard to argue that religion is not natural to human beings. You might deride the idea that religious faith rests on a sensitivity to the divine, but we certainly under- stand that that people brought up in a culture will end up believing a lot of things that are typical of that culture, including articles of religious faith. Therefore, if our attribution of delusion is sensitive to considerations about normal human psychology, we should rule out religious beliefs for the most part. Whatever their warrant may be, they are obviously part of normal human psychology. Not everyone is religious, but culturally sanc- tioned religiosity is part of human nature and not pathological in this folk sense, whereas religious claims that only a lone eccentric believes, or that depart from our expectations about normal religiosity, do trigger our models of deviant behavior.

My conjecture is that we should see part of folk psychology, broadly construed as I suggested above, as including a folk epistemology. But folk epistemology is not a vulgar version of the sort of epistemology that philosophers do. I don't think people have well-worked-out beliefs about the concept of knowledge, or about the possible significance for that concept of widespread construction of fake barns. I do, however, think that we have folk intuitions about the ways in which people form beliefs, and the ways in which they may be justified. Some intuitions that analytic epistemologists appeal may indeed be found within folk epistemology. But we do not limit our ordinary thought about normal belief formation to cases in which beliefs are epistemically justified. People believe all sorts of things that you would expect them, in the face of the evidence, not to believe. This may be explicable in terms of an emotional commitment to the truth of a proposition. Nozick (1993) imagines a mother who refuse to acknowledge that her child is guilty of a heinous crime despite evidence that suffices to convince everyone else. The criminal's mother has no evidence not possessed by others, but the cost to her of admitting her child's guilt is too great. She doesn't put it that way, since to do so would be to admit that she is believing in his innocence only for motivated reasons. She just doesn't—can't—believe that her son is guilty. In view of the lack of support for her belief and the general failure to agree with her, the mother appears to fit the *DSM* definition of delusion. But it is not clear that we should call her deluded, or even irrational. Nozick (1993, p. 86) argues that a mother in such a case is not being irrational provided that the disutility of a belief in her child's guilt is great enough to undercut what he calls the "credibility value" that would attach to a belief that her son is guilty.

Whatever you think of Nozick's conclusions, there is tremendous force to the idea that it would be normal—though not epistemically warranted— to let one's personal stake in the case outweigh the evidence. We employ psychic defenses that cause us to believe unjustified propositions. And we explain all sorts of beliefs in terms of a general tendency of people to often believe what it suits them to, whether because of their personal proclivities, class interest, or ideology or because they have devoted many years to a theory and will not give it up no matter how strong the evidence seems to *you*. Our folk psychology is alert to the operation of these defenses, at least in other people. We might think that the mother is not entitled to believe in her son's innocence in view of the evidence against him, but we can see why she might. And we don't think she is abnormal for doing so.

(However, her psychology could be so warped by the strain of keeping up the psychic defenses that we come to see her as mentally disturbed.)

Roughly, folk epistemology countenances at least three families of belief formation. The first of these families consists of beliefs that are straightforwardly derived from experience and memory—the sorts of thing that analytic epistemology is always going on about. For instance, just as all human beings assume that people act in order to get what they desire, they also think that people believe what they perceive and recall what they perceived in the past (instead of, say, currently perceiving what they recall). The second family consists of beliefs that are caused by psychological need, class position, and other sorts of motivated self-interest, as in the case of the mother mentioned above. The third family consists of beliefs picked up from the surrounding culture, such as religious beliefs or beliefs about norms (what counts as polite behavior, or the proper time to eat dinner, and so on).

In recognizing that first class of (justified) beliefs, folk epistemology is akin to analytic epistemology. But really it is part of a more general body of expectations about the causation of mental states and behavior. We do understand other people as forming beliefs through various reliable and unreliable but robust and psychologically motivated cognitive processes. Indeed, the "hermeneutics of suspicion" is a philosophically sophisticated elaboration of the basic idea that we should expect some people to believe some propositions because of who they are or where they are in society. To have a delusion is to have a belief that is not acquired in a way that satisfies the assumptions of folk epistemology. Delusions violate our normal expectations about human psychology in the specific case of belief, just as mental illness does in general. My conjecture is formulated at the intentional level—roughly, in terms of the folk psychology of epistemic processes—and is neutral with respect to mechanisms that a scientific theory of delusions might mention. In folk-psychological terms, calling someone delusional asserts that he or she is hooked up to the world in a wrong way, but it leaves open what the nature of the failure to be hooked up correctly amounts to. It may be, as on Boyer's picture, that we then run through our repertoire of models of human nature looking for a cause of the pathological behavior. My contention here is that the attribution of delusion is based on the preceding step: attributing to someone a belief that cannot be understood by means of the causal process that folk psychology recognizes. Thus, I am saying that a delusion is a belief formed in a way that cannot be understood in folk terms. That is not to say that people's behavior is incomprehensible in the sense that no belief at all can be attributed (though that may happen); we can use standard inferences from behavior (especially verbal behavior) to attribute a belief without having any idea why someone believes it.

If I am correct, we can identify an essence to delusion—but a very unhelpful, heterogeneous one, based on the language of folk psychology. And the basic idea need not be limited to delusions. Boyer's picture raises the possibility that many psychiatric conditions depend on triggering our folk assumptions that a person's psychology (even our own) is awry. If these ideas are on the right lines, much of our nosology might have grown out of folk kinds, and our diagnoses might rest on signs and symptoms grouped together by folk-psychological thinking.

The question is whether the kinds of pathology that folk psychology recognizes can play the role of regimenting scientific inquiry.

Delusions as Natural Kinds?

The suggestion I sketched in the preceding section is that delusions are attributed in a way that casts them as beliefs formed in ways that fall outside what folk epistemology countenances as normal causes of belief; these causes do not always justify belief, but they are recognizably human ways of forming a belief, no matter how epistemically suspect. What are the consequences for the scientific study of delusions if something like this is correct? More generally, if we take Boyer's project seriously, as my conjecture about delusions is designed to do, what follows for psychiatry?

One possible program immediately suggests itself. We might take the folk concept as picking out what I have called a causal signature—the same distinctive pattern showing through the diversity and leading us to an underlying causal mechanism. In this program, folk thought sets the agenda for a scientific project. Science discovers the natural phenomenon at which the folk concept aims. To do this, psychiatrists and psychologists would have to discover the normal mechanisms of belief formation; then we could rest easy—methodologically—knowing that delusions are the beliefs that fall outside this system. We could then go on to discover the causal mechanisms that do, in fact, bring about these states that are inexplicable in folk terms. I'll call this the *vindication project*, since it aims to take the folk concept of a delusion and turn it into a scientifically respectable concept that delimits a psychologically tractable kind that can anchor inquiry into abnormal belief formation.

DSM-IV-TR (American Psychiatric Association 2000) recognizes the following categories of delusion: paranoia, sin, grandiosity, reference, and somatic. These categories may be useful heuristics. We may find that they mark the main ways in which belief acquisition goes awry: by subverting normal mechanisms of learning about the state of one's body, one's social position, culturally sanctioned behavior, and so on.

The Boydian account of natural kinds lends itself well to the vindication problem in the sense that we do not, as good Boydians, have to look for a universal essence to delusion. We expect delusional subjects to only be more or less like each other, and we expect the causal process that produces delusional states to cluster, rather than to be the same in all cases. Attributions of mental illness, on this picture, depend on the failure of behavior to fit our folk theories; it may well be that in noticing that something fails to fit those theories we are noticing a failure of normal human psychology.

That is the optimistic interpretation. But if we are more pessimistic, we may note a prima facie difficulty for the vindication project. The extension of the folk concept of delusion might be a ragbag of different abnormalities in belief acquisition that have nothing in common. There may be little reason to assume that the folk concept picks out any scientifically significant set of natural phenomena, since "weird ways of coming to believe something" may not designate a natural kind. There may be an indefinitely large number of different, largely unrelated ways in which beliefs can fail to form normally according to folk canons. Remember, for delusions to constitute a natural kind in Boyd's sense it is not enough that there be clusters of characteristics that strike us as similar across cases. There must also be shared causal processes. The vindication project argues that folk thought can spot the clusters of properties that imply the existence of those causal processes. I want to draw attention to that move. To defend psychiatric diagnoses we need more than a better conception of natural kinds. (I am happy to endorse Boyd's.) We also need reasons to believe in the vindication project. Our attribution of mental illness is a function of folk thought, and it is the usefulness of folk thought as a guide to how the mind works that is in question.

So, to return to delusion, we may confront myriad different failures of what folk epistemology groups together as psychologically similar processes when in fact they are not scientifically similar at all. On this pessimistic reading, the vindication project is doomed to failure because there is no genuine causal signature underlying the cluster of properties that guide the attribution of delusion: the properties cluster because they respond to human ways of grouping salient phenomena rather than a common basis in similar natural processes. The causal signature is illusory.

In his defense of seeing delusions as a natural kind, Samuels (2009, p. 76) argues against an objection like this. He says that delusions may constitute a *generic* kind, like metal. A generic kind is a genuine natural kind, and there are further, more specific natural kinds in its extension. The generic kind metal, in Samuels' example, includes magnesium as a specific kind. This is how things would be if, as I speculated above, current categories of delusion are genuine subtypes of the generic category.

The worry is that if human interests or human responses hold the generic category together we do not have a natural generic category at all. We may have a generic kind that shares a lot of properties that strike humans as relevant—more like "shiny things" than "metals." There are presumably physical facts in virtue of which things look shiny to beings like us, but they are unlikely to map on to a natural category.

If Boyer is correct, the vindication project rests on the wager that folk attributions of mental disorder track genuine causal signatures, rather than just imposing a unity dictated by how other people strike us. This implies optimism about the scientific credentials of folk psychology that may not turn out to be the way to bet. It may be that many psychiatric diagnoses have inherited from folk thought a belief that certain kinds of deviance can be grouped together on the basis of a shared underlying process that is not in fact there. This does not mean that there are no natural kinds in psychiatry. There may well be genuine causal signatures and genuine causal mechanisms. But it may not be folk psychology that detects them.

References

American Psychiatric Association. 2000. *Diagnostic and Statistical Manual of Mental Disorders*, fourth edition, revised (*DSM-IV-TR*).

Beebee, H., and N. Sabbarton-Leary. 2010. Are psychiatric kinds "real"? *European Journal of Analytic Philosophy* 6 (1): 11–27.

Bentall, R. 2003. *Madness Explained*. Penguin.

Boyer, P. 2010. Intuitive expectations and the detection of mental disorder: a cognitive background to folk-psychiatries. *Philosophical Psychology* 23: 821–844

Boyd, R. 1990. What realism implies and what it does not. *Dialectica* 43: 5–29.

Boyd, R. 1991. Realism, antifoundationalism, and the enthusiasm for natural kinds. *Philosophical Studies* 61: 127–148.

Churchland, P. M. 1981. Eliminative materialism and the propositional attitudes. *Journal of Philosophy* 78 (2): 67–90.

Ghaemi, S. 2003. *The Concepts of Psychiatry*. Johns Hopkins University Press.

Hopkins, D. 2002. *The Greatest Killer: Smallpox in History*. University of Chicago Press.

Horwitz, A., and J. Wakefield. 2007. *The Loss of Sadness*. Oxford University Press.

Kendler, K., P. Zachar, and C. Craver. 2010. What kinds of things are psychiatric disorder? *Psychological Medicine*, September 22: 1–8.

Kleinman, A. 1987. Anthropology and psychiatry: The role of culture in cross-cultural research on illness. *British Journal of Psychiatry* 151: 447–454.

Murphy, D. 2006. *Psychiatry in the Scientific Image*. MIT Press.

Nozick, R. 1993. *The Nature of Rationality*. Princeton University Press.

Ryder, A. G., J. Yang, X. Zhu, S. Yao, J. Yi, S. Heine, et al. 2008. The cultural shaping of depression: Somatic symptoms in China, psychological symptoms in North America? *Journal of Abnormal Psychology* 117 (2): 300–313.

Sadock, B., and V. Sadock. 2007. *Kaplan and Sadock's Synopsis of Psychiatry*, tenth edition. Lippincott Williams & Wilkins.

Samuels, R. 2009. Delusion as a natural kind. In *Psychiatry as Cognitive Neuroscience: Philosophical Perspectives*, ed. M. Broome and L. Bortolotti. Oxford University Press.

7 Being a Mental Disorder

George Graham

Are there—in addition to the beliefs, desires, wants, memories, and so on that help to constitute the minds or mental states or attitudes of persons—mental disorders or illnesses? We certainly act and talk as if there are mental disorders or illnesses.[1] We visit psychiatrists to get help for them. We take medication to ameliorate them. We write memoirs to share experiences of them. It is useful to divide the answers to this question into two broad classes. One, to use a term in its ontologically technical sense, is *realist* about mental disorder. The other is, to use a contrarian technical term, *anti-realist*.

To believe that it is accurate and veridical to describe certain mental states, processes, or conditions as mental disorders or illnesses is *realism* about mental disorder. A mental-disorder realist claims that mental illnesses are real or exist. They have being. We act and talk as if there are mental disorders, and there are such conditions.

To believe that an accurate, veridical psychology does not and should not use concepts of mental disorder or illness to describe any sorts of mental states or conditions whatsoever is *anti-realism* about mental disorder. To a mental-disorder anti-realist, a mental-disorder concept is a certain kind of concept, to be sure, but it fails to identify or denote anything. It has a null denotation. Mental disorders have no being. They are fictions or myths. We act and talk as if there are mental disorders, and that persons are possible subjects of them, but there are and can be no such conditions.

Realism about mental disorder is orthodoxy in psychiatry, of course. Without commitment to the existence of mental disorders there would be no psychiatry, no psychopathology, and no mental-health clinics. Orthodoxy notwithstanding, however, providing grounds for the conviction that mental disorders really do exist is not a gratuitous exercise. Anti-realism about mental disorder has had vocal advocates, among them Thomas Szasz

(1974, 2001) and Ethan Gorenstein (1992). A commitment to realism faces serious conceptual and scientific challenges.

The chief challenge is to describe the meaning of mental-illness realism's central concept or category: the concept or category of mental disorder or illness. If such a condition exists, what is it like? How is it best described? This challenge is complicated by the fact that among realists there is no stable, uniform, or received description of just what a mental disorder is supposed to be. Realists are not all cut from the same conceptual cloth. The two main current schools of realist thought—the symptom-based conception of a mental disorder (promoted by the third, fourth, and fifth editions of the *Diagnostic and Statistical Manual of Mental Disorders*) and the broken-brain or brain-disorder conception (often advocated in neurology, neuropsychiatry, and cognitive neuroscience)—are incompatible with each other and produce different taxonomies of disorder. (See Murphy 2009 and Radden 2009 for helpful discussions.) The *DSM* promotes a nosology or classification scheme for disorders that is focused on clusters of clinically presented symptoms, and not on descriptions of their proximate causes, sources, or origins (or distal or etiological influences). The broken-brain classification scheme emphasizes the purported neurobiologically or neurochemically destructive causal details thought to be proximately responsible for the onset, the primary symptoms, and the progression of a disorder.

A second and related challenge that a defense of realism faces is not so much bound up with the meaning of the concept of mental disorder as it is bound up with the warrant or evidentiary grounds for the clinical attribution of mental disorder. What are those grounds? Mental illnesses may not satisfy the epistemic standards for attribution that are in force in chemistry and physics, although they may satisfy evidentiary standards operative in clinical practice and psychiatric discourse. So are mental illnesses *truly* real and knowable to be real, or is their reality subordinate to observer-dependent clinical classifications, taxonomic practices, or conventions that may be in place to label or classify them? What is required for *being* and *being known* or interpreted as a mental disorder?

To put the second challenge in somewhat different terms: What keeps mental disorder from being a mere (though potent) myth, in a technical sense of that term—a way of interpreting ourselves to ourselves, in clinics and elsewhere, a manner of understanding some of our problems in living, but an interpretation that does not truthfully or objectively apply to anything. What makes a disorder "out there," objectively in the world? Here is the answer that I propose:

Realism about Mental Disorder (RMD) A mental disorder is an *act-of-classification-independent* and, more specifically, an *inherent* condition of a person. Act-of-classification independence and inherence are the touchstones of mental-disorder realism. The successful application of the concept of a mental illness is not just a question of deploying an otherwise pragmatically useful concept or description. It also is a question of whether an act-of-classification-independent and inherent condition of a person is denoted by the concept.

This chapter is about what the italicized terms in the above definition mean and about how not just to understand realism in RMD terms but to defend it—to argue for the existence of mental disorder. I do not discuss types of proximate causal explanations required for understanding the emergence of a mental disorder or how an otherwise good mental-disorder concept may itself be constructed. Those are two topics that far exceed the limits of a short chapter, although they are crucially important for a fully systematic discussion of RMD and defense of mental-disorder realism, which this essay is not. (For detailed explorations of those topics, see Graham 2013a and Graham 2013b.) But in the present chapter I do employ a concept of mental disorder, for illustrative purposes. (The concept employed, which is my own, is described and defended in the works cited in the parenthetical sentence above.) I use the concept or illustration in this chapter to help to distinguish between two different ways in which to argue for the existence or reality of mental illness or disorder, one of which I call *mediated* or ontologically derivative and one of which I call *unmediated* or not derivative. I intend to describe why the second method of argument or defense is a genuine alternative to the first and should be taken seriously. An unmediated defense, if successful, brings mental disorder within the folds of clinical practice and medical-scientific discovery and investigation. And it does so without implying or suggesting that there is something defective or incomplete about the category of mental disorder if mental disorder or illness fails to qualify, in its particulars, as a brain or neurological disorder, a natural kind, or a biomedical disease.

I

What is required for the proper application of the word "real"? Hypotheses as to what makes for being real come in many varieties. The first thing to notice about being a mental disorder is that the reality of mental disorder is not, of course, something mind independent.

Molecules are real. They exist. They depend on no mind whatsoever for their existence. They are mind independent. If no minds were to exist, molecules still would exist. Not so mental disorders. Mental disorders are conditions of minds of persons. If no minds existed, mental disorders could not exist. Thus, mental disorders, if real, are not real in the same mode or manner as molecules (or as the states or conditions of molecules). In what mode or manner, then, do disorders exist? What sort of nature or reality belongs to them?

Perhaps disorders exist in the same mode or manner as, say, Father's Day or "proper day for a Valentine's card." This would be a socially or culturally assigned category and thus a species of a mind-dependent mode of existence. The existence of special days such those mentioned above depends on how we describe or classify the passage of time. If mental illnesses exist in the manner of Father's Day or Valentine's Day, then being a mental illness depends on facts about how we think about or classify and label certain conditions of persons as mental illnesses. If such an act-of-classification dependence holds, and I say that a certain person has a mental disorder, the claim is true (or false) only relative to a convention or practice that is in place for referring to specific conditions rather than others as mental disorders. Absent the convention or cultural practice, nothing is a disorder. Being a disorder depends on the existence of relevant labeling conventions.

Molecules and their states or conditions, by contrast, exist whether we label them as such or not. Indeed, we may aptly ask if we classify, think about, or understand molecules correctly. The truth or falsity of our claims about molecules is conferred on those assertions by their foci or objects of reference—that is, by the bits of matter or conditions that they are about. I may make a true or a false claim about the behavior of a molecule. There are act-of-classification-independent facts about molecules. But Father's Day? If you look at the date of Father's Day, you will not find any feature of a year that picks this day out independent of the classification activities of human beings. Father's Day is a kind of "social construct" in the sense that assigning a date to the expression "Father's Day" is a social convention. This is not to imply that the assigned date for Father's Day is arbitrary. It may be, but it doesn't have to be. Some aspects of the day may encourage its choice as Father's Day. But the property of being Father's Day is a property that exists only relative to social labeling conventions or classification practices. A change in practice changes the day. To eliminate the labeling practice is to eliminate the day.

Do mental illnesses exist whether or not we classify, categorize, or recognize them? Are they act-of-classification-independent conditions? (Hereafter, for brevity, I shall abbreviate "act-of-classification" to AC.)

A mental-illness realist (or a realist of the stripe that I am describing as a realist) says "Yes, mental disorders are AC-independent conditions." It doesn't matter how we persons in fact classify our mental states or condition.[2] Some conditions are mental disorders or illnesses. Others are not.

How so? How is it that some mental conditions are AC independent? One answer goes as follows: If a mental disorder is a *brain* disorder, then it qualifies as AC independent. Consider, for example, a list of brain disorders—say, Alzheimer's dementia, epilepsy, and Parkinson's Disease. Whether a person suffers from one or more of these conditions does not depend on whether his or her condition is labeled with one of these terms. Human beings were subjects of these neural disorders long before medicine recognized them. Brain disorders are AC independent. Now consider a list of mental disorders—say, delusional paranoia, learned helplessness depression, and dissociative identity disorder. According to the brain-disorder line of thought, if these conditions are brain disorders they are AC independent. Their existence does not derive from labeling conventions.

Many realists about mental illness assert that mental disorders are brain disorders. As Nancy Andreasen crisply puts it, mental disorders are "cells in our brains [gone] bad [and] expressed at the level of systems such as attention and memory" (2001, p. 7). To be a mental disorder is to be a brain disorder, and insofar as brain disorders are AC independent, so also are mental disorders. But are mental disorders aptly described as brain disorders—as cells gone bad?

Substantial immaterial minds are not a theoretical option in medical science or psychiatry. It seems best to think of mental disorders as having a biological basis in the brain. But this does not entail that mental disorders are brain disorders any more than the proposition that economic and cultural activities have their ultimate bases in the activities of physical particles and forces entails that there are no cultural phenomena or economic systems. (See Stephens and Graham 2009 and Graham 2013a.)

A disordered mind may be based in the brain or the central nervous system without the brain being disordered (damaged, neurologically impaired, dysregulated, with cells gone bad, etc.). Or a disorder may be in the brain and the central nervous system without being a brain disorder or a disorder of the brain. To appreciate this point, think of a comparison with somatic illnesses. Illnesses in the body are not necessarily illnesses of the body or instances of a body that biologically has gone bad. Many somatic illnesses are, of course, illnesses of the body (and not just in it), but some are not. Consider the body of a pregnant woman experiencing morning sickness. The ailment or source of discomfort (the nausea and so on) is in the body, certainly, but is this an illness of the body? Is the body damaged, functioning improperly, or in a biologically wrongful manner? Morning sickness may well be an evolved somatic defense mechanism against the harmful effects on the vulnerable embryo of ingestion of plant and animal toxins, which were abundant in the natural environment of our foraging prehistoric ancestors (Profet 1992). Morning sickness may, overall, be a "healthy condition" in the technical biological or adaptational sense that it has been selected for by Mother Nature to ensure that pregnant women are cautious about what they ingest, even if in certain extreme circumstances, because of a case's unpleasantness or severity (some cases induce malnutrition and extreme dehydration), the condition requires medical attention and may merit being classified as an illness of the body.

The question whether mental disorders are best understood as brain disorders is similar to various other questions sometimes asked about mental disorders, such as these: Are mental disorders or illnesses biomedical diseases? Are mental disorders "out there," as cancer or malaria is? Are disorders natural kinds? Are they "out there," as chemical substances are? Like salt and sugar and other natural kinds? If mental disorders are a type of disease or natural kind, then, again, they qualify, I assume, as AC-independent conditions. Cancer and malaria are diseases. Cancer and malaria are not dependent on human classification practices for their reality or being. Salt and sugar are natural kinds; they are not dependent on human classification practices for their existence.

Like the proposal that mental disorders are brain disorders, any proposal that mental disorders are natural kinds or diseases requires specific argumentation. Just to say that they are physically based does not settle the issue. It is ill-considered to assume that being physical means that a mental disorder is a disease, a natural kind, or a brain disorder. Thus, if one worries whether mental disorders can be AC independent without being brain disorders, natural kinds, or diseases, that particular worry is misplaced. (Later in the chapter I will try to explain why mental-disorder realism may not require a mental disorder to be a brain disorder, a natural kind, or a disease.)

II

It is important to be clear about why realism requires act-of-classification independence of a disorder. In response to a mention of a possible role for classificatory acts or practices in the existence of a mental illness, someone may claim that there is a form of realism that insists that mental disorders do exist, provided that cultural (medical and so on) conventions are in place for classifying or describing them. A theorist may wish to call this position about the nature of disorder AC-dependent realism. Talk of mental disorder is taken to be factual, but to be reducible to discourse about cultural conventions.

AC-dependent realism is not without motivation. It is not unbelievable. Since there is no detailed consensus about the meaning of the central concept of a mental disorder, even among mental-health professionals, it is conceivable that the very category of a mental disorder is act-of-classification relative or clinical-observer relative. (In Graham 2013a, I identify six distinct concepts of mental disorder that are available in the literature.) Reference to such relativity may help to explain why there is no stable, received concept of a mental disorder. Different clinicians or observers make incompatible judgments about the nature of a mental disorder. If that's all there is to being a mental disorder, viz., different judgments or acts of classification, it is no mystery that there is no standard or uniform concept of a mental disorder. There is no uniform concept because mental disorders are AC dependent.

Judgmental differences and variability aren't sufficient to warrant AC-dependent realism, however. Clearly, the way in which we do *in fact* draw categorical boundaries around behaviors and mental conditions often expresses classification conventions and the different interests or purposes that motivate those conventions. This admission, however, does not imply that the nature of a mental illness is itself a *mere* classification or taxonomic convention, for a main aim or purpose of our classifying mental states or conditions as disorders is to properly understand these conditions so that that our classifications will be correct. We are interested in getting classifications to match conditions of mind and behavior, not in getting them to mesh with other labeling conventions (unless we have good reason to antecedently or independently trust those other conventions). We are interested in types of illness. We want our conventions to represent proper types.

I assume that, if mental disorders exist, they possess whatever it takes, in an AC-independent manner, to be a mental disorder. Mental disorders, if real, are not (as it were) Mental Disorder Days.

III

What does it take for a mental disorder or illness to exist in an AC-independent manner and to be real? In defining RMD above, I referred to a mental disorder as not just AC independent but also an *inherent* condition. The inherence of a disorder in a person is what it takes to be AC independent and to be real. To understand what I mean by the inherence of a mental disorder, consider keys, locks, and the idea of being intrinsic.[3] Suppose that a metal key is of a particular shape and that it opens locks of a complementary shape. The capacity or power to open a complementarily shaped lock is a feature of the key. (The power is based in the key's rigidity and possessing a particular shape.) By this I mean that the key has it "intrinsically"—that is, separately from the *actual* existence at any *particular* moment of complementary locks. At any particular moment, there may be no complementary locks for a key to open. If, however, a key is to manifest, exhibit, or exercise this power, the exercise requires that it interact with a complementary partner—in this case, an actually existing lock of a certain shape.

We may suppose that a mental disorder is, in some respects, like a key. An individual or person may have a disorder when, in this or that situation, it is not being exercised. We may also suppose that a disorder is manifest only in interaction with certain circumstantial and contextual or complementary partners and not in other circumstances. Thus, the important question is not whether a person can have or harbor a disorder if it is not manifest or exercised, for the answer to that question (subject to some important qualifications) is affirmative. The important question is "What must be true of an environment or circumstance for it to be a complement or partner for a disorder?"

Perhaps if my paranoid delusional disorder is to exhibit itself I must be near colleagues at work. Perhaps if my addiction to gambling is to be exercised I must be at a race track or in a casino. In order for my major or clinical depression to be manifest, I may have to be faced with a negative threat or stressor that seems looming and inevitable. The more serious, pronounced, or grave a disorder, perhaps the wider and more variegated its range of complementary or contextual partners. Perhaps when a case of major depression truly is severe a whole range of social circumstances or contextual landscapes may help to manifest its presence. This does not necessarily mean that a complementary social or external circumstance causes the disorder or depression (or paranoia, etc.). Helping in the exercise of a condition is not helping to cause the condition. A complementary lock does not cause a key. Rather, circumstances or contexts (colleagues, threats, and so on) contribute to or help to elicit a disorder's activation, exercise, or exhibition. Circumstances serve as prompts or stimuli as well as scaffolds, props, or enablers for a disorder (Graham 2013a; Horwitz

2002). If I am depressed and in bed, I may fail to get out of bed. If I am at a race track and addicted to gambling, I may bet my entire paycheck on a long shot.

If a mental disorder (say, major depression) is an intrinsic or circumstantially separable feature of a person, had by a person as the subject of (or object with) the condition, then this is what I mean by referring to a disorder as an *inherent* condition. The *object* (or subject) in which the disorder is housed, is seated, or inheres is, as it were, the person.[4] To draw a circle around a person is to draw a circle around the object that has the disorder. Readers of science fiction may like to think of inherent conditions of persons as conditions that would be duplicated if a person were to be duplicated by passing through a duplication machine. A person's tenure as an associate professor of economics would not be duplicated, nor would his or her birth date. Such features of persons do not "inhere" in persons. They are not intrinsic to them.

So what is it, then, if real? A mental disorder? A mental disorder is a special type of psychological incapacity, or impairment, or disability. And incapacities or impairments, just like capacities or powers, may be harbored in, may be based in, or may exist in persons even when the circumstances in which they are manifest do not in fact obtain. They are circumstantially separable. Just as a key is *capable* of opening a lock if a relevant lock appears, although a relevant lock may not appear, so a deluded paranoid person may be *incapable* of, say, trusting colleagues if colleagues appear, although they may not.

I do not mean to suggest that mental disorders and circumstances are utterly separable or disconnected phenomena. In several respects or along other dimensions, disorders and circumstances certainly are not separable. Although a person may harbor a disorder when it is not manifest, or when no scaffolds or prompts for its symptoms are present, circumstances otherwise are intimately relevant to disorders as well as to our understanding of them. Let me count the ways. I will mention five. If there are others, I have not thought of them.

• It is unwarranted to assert that it can be known or evidenced whether a person has a mental disorder if it is not manifest or exhibited in at least some circumstances. However, we must not fuse together the nature of a disorder with its epistemology or equate its being with its being known. Being a disorder is one thing; being active or manifest and therein epistemically or evidentially accessible is another.
• Social or external circumstances may figure in the etiology or the causal genesis of a disorder, prior to any specific roles that circumstances or

contexts may play in a disorder's manifestation or exhibition. My history of entrapment as a prisoner of war may be responsible for my being clinically depressed when I return home. The variable-ratio schedule of reinforcement to which I was exposed at a horse track may help to explain my addiction to gambling. But once a disorder is mine or is intrinsic to (or inheres in) me, it may fail to be manifest or evident when no suitable environmental partner appears. I may be a subject of major depression without acting sad or forlorn here and now, just as a key may open doors, having been designed to do so, even if no relevant door exists here and now.[5]

• Circumstances may also be relevant to the phenomenological or conscious representational content or experience of a disorder. For example, the content (feelings, moods, attitudes, and so on) of a case of major depression may project onto the contexts or surroundings in which it is manifest or exercised. "Everything is getting meaner and grayer," says a depressed character in Ingmar Bergman's film *Scenes from a Marriage* (quoted on p. 174 of Church 2003). "Music, scents, people's faces and voices." A depressed mood may paint over a depressed person's perception of and feelings toward the world—music, faces, and so on. One former patient with depression wrote that the very air he breathed felt "thick and resistant, as though it [was] full of mushed-up bread" (Solomon 2001, p. 50).

• The harmfulness for its subject of a disorder is environmentally contextualized. Being depressed and not getting out of bed, I lose my job. Subject to paranoid delusions, I am friendless.

• The separability of disorder and circumstance, no doubt, is a kind of bounded or contextualized separability. A disorder, to be a disorder, must be manifest in some normal or relevantly possible courses of events, viz., contexts in which a manifestation partner is present. Without ever being manifest, without symptoms, without effects on behavior, a condition or an incapacity can't claim to being a disorder. If it doesn't harm a person, there is no pathology to it, as it were.

Thus, when I distinguish between the inherence of a disorder and its manifestation I do not mean to distinguish between a disorder and any and all forms of environmental or circumstantial dependence. I mean only that being a mental disorder, a manifestation of a disorder, and a complementary context or external circumstance for a disorder's manifestation are three distinct things. Such distinctions are useful for describing what is meant by speaking of a person as the subject of a disorder and by speaking of a disorder as a real or existing condition.

IV

Realism about mental disorder says that among AC-independent and inherent conditions of persons are mental disorders or illnesses. So now, if one is a realist about mental illness or disorder, how should one go about arguing that mental disorders exist? In the remainder of this chapter I plan to discuss how this can be done. My discussion will be brief, quite truncated in fact. For more detailed discussions, see Graham 2013a and Graham 2013b.

There are, I propose, two different ways to conceive of the defense of realism. These I label *mediated* and *unmediated* defenses of the existence of mental disorder. (Those are my terms of art; they are not used elsewhere in the literature as I use them here.)

First, what is a mediated defense? I began to discuss mediated defenses above in my brief remarks about whether mental disorders are brain disorders. A mediated defense—construed broadly—says that mental disorders are real or exist if they qualify as members of one or more of the following three categories of conditions: biomedical diseases, brain disorders, natural kinds. Thus, it may be said that malaria is a disease and real (an AC-independent and inherent condition of persons). If mental disorders are relevantly like malaria, they are diseases and thus real. Alzheimer's dementia is a brain disorder and real. If mental disorders are relevantly like Alzheimer's dementia, they are brain disorders and thus real. Sugar, salt, and gold are natural kinds and real (AC independent and with their own inherent natures). If mental disorders are relevantly like sugar, salt, or gold, they are natural kinds and thus real.

Such is the central presumption behind a mediated defense of mental-disorder realism. I call the specific stratagem *mediated* because, according to this type of defense, the reality of a disorder is a function of satisfying the terms of a special subsuming or mediating category—specifically that of a disease, a brain disorder, or a natural kind. Mediated defenses appear in various guises in the literature on mental disorder. Sometimes they appear explicitly, as in Samuels' (2009) defense of the proposition that delusions are natural kinds or in Andreasen's (2001) discussion of how each of the categories of disease and brain disorder apply to mental illness. Sometimes they appear implicitly—for example, Stein et al. (2009) do not directly argue that mental disorders are brain disorders (or "brain-mind disorders," as they put it), but they suggest that this may have to be the case if Cartesian dualism about the mental is to be avoided (as, they assume, it should be). I have little or nothing to say about the surrounding literature on mediated defenses here. My interest is in a outlining a methodological challenge to a mediated defense, not in any particular mediated defense or specific mediating category.

If we are to demonstrate that a mental disorder is a natural kind in hopes of showing that it is AC independent and inheres in people, we must first possess a sound and sensible theory of natural kinds before we can know whether such a demonstration succeeds. We must think of natural kinds not, as Paul Churchland describes them, as "at most a tiny elite of very basic physical properties," and in a set that "may indeed be entirely empty" (1989, p. 294), but as potentially inclusive of mental disorders or illnesses. This methodological challenge of requiring a first possession of another theory (not a theory of mental disorder, but one of, say, natural kinds) applies to the other two mediating categories. If aspiration for establishing the reality of mental disorders somehow hinges on their being diseases or brain disorders, satisfying theoretical accounts of such categories of phenomena are needed.

Is a mediated strategy or defense right or proper? Is focusing on one or more of the mediating categories desirable for realism about mental disorder?

Mediation, if successful, would help to defend realism. Tethering disorders to a non-suspect or previously settled category would disarm the worry that there is a special problem of act-of-classification dependency or clinical observer judgmental relativity about a mental disorder. However, unfortunately, just as there is no stable, received interpretation of the idea of mental disorder, there are active controversies and heated debates in the literature over concepts of natural kinds, brain disorders, and diseases. Thus, even if we allow that concepts for such categories may somehow eventually permit mental disorders to be categorized as natural kinds, brain disorders, or diseases, it may strain both clinical patience and theoretical credibility to believe that such controversies and disagreements should first to be resolved in order to help to justify asserting that mental disorders exist. Remember, the focal concern of mental-disorder realism is to defend the proposition that mental disorders exist. It is not to explicate concepts such as those of natural kinds, brain disorders, or biomedical diseases with various interpretations or with analyses specific to them when applied to mental disorder.

Of course, if notions of natural kind, brain disorder, or disease do not readily apply to mental disorders, this does not preclude making accommodating semantic designs or revisions in one or more of these concepts so as to permit talking of mental disorders as natural kinds and so on. But what happens, then, to the stratagem of a mediated defense? It evaporates or dissolves, does it not? Rather than employ a prior or independent notion of a natural kind, brain disorder, or disease to warrant thinking of mental disorders as AC independent and inherent, one or more of these notions would be transformed or semantically retextured under the separable and independent assumption that mental disorders are real conditions of persons. Mental disorders have being, so an individual may be said to have a mental disorder even if we are unsure or doubtful, at the time, whether this condition is also a natural kind, a brain disorder, or a disease.

V

Without downplaying the possible wisdom or lessons to be learned from examination of whether notions of brain disorder, of disease, or of natural kind apply to mental disorders, perhaps we also need or could use a different type of defense of realism. I propose that there is room in theoretical or argumentative space for arguing for the existence of mental disorder that does not aspire to show that mental disorders are brain disorders, diseases, or natural kinds. This is what I refer to as the unmediated method. For example, we may lack closure or decisiveness on whether mental disorders possess sortal essences of the sort that chemicals (on one model for natural kinds) possess, but still aptly categorize certain cases of depression as mental disorders. Or we may be undecided as to whether mental illnesses possess destructive etiologies of the sort found in prototypical diseases, but still aptly think that delusional paranoia is a mental illness. Or we may admit that a mental disorder is a disorder based *in* the brain without also being a disorder *of* the brain or a brain disorder, and yet wisely classify delusions that fail to reflect brain damage as mental disorders.

There can be variations in the unmediated manner by which mental disorders may be shown to be real conditions of persons.[6] Much, of course, depends on just which concept of a mental disorder is in play.

The details of the particular unmediated method that I favor turn on the concept of a mental disorder that I prefer, although the program of an unmediated defense is detachable from my specific concept. It requires only that a mental illness is not presumed or presupposed to be (if real) a disease, a natural kind, or a brain disorder. My particular concept or idea of mental disorder goes, in outline, something like this (see Graham 2013a and Graham 2013b):

Concept of Mental Disorder (CMD) The very idea of a mental disorder or illness is the notion of a type of impairment or incapacity in the rational or reason-responsive operation of one or more basic psychological faculties or capacities of persons. The proximate or immediate causal forces or propensity conditions responsible for this type of incapacity are best described in mixed terms, as a composite of personal conscious and Intentionalistic processes and activities, on the one hand, and sub-personal brute a-rational mechanisms, on the other. Since a disorder is a type of impairment or incapacity, normative conditions or the failure to meet them are essential to being a disorder. The psychological capacities, whose impairments constitute the essential features of a mental disorder, do not operate or function as they should. Clinically depressed persons, for example, are unreasonably or irrationally and uncontrollably aware of negative aspects of themselves and of the world, and often are tormented "by memories of enterprises that have ended in failure" (Bentall 2007, p. 130). Subjects of delusional paranoia, for another example, are unreasonably or irrationally and uncontrollably distrusting of others. They are imprudently hyper-vigilant for perceived threats to their person or self-interest. Our human capacities for emotional care and commitment, amiss in clinical depression, as well as for social understanding, awry in paranoia, are critical for us as human beings. Unless these capacities are in proper order, it is immensely difficult, indeed often impossible, for us to lead decent or satisfying lives. In depression and paranoia the relevant capacities do not operate as they should. In other types of mental disorder, other equally important capacities are impaired, and the capacities or faculties just mentioned may also be impaired in other forms of mental disorder. Harms typically result from such incapacitations.

I do not claim uniqueness for CMD. Virtually everything in it may be found in some other theorists' thoughts about mental disorder. I believe, however, that my particular constellation of elements, and perhaps the order and significance that I attach to them, helps to shed led light on a number of challenges about mental disorder. (For a discussion, see Graham 2013a.) The challenge of defending the existence or reality of mental disorder is among them.

Given CMD, how is an unmediated defense of the existence of mental disorder to be conducted? To what does the method of defense appeal? What facts or forms of evidence are germane if belief in the existence of mental disorder is supported?

To begin with, it should be noted that some people are much worse off, psychologically and behaviorally, than others. In some cases a person's being much worse off is due to the fact that one or more of his or her basic psychological capacities (for social understanding, emotional commitment, and so on) is or are impaired or incapacitated. Such a person falls into harm's way and is unable to respond effectively to good reasons to avoid the harmful consequences of behavior that stem from the incapacity. Most, if not all, typical forms of such reason-unresponsive psychological incapacitation or impairment are constituted, in part, by various forms of disturbance in the conscious or phenomenal experience of a person—generalized distrust, persistent global sadness and pessimism, anxiety and fearful distress, and so on. Additionally, the incapacitation possesses a proximate causal source or explanatory foundation that is, again, partly psychological in nature or content. Wide-ranging, chronic, negative evaluations of one's very own person or self, for instance, may be partly responsible for persistent global sadness and pessimism about the future. A person in the grip or the throes of such incapacitating psychological states or conditions may also have strong incentives (whether or not the person is aware of them) to seek or welcome medical or mental-health assistance or help from others in managing at least one central aspect of his or her life.

Given that psychologically incapacitated conditions of the above sort exist, and qualify as AC-independent and inherent conditions of persons, they warrant being categorized as cases of mental disorder. Categorization as a disorder is not warranted because a condition has been shown to be a natural kind, a biomedical disease, or a brain disorder. It is warranted because of the harmful, complex, and specific nature of a relevant condition, however much the condition is unlike cases of sugar, malaria, or Alzheimer's dementia.

I could continue to detail the unmediated method at an abstract level of description, but I prefer, in the short space remaining, to illustrate the method with a quick example. Suppose that I am the subject of a condition, a spiritual delusion perhaps or state of psychosis, in which I believe or am convinced that I am God. Suppose that eminently sound and sensible norms of rational belief are violated by this conviction, of course, and that my conviction, together with my resistance to obvious contrary evidence, indicates that my psychological faculties for self-comprehension and prudent self-care are impaired or incapacitated. As a result I harm myself. I try to walk on water and, but for the swift action of a lifeguard, nearly drown. I refuse to pay a medical premium for the birth of my child, claiming that his was a virgin birth and that no premium should be necessary for a son of God. I buy a loaf of bread and a fish. I try to live off of them for a month, claiming to multiply each item miraculously to satisfy my nutritional needs, only to lose 40 pounds and require hospitalization for malnutrition. You try to reason with me about my behavior, but I am defensive and unresponsive. My family and friends point to striking incentives for me to improve my way of thinking and behavior and to curtail its harmfulness. I am unmoved.

The normative drift? There is something *wrong* with me, certainly. I am in harm's way. I am not as I should be. I am incapacitated or impaired. I need help.

Suppose I am diagnosed as the subject of a delusional disorder of the religiously grandiose variety (Munro 1999). Suppose that there is no evidence that my brain cells have gone bad or that I am the victim of a neural dysfunction. Brain imaging, neurochemical analyses, and so on evidence no brain damage or neural toxins. Suppose I soon develop paranoid delusions on top of the religious ones. On questions of who I am or how I should lead my life, I am, to put things crudely, not in properly reason responsive self-control.

Suppose, too, that although there is no apparent one-one relation between either my grandiosity or paranoia and an underlying neural kind, as there may be in a case of the behavior that stems from some neurological/brain disorders (such as a blinding brain lesion), there are a number of intriguing one-many relations between my psychological condition and the myriad brain systems that we have independent evidence are responsible for modulating such psychological activities as attention, arousal, and feelings of euphoria and fear. It isn't that my condition is understandable exclusively or exhaustively in brain science terms (remember, we are not assuming that I have a brain disorder[7]), but there exist, let us assume, various questions about my condition that are best answered in the vocabulary of neuroscience. Why is it, for example, that my periodic outbursts of florid paranoia are triggered by the presence of certain people rather than others? Why, for example, am I floridly distrustful of my parish priest, but not of the neighborhood grocer? Part of the answer may lie with my religious preoccupations and therein may require reference to my thoughts about the religious significance of the priesthood (as opposed to the job of being a grocer). But perhaps part of it must be addressed by explanatory reference to information processing connections between the face-recognition area of the brain and the limbic system or other sub-personal mechanisms that help to modulate my fluctuating patterns of emotional arousal.

In view of the grandiosity and paranoia just outlined, it is fit and proper, I propose, to say that I am the subject of a mental disorder. The harmful or wrongful condition that I am in or harbor is an AC-independent and inherent feature of me. The attribution of a mental disorder, all things considered, is a warranted hypothesis, even if we may have good reason to doubt whether the condition is a natural kind, a disease, or a neurological disorder.

An "unmediated" categorization of a condition as a mental disorder is, of course, not indisputable. Just like a mediated attribution of a disorder, it is an empirical hypothesis, not a demonstrative proof from unquestionable axioms. True, it places the burden of defense for realism on the shoulders of someone who wishes to say that a person has a mental disorder, without also showing that the condition is a natural kind, that it is a biomedical disease, or that it reflects brain damage.

I do not have the space here to detail each of the necessities or essential ingredients in the unmediated manner of defending the attribution of a mental disorder. A fully adequate or complete defense requires, for me, given CMD, providing a plausible rendering of the concepts of basic psychological capacities, incapacity-tethered unresponsiveness to reason, and harms to persons. It also requires coming to grips with the fact that the topic of "objective norms" for the proper function of basic psychological capacities is a subject of heated debate in the mental-health literature. The epistemic objectivity of health and illness norms is a subtle and rather daunting issue, but, I believe, not one that undermines or defies effective analysis. The conditions of persons that qualify as mental disorders are prototypically irrational or unreasonable in various distinctive ways and along different dimensions of mind and behavior. This "distinctive-to-disorder irrationality" helps to constitute their pathology or the presence of something *wrong* with a person, and is something that makes certain people markedly worse off than others.

VI

In this chapter I have outlined in broad brush strokes a view about being a mental disorder or illness, and about two distinct methods for warranting the claim that mental disorders exist. One is mediated by one or more of three specific categories. The other is not.

No doubt some readers may prefer a mediated defense of the existence of mental disorder. They may be skeptical of an unmediated argument. An unmediated argument may not offer, to their way of thinking, a sufficiently solid or genuine place in nature for mental disorder. However, the main purpose of this chapter is not to promote the unmediated method (although I prefer it) or to try to raise devastating objections to mediation.

It is to describe, once we are clear about just what it means to be a mental-disorder realist, why mediated and unmediated defenses of the existence of mental disorder constitute different types of defense.

If mediated defenses prove ineffective, we may still recognize the reality of mental disorder in a more direct and less ontologically processed manner. When all is said and done, perhaps a bout of major depression is one general sort of state or condition. The dissolution of a cube of sugar, a fit of malaria, or the progressive development of neuritic plaques and neurofibulary tangles in the cortex of a victim of Alzheimer's dementia (see Macciochi and Barth 1999, p. 258; compare Terry 1992) are entirely different sorts of real-world conditions. Each is, in its own way, an AC-independent and inherent state of affairs, but neither may be a proper or wise model for being a mental disorder.

Acknowledgments

I would like to thank Richard Garrett, John Greenwood, Ralph Kennedy, Neil Levy, Jeffrey Poland, G. Lynn Stephens, Şerife Tekin, and Peter Zachar for useful feedback on an earlier version of this chapter. The earliest version was delivered at a helpful and informative workshop on mental disorders and natural kinds some years ago at UAB. This version is so different from that one that it turns versions into the most motley of unnatural kinds.

Notes

1. I use the expressions "mental illness" and "mental disorder" interchangeably.
2. I do not wish to be read as suggesting that things (states, conditions, etc.) that are constituted by social conventions are *necessarily* unreal. Someone can be a baseball player or a professor only relative to certain conventions, but neither baseball players nor professors are unreal. So, too, a mental state or condition can be, say, a feeling of guilt or an attitude of embarrassment or shame only given certain conventions (about moral duties and social norms for appropriate behavior), but guilt, embarrassment and shame are not for that reason unreal. What I am saying in this chapter is that, for mental-disorder realism, mental disorders or illnesses are not constituted by *sheer* acts of (collective, social) classification of them. If we all say that a certain day is Father's Day, it is Father's Day. If we all say that a certain condition is a delusional disorder, it isn't necessarily a delusional disorder.
3. Metaphysicians sometimes use the adjective "intrinsic" to refer the inherent features or properties of things. See Heil 2003, especially p. 124. I am indebted to Heil for the lock-and-key example.

4. How, or precisely wherein, is a disorder harbored? I suppose that the basal mechanism is the embodied brain and central nervous system. Exploring that particular "how" question would require a discourse on the neural bases of mental disorder, a topic that I cannot even begin to approach here. Perhaps I should add, though, that by "inherent" I do not mean being ineliminable. Just as a key may lose its shape and thus lose its ability to open locks so a person may become free of a disorder. To inhere is not to forever be stuck.

5. To some ears what I have just said above may seem mistaken or confusing. "I can be the clinically depressed without acting or feeling depressed? That is outlandish!" It is not outlandish. Somatic illnesses often are conditions that a person may be in or possess even when not manifest. For example, I may have a cardiovascular disease that is not symptomatically manifest while I am resting on a couch. It isn't that the illness merely is latent. I actually have it. But none of its symptoms may be evident while I am reclining.

6. Other attempts at unmediated defenses of the existence mental disorder or of psychological ill health are available in the literature, although not under the label "unmediated." One is offered by Richard Bentall (2004) in connection with his critique of a biomedical disease model of disorder. Bentall calls his a symptom-based or complaint-based psychiatry (although this certainly is not to be confused with *DSM*'s symptom-based nosology). "Complaints," he writes, "are all there is." There is, he asserts, no "ghostly illness" that requires an explanation. I don't have space to discuss Bentall's approach here, but I believe his position may be aptly reconstructed as an unmediated construal of what it means to be a (ghostless) mental illness or disorder. (Bentall's view is discussed in Graham 2013a.)

7. One of the claims made in Graham 2013a and in Graham 2013b is that mental disorders *qua* mental possess (in part) mental or psychological (proximate) causal-explanatory foundations, whereas brain disorders do not. As long as a disorder is a brain disorder, and not just in the brain but of it (to use a terminological distinction noted earlier in the chapter), the language of brain science is sufficient unto the explanatory day or neurological purposes thereof. Psychological language, however, is required (along with brain science) to help to understand the immediate origins of a mental disorder. Or so I argue in the two works cited here.

References

Andreasen, N. 2001. *Brave New Brain: Conquering Mental Illness in the Era of the Genome*. Oxford University Press.

Arpaly, N. 2005. How it is not "just like diabetes": Mental disorders and the moral psychologist. *Philosophical Issues* 15: 282–298.

Bentall, R. 2004. *Madness Explained: Psychosis and Human Nature*. Penguin.

Bentall, R. 2007. Clinical pathologies and unusual experiences. In *The Blackwell Companion to Consciousness*, ed. M. Velmans and S. Schneider. Blackwell.

Church, J. 2003. Depression, depth and the imagination. In *Imagination and Its Pathologies*, ed. J. Phillips and J. Morley. MIT Press.

Churchland, P. M. 1989. Conceptual progress and word-world relations: In search of the essence of natural kinds. In *A Neurocomputational Perspective: The Nature of Mind and the Structure of Science*. MIT Press.

Gorenstein, E. 1992. *The Science of Mental Illness*. Academic Press.

Graham, G. 2013a. *The Disordered Mind: An Introduction to the Philosophy of Mind and Mental Illness*, second revised edition. Routledge.

Graham, G. 2013b. Ordering Disorder: Mental Disorder, Brain Disorder, and Therapeutic Intervention. In *Oxford Handbook of Philosophy and Psychiatry*, ed. K. Fulford et al. Oxford University Press.

Graham, G., and G. L. Stephens. 2007. Psychopathology: minding mental illness. In *Philosophy of Psychology and Cognitive Science*, ed. P. Thagard. Elsevier.

Heil, J. 2003. *From an Ontological Point of View*. Oxford University Press.

Horwitz, A. 2002. *Creating Mental Illness*. University of Chicago Press.

Macciochi, S., and J. Barth. 1999. Dementia. In *The Blackwell Dictionary of Neuropsychology*, ed. J. Beaumont, P. Kenealy, and M. Rogers. Blackwell.

Munro, A.1999. *Delusional Disorder: Paranoia and Related Illnesses*. Cambridge University Press.

Murphy, D. 2009. Psychiatry and the concept of disease as pathology. In *Psychiatry as Cognitive Neuroscience: Philosophical Perspectives*, ed. M. Broome and L. Bortolotti. Oxford University Press.

Profet, M. 1992. Pregnancy sickness: a deterrent to maternal ingestion of teratogens. In *The Adapted Mind: Evolutionary Psychology and the Generation of Culture*, ed. J. Barkow, L. Cosmides, and J. Toobey. Oxford University Press.

Radden, J. 2009. Is this dame melancholy?: Equating today's depression and past melancholia. In *Moody Minds Distempered: Essays on Melancholy and Depression*, ed. J. Radden. Oxford University Press.

Samuels, R. 2009. Delusion as a natural kind. In *Psychiatry as Cognitive Neuroscience: Philosophical Perspectives*, ed. M. Broome and L. Bortolotti. Oxford University Press.

Solomon, A. 2001. *The Noonday Demon*. Chatto and Windus.

Stein, D., K. Phillips, D. Bolton, K. Fulford, J. Sadler, and K. Kendler. 2009. What is a mental/psychiatric disorder? From *DSM*-IV to *DSM*-V. *Psychological Medicine* 40: 1–7.

Stephens, G., and G. Graham. 2009. Mental illness and the consciousness thesis. In *The Neuropsychology of Mental Illness*, ed. S. Wood, N. Allen, and C. Pantelis. Cambridge University Press.

Szasz, T. 1974. *The Myth of Mental Illness*. Harper and Row.

Szasz, T. 2001. Mental illness: Psychiatry's phlogiston. *Journal of Medical Ethics* 27: 297–301.

Terry, R. 1992. The pathogenesis of Alzheimer's Disease: What causes dementia? In *Neurophilosophy and Alzheimer's Disease*, ed. Y. Christian and P. Churchland. Springer.

8 Defensible Natural Kinds in the Study of Psychopathology

Harold Kincaid

In this chapter I argue for two main theses: that there are some types of psychopathology that can reasonably and usefully be thought of as constituting natural kinds, given a naturalist take on the latter, and that those kinds are best thought of as categorical rather than dimensional. I also make some arguments about what must be done—but largely has not been done—methodologically to identity psychopathologic kinds of the sort I defend. In section 1, I argue for one picture of natural kinds, theories, and explanation appropriate for the social and behavioral sciences. In section 2, I look at a number of arguments that psychopathology must be thought of as dimensional. I either reject them or show how they are compatible with categorical approaches. In section 3, I apply the perspective of section 1 and insights from section 2 to argue that there is a plausible case to be made that certain types of depression constitute natural kinds in my favored sense.

1 Natural Kinds, Theories, and the Social and Behavioral Sciences

Why are we interested in whether various behaviors we label as psychopathologies are natural kinds? I take it that our basic motivation is to show that our accounts of these behaviors provide objective explanations and successful predictions of behavior—explanations that ideally give us guidance in intervening.

Although the word "objectivity" has multiple independent senses and uses (Douglas 2004) and can be fodder for grand philosophical theses, my usage is more commonsensical and practical. When we ask if we can produce objective explanations of behavior labeled psychopathological, we want to know if the explanations we provide result from reliable processes—that is, processes that give us fallible evidence that our explanations are true. With that goal in mind, the first task is to explain when invoking natural kinds succeeds, both as a general philosophical account of science or as specific explanations for behavior. There is a traditional answer to that question that still carries considerable sway. After sketching that traditional answer and its problems, I will present an alternative vision.

The traditional approach to natural kinds, following in positivist footsteps, sees theories as central to science, laws as the main component of theories, and laws as regularities relating natural kinds. Natural kinds are captured by definitions that give the individually necessary and jointly sufficient traits picking them out. In our best science, this results in measurements of quantities that are then related in systematic ways by the laws of science, as temperature, pressure, and volume are related by the gas laws. Laws pick out natural kinds when they support counterfactual assertions. Thus, identifying the natural kind "copper" allows to us assert the real law that if a certain sample were heated to 1,084°C it would melt. Generalizations without natural kinds do not support counterfactuals. The generalization "all the coins in my pockets are pennies" does not allow me to infer that if there were other coins in my pocket they would melt at 1,084°C. Philosophy of science can contribute to all this by clarifying and formalizing these interlocking components by, for example, giving the necessary and sufficient conditions for concepts of law and natural kinds themselves, formalizing the correct criteria for specific natural kinds, and giving the logical formulation of the laws that natural kinds ground.

It is natural step from these ideas to normative judgments about good science. On this traditional view, successful science requires showing that the domain to be investigated consists of natural kinds. Thus, there may well be some misguided attempts at science in domains that have no natural kinds. Again, philosophy can help in the process of deciding which inquiries can be successful sciences by determining whether they meet the requirements for having natural kinds and thus for laws and theories. Some areas of inquiry can be shown to be dead ends as sciences because their basic concepts cannot be natural kinds.

Applied to the study of psychopathology, this perspective on natural kinds shows up in some common projects. One says that to study psychopathology we need to start with a clear concept of disease. We can get a clear concept by looking at proposed definitions tested against intuitive examples. The presumption is that "disease" is a natural kind that we can clarify and for which we can find necessary and sufficient conditions. A predominant strand in this tradition argues that an adequate concept of disease must be explained in terms of deviations from normal functioning. With such an analysis in hand, we can then go on to ask which, if any, of the behaviors currently labeled psychopathological pick out disease natural kinds. The scientific standing of and prospects for progress in psychiatry and whatever other areas study psychopathology allegedly depend on the answer. Horwitz and Wakefield (2007) proceed in roughly this way as they attack the classifications of depression in the fourth edition of the *Diagnostic and Statistical Manual of Mental Disorders*. They conclude that some individuals labeled depressed constitute a real natural kind but that many others do not and are not the proper objects of investigation by psychiatry.

The general positivist perspective on natural kinds also informs contemporary psychometric approaches to psychopathology. Here the main thought is that studying psychopathology is best done by finding measurable quantities or attributes. These attributes vary along continuous dimensions and are latent variables inferred primarily from observed responses to questionnaires. A mature science of abnormal behavior would show how variations in one attribute are related to variations in another—in short, would produce laws in the positivist sense. The positivist influences also show up in this approach in that *laws* as universal regularities relating quantities are the ideal, whereas there is relatively little mention of causation and mechanisms. Though latent-variable models of the kind used in psychometrics can be interpreted as full-fledged causal models, they seldom are. Taking a causal picture seriously would mean trying to rule out alternative models that might be consistent with the data by, for example, confronting the simple causal picture of item-response theory with its local-independence assumptions against other more complicated models.[1] However, such attempts are not made.[2]

By emphasizing conceptual analysis and a logic of scientific inference, the positivists (and, later, analytic philosophy) claimed more for philosophy— and in a sense more for science—than can be achieved. It is a mistake to think that once we acquire a concept we are in a position to determine its essence—its necessary and sufficient conditions—by tests against intuitions and linguistic practice. Most successful concepts, including scientific ones, have a much more complex relation to evidence and reality that has to be worked out in the actual practice of the science itself—an ongoing process, as Mark Wilson (2008) shows in wondrous detail for important part of physics. Science does not first get clear on its basic concepts and then do the science, nor does science wait for philosophers to clarify their domain and determine whether they meet the standards for good science. Conceptual clarification, establishing standards of good research, and empirical investigation are ongoing, interactive processes.

There is good reason to think that most ordinary concepts and many scientific ones are best understood as identifying prototypes that anchor family resemblances between applications. The concept of the gene is very instructive in this regard and has important implications for thinking about psychopathology. There is still no agreed-upon definition in terms of necessary and sufficient conditions of "gene" (Moss 2003). Instead, different variations of the concept work in different applications. The population genetics concept that has its roots in nineteenth-century developments identifies a "factor" or "elements" that explains patterns of inheritance of phenotypic characters. For some time, molecular biology worked with a definition in terms of a strand of DNA that codes for a protein. However, reality has been recalcitrant, and the actual biology is far more complicated and variegated than this simple "beads on a string" picture. Nonetheless, biology continues to make great progress using the gene concept.

Furthermore, tests of potential concepts against intuition are of dubious value. First, as we just saw, concepts can be quite useful without being strictly definable. Furthermore, we have to ask whose intuitions we use and how it is that intuitions tell us about how the world works. Intuitions vary across groups, and there surely is no reason to think that those of analytic philosophers should be privileged. However, even sticking to disciplinary experts will not ensure agreement on matters of linguistic usage. In the end, science progresses by settling disputes over concepts by sustained and diverse attempts to tie them to the world, not by achieving semantic consensus over intuitions.

Another classic problem for the positivist picture of natural kinds is that it is an uncomfortably small circle. Laws are distinguished from accidental generalizations by their ability to support counterfactuals. Statements support counterfactuals when they pick out natural kinds. Natural kinds are picked out by those categories that figure in natural laws.

Of course, if the goal is not to give a reductive analysis, this circle could just be a fact of life, not necessarily a problem. However, investigating this circuit further raises doubts about whether its elements ground clear distinctions even if we ignore the smallness of the circle. I would argue (Kincaid 2004; see also Ladyman and Ross 2007) that the ability of a categorization and its related generalizations to support counterfactuals is a matter of degree, depending on what we hold fixed and what we know about causal processes. If my pants pockets are such that only pennies will go in them, then generalizing about the coins in my pocket will support counterfactuals because we can provide a causal mechanism behind them.

A related issue with the positivist circle is that the emphasis on laws and on theories composed of them badly describes the way some important science works. Rather than having universal laws related in systematic ways to constitute a theory, much science provides piecemeal causal explanations inferred from interventions and observations. What we get is a batch of mechanisms that have to be tried out and modified for new applications. An axiomatizable theory that defines and interweaves fundamental kinds across a broad domain is not on the books. I have argued for this conclusion, for example, in cancer research (2008). Molecular biology in general is about identifying factors—mostly molecules and organelles— and their roles in complex causal networks.

The above considerations raise serious doubts about the program in philosophy of medicine and psychiatry that seeks a universal account of disease that is then used in a normative way to judge the worthiness of accounts of specific diseases. There is little reason to think there is one disease concept, even after pruning, and equally little reason to think that we can learn much about the scientific issues—rather than value and policy issues— by searching for it. This was precisely the conclusion that a task force of scientists reached when asked to advise on whether obesity should be considered a disease (Allison et al. 2008).[3]

Most of what I have said so far has been negative. I want to turn now to a positive conception that is useful in thinking about natural kinds and psychiatric classification. The conception will be defended and applied in sections 2 and 3.

Psychopathology is amenable to applications of natural-kind classifications in that (1) we can sometimes pick out a distinct group of individuals falling into a category and (2) we can use such categorizations to pick out real patterns in the sense of Dennett 1991 and Ladyman and Ross 2007. In connection with point 1, the idea is that the traits of a heroin addict who has made repeated unsuccessful attempts to quit the drug at great cost to himself and others, as well as the traits of the person experiencing major depressive disorder who can only sit in a darkened room staring into space, are not just attributes continuously displayed in various degrees by all members of the population. In other words, some psychopathology is a natural kind in that there is a qualitative difference between individuals who fall into a category and those who do not. Thus, I am defending a categorical view of some psychopathology rather than a dimensional view.

The dialectic in the debates over mental kinds as natural kinds and those over categorical vs. dimensional views of psychopathology is subtle. Dimensional traits such as temperature, pressure, and volume certainly are fine candidates for natural kinds in the science—they fit into laws in the ways expected of natural kinds. However, natural kinds can also be about grouping entities rather than measuring traits. I believe that the dimensional view of psychopathology has sometimes been a real hindrance to making the case for psychopathologies as natural kinds.

If taken seriously, dimensional accounts are really considerably more demanding than categorical accounts, though this is often not recognized for various reasons. For one thing, as I argue below, it is common to hoist unnecessary demands on categorical accounts so that the relative stringencies of dimensional accounts are downplayed. Moreover, the psychometric tradition has generally claimed to be measuring dimensions while using a notion of measurement (assigning a number) that has a dubious ability to pick out natural kinds in the way other sciences can. An attribute such as temperature has properties that make measurement in the basic sense possible (e.g., additivity); assigning a number in the psychometric tradition falls short of that (Michell 1999). So the actual dimensions that are defended over categorical approaches are anemic ones.

This situation has led to a somewhat weird circumstance. Those trained in the psychometric tradition argue that psychiatry's traditional categorical nosology is misguided because psychopathology, like all psychological characteristics, is dimensional. Yet their own dimensional construals of psychopathology are easy targets for critics who think of dimensions as natural kinds of the sort that the physical sciences produce (Borsboom 2009). The upshot is supposed to be that psychopathology cannot successfully be described in terms of natural kinds. The picture of psychopathology offered in contemporary psychometrics is a very demanding one: science has to describe fundamental traits that meet the requirements of fundamental measurement (e.g., they support interval scales and show law-like relations among them). The causal mechanisms described by modern molecular biology, for instance, are not generally expressible in these terms. The psychometric ideal threatens to let the best become an enemy of the better. Thus my goal is to show that there is a plausible categorical sense of psychopathology that is not committed to the strong claims that a defensible dimensional conception would entail.

In addition to dividing individuals into distinct groups, the second element in the view of natural kinds I defend says in simple terms that there are discernible patterns in people's lives, often causal in nature, that we can identify by means of categorizations of psychopathology. Dennett uses the notion of a real pattern to denote nonredundant information-bearing relations, which are relative to a type and scale of description. Kindred notions are Goodman's twins of projectability and entrenchment, predicates that travel beyond their original domain successfully. On this view, we have defensible natural kinds in the study of psychopathology if we have evidence that our classifications pick out distinguishable groups of individuals and that those classifications allow us to identify well-grounded patterns between membership in that group and other variables.

This conception of a natural kind is a liberal one, but that does not mean it makes natural kinds as matter of convention or subjective. Immediately below, and in section 3, I will discuss rigorous methods for establishing the existence of natural kinds of psychopathology in the sense I have sketched. My natural kinds admit a certain sort of pluralism. The patterns picked out may be more or less generalizable and informative, and there may be multiple consistent ways of assigning individuals to predictive and explanatory categories. I am a realist about natural kinds in psychopathology; however, it is a kind of "rainforest realism," to use Don Ross's (2000) phrase. In view of the very significant causal complexity in the determinants of psychopathology, it would not be surprising to find that there were multiple different but consistent ways of delineating it.

The account I am relying on also need not entail that there is a single identifiable cause or basis of category membership or that membership is an all-or-nothing affair. There may be multiple different systems interacting in different ways, picked out by cognitive neuroscience and neurobiology, that produce the same or similar kinds of psychopathology. Fuzzy-set descriptions in which there is a degree of membership (running from "not in" to "in with some significant probability" to "definitely in," for example) might also characterize the psychopathological kinds I am defending. These empirical issues are beyond my purview here.

I want to finish this section by providing more substance to the notion of categorical groupings that support objective predictive and explanatory accounts of psychopathology. I want to show that it can be reasonable to assert that kinds of psychopathology can be classified in such a way that putting individuals in kinds or categories allows for reliable evidence about regularities and/or causes. By reliable evidence I mean evidence that is produced by independent measures and tests—that is, measures and tests that do not depend on one another for evidential value. A PET scan and an fMRI scan are independent in that they rely on different physical quantities; a correlation found in one population and replicated in another are independent in that the success of one does not depend on the other. These independent tests provide evidence for regular associations and causal relations. Comorbidities between different diseases are one kind of association; differences in relapse rates between those in a category and those not in a category, with other probable factors controlled for, may be a causal relation.

In the psychometrics tradition there is extensive discussion of related issues under the heading of "construct validity," distinguishing many elements of validity. One broad notion identifies the "nomonological validity" that may result when a categorization is connected in a law-like way with other important variables and measures. That can happen through "convergent validity" (correlating with things it ought to correlate with) or through "discriminant validity" (not correlating with things that should be irrelevant). Obviously these notions point to something similar to what I am getting at with my demand for categories that support objective predictive and explanatory accounts of psychopathology.

However, for several reasons, traditional psychometric approaches to "validation" are often unhelpful for projects of the kind I am pursuing. The various types of validity described are not used entirely consistently, and more time is spent on identifying these subspecies than on developing concrete tools that realize them. The literature also depends on assumptions I do not want to make: classifications use observable indicators to measure unobservable traits that are dimensional in nature. The distinction between observable indicators and unobservable latent variables is too simple for the same reasons that the distinction between observable and unobservable distinction is too simple, though contextual local variants can be defensible. Moreover, the view I am defending does not require that categories pick out dimensional traits that meet the demands of numerical measurement.

This image of defining a construct and then going on to validate it also easily becomes the too-simple positivist picture of first defining concepts in terms of necessary and sufficient conditions, then identifying measures of those conditions, and then showing that they instantiate universal laws. In a recent review article on the validity of psychological constructs promoting this picture, Strauss and Smith (2009, p. 112)—quoting Bryant (2000)—write:

Imagine, for example, that you created an instrument to measure the extent to which an individual is a "nerd." To demonstrate construct validity, you would need a clear initial definition of what a nerd is to show that the instrument in fact measures "nerdiness." Furthermore, without a precise definition of nerd, you would have no way of distinguishing your measure of the nerdiness construct from measures of shyness, introversion or nonconformity.

Although it might be nice if things proceeded this way, scientific progress often occurs without meeting these demanding standards and may well be hindered by seeking them. I have already mentioned the work by Mark Wilson that shows just how complex and contextual the application of scientific concepts often is. Hasok Chang (2004) makes a similar case for temperature, the foundational concept for the gas laws and something thought to be a paradigmatic and exemplary case of scientific measurement. Chang shows the actual story to be far messier. Scales were developed without any clear definition or theory of what heat was. The fixed points of boiling and freezing were not so fixed and admitted multiple definitions. Linearity across the range was largely assumed, not justified. Dealing with very high and very low temperatures required different scales not easily related to one another. Far from starting with a precise definition of heat and using its conditions to build measurements that provided gold standards, the science progressed fitfully, with much mutual justificatory dependence between proposed scales and instruments.

Finding evidence for what I think is currently doable in the study of psychopathology—categorical groupings that support objective predictive and explanatory accounts of psychopathology—does not require numerical measurements of latent traits. Rather, I think, progress can come from showing that there are some categorizations of psychopathology that group individuals together (rather than measuring abstract properties) in a way that allows for the piecemeal identifying of causes and explanatory associations, rather than universal laws between attributes.

Let me say something more concrete and positive about the process of identifying explanatory categorizations. Though the distinction is not sharp, for our purposes we can break the process of identifying categories into two parts: providing evidence that we have found a real categorical distinction between having a certain kind of psychopathology and not having it and showing that the categorical distinction in question allows us to identify putative associations and causal relations.

We can provide evidence that we have a real grouping by showing that we have independent items or indicators that pick out the same individuals. For the psychopathology of depression, as we will see in section 3, various independent measures are available. Among these measures are answers to items on questionnaires (which themselves will get at different behavioral and attitudinal characteristics), the results of various cognitive tests, and different kinds of physiological measures. To the extent that informationally distinct indicators classify individuals similarly, we have evidence for a relevant grouping.

Finding that scores on different continuous scales purportedly measuring the same construct correlate with one another is one way to achieve the first step of showing that there is a distinct group. If the scales come with cutoff scores and agree among themselves when assigning individuals to categories, this categorization can also be evidence. However, this common practice has several limitations. The screens used may overlap considerably in the items used, compromising informational independence. The cutoff scores may have limited justification and thus may be arbitrary. The screens may have an ambiguous relation to theoretically motivated characteristics of the disorder and/or to *DSM* criteria.

In addition to these problems, if our goal is to find categorical distinctions in nature rather than to measure continuously distributed attributes, indicators that are highly correlated can be an obstacle rather than a virtue. Correlated indicators are a virtue if we think there is an underlying common cause of indicator scores, because low-level correlations suggest that there are other causes of the indicators scores and thus raise doubts about the existence of a single underlying trait causing them. However, if our aim is to show that individuals fall into distinct groups rather than to measure a continuous trait—and it is the former I am advocating as a reasonable goal at this point in the study of psychopathology—then we are not committed to some underlying unobserved single factor causing scores on indicators. In fact, some of the best methods for grouping individuals if there are qualitatively distinct categories—what are called taxometric methods (Ruscio et al. 2006)—work best if indicators are *not* strongly correlated.

Taxometric methods are a distinct set of potentially powerful ways of establishing the first step of showing that there are objective classifications that ground predictive and explanatory generalizations. They provide important evidence for the conception of psychopathological natural kinds I am urging, so it is useful to outline the basic intuitions behind them.

Taxometric methods, developed by Paul Meehl and others (Meehl and Yonce 1994, 1996; Meehl 2004; Ruscio et al. 2006), have implementations in the R programming language (Ruscio et al. 2006). The procedures examine sets of indicators in different subsamples of data, looking for correlations between those indicators that would obtain as the subsamples approached an equal division between individuals in a taxon and those in its complement. If such subsamples are not found, the evidence supports dimensionality. So, for example, if we randomly sample from a population of men and women and regress their heights on baldness measures, we expect to see maximum slopes in subsamples composed equally of men and women and slopes of zero in subsamples consisting in only men or women. No such difference between equally mixed and skewed samples would be seen if gender were continuously distributed. Such methods for picking out groups have been extensively studied in simulations with known data, and there is a fairly good grip on the relative sensitivity and specificity of various taxometric procedures. Several independent algorithms are able to identify the presence or the absence of a qualitatively distinct group quite accurately.

Taxometric results can be further strengthened by combining them with other statistical investigations. It is common in psychology to approach classification by means of factor analysis and related techniques. As I will explain in the next section, these tools are not well suited for deciding whether a certain classification is best thought of as categorical or as dimensional. However, these tools do provide evidence for whether a single dimension or multiple dimensions best fit a given set of data, on the assumption that the phenomena are dimensional. If taxometric methods lead to a categorical result, then a multi-dimensional model can be tested against indicators scores in the nontaxon group to see if it explains the data well. Bernstein et al. (2010) used taxonic methods to investigate anxiety sensitivity and found evidence of a taxon. They then showed by confirmatory factor analysis—which is really just a specific kind of structural-equation modeling where an underlying factors are unobservable causes of indicator scores—that a four-factor model fit the complement, nontaxonic group well. This provides supporting evidence for the hypothesis that individuals with severe, qualitatively distinct conditions had been lumped together with individuals with quite varying and multifaceted attributes.

Though there is much talk about validity in the literature, *detailed accounts* of the second component—of what has been called nomological validity or the ability to use objective categorizations to explain and make predictions—are hard to find. I think this is in part because the concept itself has positivist hangovers that take law-like generalizations as essential. But law-like generalizations without causal mechanisms can lead to a host of non-explanatory connections. The obvious solution to such worries is to try to find evidence backing up explicit causal claims and models based on assignment of individuals to psychopathological categories. That is indeed the ideal, I think. But because of the positivist hesitancy to talk of causes at all in the social and behavioral sciences, this route has not been vigorously pursued.

Although systematic discussions of nomological validity are scarce, in practice researchers do make arguments for, and have methods to identify, nomological validity. We can flesh out that concept by briefly describing some of these approaches. As was noted above, evidence can come from showing associations where they are expected and showing no associations where they would not be expected. We call upon specific background knowledge to tell us what to expect. That knowledge may simply come from known past associations without any plausible causal story behind the correlation, or it may involve information for which there is evidence that some kind of causal process or mechanism lies behind the association. Obviously the latter makes for more convincing evidence. For example, we might expect substance abuse and depression to covary, because substance abuse may be a form of self-medication, because abuse may lead to stresses that make depression more likely, and so on. We have no similar background information suggesting that schizophrenia and bulimia should covary.

Some of the methods used most often in trying to show that a given assignment of individuals to distinct categories fits into a nomological network are listed below.

(1) Look at the predictive value of a bivariate regression with category status as the independent variable. If we were, for example, trying to show that a classification of individuals into addicted/non-addicted or major depressive disorder is valid, we might treat relapse rate as the dependent variable and category status as the independent. The size of the standardized regression coefficient would be taken as measuring the size of the association, and a test of statistical significance would argue against the hypothesis that this association resulted from random sampling variability.

(2) Look at the predictive value of a multivariate regression with category status as an independent variable along with some other variable(s) that might confound the relationship between category membership and the

independent variable. If we were trying to show that a classification of individuals into major depressive disorder is valid, we might again treat relapse rate as the dependent variable, category status as an independent variable, and family history as a further independent variable. The size of the standardized regression coefficient would be taken as measuring the size of the association, and a test of statistical significance would argue against the hypothesis that this association resulted from random sampling variability.

(3) Do both (1) and (2) with something category status should *not* predict. If we take obsessive compulsive disorder to be something distinct from addiction, we might use a diagnosis of compulsive disorder as the dependent variable and addiction or depression status as the independent variable, and vice versa.

These methods try to establish expected correlations and noncorrelations of group membership. Variations on these methods are common for identifying construct validity.

I think these methods provide good tools for the project, but it is, of course, an empirical matter whether they succeed, and they certainly could be developed into a more comprehensive and integrated set of procedures. Thus, I do not share the pessimism expressed by Jeffrey Poland in this volume. Poland argues that whatever correlations we find between *DSM*-related measures and other variables connected to psychopathology are mostly spurious—they result from other elements affecting some subset of those labeled with the *DSM* diagnosis. As I have mentioned and will discuss in more detail below, screens used for categorization certainly can have many problems that may cause confounding. Nonetheless, multivariate techniques do look for other factors that might explain observed correlations; they can potentially tell us when there is some characteristic true of only a subset of individuals that accounts for correlations between the *DSM*-type classification and other variables. Multivariate regression is precisely looking for subsets of each independent variable that have predictive power. If such subsets exist, then spurious correlations will be reduced or eliminated. There is no *a priori* reason why Poland's worries cannot be answered.

I have also noted already that the various methods cited above would be most compelling if they were formulated as full causal/measurement models, and that there is indeed a risk of spurious correlation—and spurious noncorrelation—without them. In the abstract, there is no way of systematically eliminating such possibilities or confirming them—we need specific causal models to identify and investigate these possibilities.

Some authors who focus specifically on the categorical-vs.-dimensional debate also would like to go beyond showing just that a category fits into a nomological web by testing a categorical classification directly against a dimensional one. They do so by including a dimensional measure along with categorical status in the first three tests above. If the taxon variable retains its size and significance after the dimensional variable is added, then the interpretation is that category membership has independent explanatory power; if the dimensional variable is small and/or nonsignificant, the conclusion is that it has all the explanatory power. If the reverse holds for the dimensional variable, it is concluded that the phenomena are dimensional.

I do not think these tests are reliable. Like general tests for nomological validity, these tests need an explicit causal model before inferences can be drawn. To see this, let me sketch what I take to be a reasonable abstract general causal model of psychopathology embodying the categorical approach (figure 8.1).

Suppose that there are identifiable neurological changes in severe alcoholics such that we can divide the population of drinkers—perhaps based on a previous taxonomic analysis or other evidence—into three groups: those with severe disease, those with problems, and those with no problems. Belonging to those different groups is then a causal factor explaining scores on observed indicators such as withdrawal, but it need not be the only cause of those indicators (and indeed should not be if we want dimensional differences in indicator scores to matter). The phenomena these indicators measure may, in turn, influence outcome variables such as relapse, response to treatment, and comorbidity. Category membership may also directly influence outcomes. Predictors of category membership are then distal causes.

This first-pass model can, of course, be enhanced with more variables and causal arrows, but in its skeletal form, as presented here, it shows how the associational procedures described above may mislead. Regressing outcomes on group membership and dimensional severity scores makes sense if we think the causal relation among group membership, a dimensional factor measured by the indicators, and predicted outcomes is as characterized by one of the two structures illustrated in figure 8.2. If one of these is the true structure, using the kinds of regressions described above to test dimensionality against categorical interpretations will provide us with evidence about which of the two structures is more plausible. However, these are not the only possible models, as figure 8.1 demonstrates. If the true structure is something like the one illustrated in figure 8.1, then the

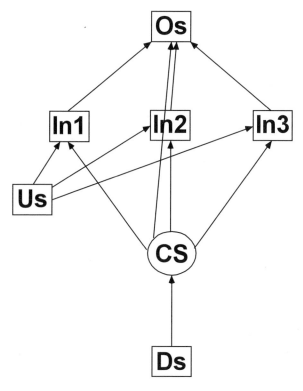

Figure 8.1

A first-approximation causal model of addictive phenomena. In1, In2, and In3 represent observable indicators or symptoms (circles representing observables and squares nonobservables). CS (categorical status), the group-membership variable, can take on three values: severe, moderate, and problem free. Arrows represent the direction of direct causes. Ds represents distal causes of group membership, e.g., drug exposure, and Os are outcomes variables, such as comorbidity with depression. Us represents other factors besides category membership that influence scores on indicator variables, allowing for the possibility that there is a dimensional aspect that plays a causal role. Distal variables cause category membership and may also cause outcomes directly.

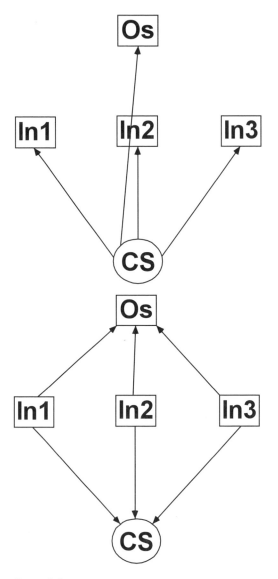

Figure 8.2
Top: A pure categorical model. Category status (CS) alone determines outcomes (Os).
Severity on indicator scores is causally irrelevant. Bottom. A pure dimensional
model. Category status (CS) has no independent effect on outcomes (Os), which are
determined by severity on indicator scores.

procedures used in trying to test dimensionality directly against categoricity will tend to cause us to underestimate the size of the coefficients on group membership and to find it insignificant. That happens because in this model severity is an intervening variable and conditioning on an intervening variable screens off causes prior to it, but that is exactly what the regression methods described above for testing dimensions versus categories do. Likewise, regressing group membership on distal variables and severity will result in the distal variables being screened off. Thus, direct tests of categorical versus dimensional approaches that work on statistical grounds alone without an explicit causal model must be interpreted with caution, whether they claim to find evidence for or against categories or dimensions. They presuppose quite unsophisticated models of the relations among category status, degree of symptoms, and other related causal variables.

2 Dispelling Confusions about Objective Categories

In the preceding section, I gave a brief introduction to my take on natural kinds as mental kinds: Psychopathological kinds are defensible natural kinds insofar as we have evidence that psychopathological individuals form qualitatively distinct groups that ground explanations and predictions. However, there are various common arguments in the literature that psychopathology must be understood as a dimensional phenomenon, not a categorical one. This section rebuts those arguments.

First, it is important to keep from framing issues in all-or-nothing fashion (as is often done). Some of the behaviors that get described as psychopathological may actually represent qualitatively distinct phenomena that allow for objective groupings, as I am arguing; others may best be thought as dimensional attributes with a continuous range, and others perhaps as largely social constructions in the sense of heterogeneous behaviors having only social status in common.[4]

Moreover, the restricted view of natural kinds I am defending is not subject to various criticisms of categorical views that demand more than of them than is reasonable (or is more than attributed to them by their advocates). Thus, it is not uncommon to assume that if objective categories are to be identified successfully they must constitute a system that is exhaustive and exclusive (Bailey 1994). On this reading, every individual with psychopathology ought to fit into one and only one category, just as each organism must fit into one and only one species. The second half of the requirement—fitting into only one category—is often pressed against categorical views by dimensional critics who point to the fact that individuals with one *DSM* diagnosis may also have a second diagnosis simultaneously and that the criteria for one *DSM* diagnosis may overlap with that of others.

Systematicity is great when you can get it, but it comes in degrees, and finding objective predictive categorizations for some kinds of behavior we think of as psychopathological is progress even if much of our understanding of psychopathology is in a disordered state. Moreover, the demand that any legitimate categorizations must be exclusive—one per person with no overlapping symptoms—is unreasonable and even undesirable. It is unreasonable in that it is a demand not made of medicine in general, where multiple disorders are common in single individuals (for example, HIV and TB) and different disorders may share some of the same characteristics (e.g., joint dysfunction in osteo-arthritis and rheumatoid arthritis). The demand for exclusivity is undesirable in that we have good evidence for thinking that some disorders *ought* to overlap in just the ways we see. For example, we have good physiological and cognitive-behavioral evidence that addiction and depression involve overlapping brain areas conceived both structurally in terms of localization and functionally in terms of cognitive roles. We also know that there can be direct causal connections between the two disorders—some addictions may result from self-medication for depression. Finding overlap thus can be positive evidence that we are on the right track, not that things have gone amiss. Hence, it may be necessary to rethink the common practice of excluding individuals with comorbidities from clinical and other studies.

Another common argument for thinking of psychopathology as dimensional rests on the alleged fact that psychopathology must be the result of many small causes. This observation comes largely from the results of geneotyping studies. Such studies often show inconsistent results and/or small associations between candidate genes for psychopathology, and so it is concluded that psychopathology is (in genetics-speak) a "complex" trait—that is, one that doesn't follow nice Mendelian rules and that depends on environmental interactions with vulnerabilities.

We can grant that psychopathologies are complex traits but deny that it follows that psychopathology can only be treated dimensionally. Diabetes and cancer are also complex traits with many small interacting causes and environmental influences, yet categorical approaches seem well warranted in their study. Only through the lens that dominates psychometrics—where the psychological world is populated by attributes that vary in degrees (and the number of which seems a function of how many "instruments" we can make up)—do complex causes mean that there are no qualitative groupings. Indeed, if we think of complex causes as providing binding constraints, thresholds, necessary but insufficient causes, and so on, complexity can equally argue against smooth dimensions.

The dimensional lens of psychometrics is also behind another kind of evidence commonly provided for thinking of psychopathology in terms of continuous properties. It is common to report that a questionnaire producing a continuous score has "good psychometric properties" and that therefore we have reason to believe in the proposed latent dimension. Two standard good properties are the goodness of fit of a factor analysis and the internal consistency of the items in a questionnaire. Factor analyses ask if the variations in a set of ordinal or numerical items are consistent with the variations of an underlying latent factor or cause. Internal consistency concerns how well the various indicators correlate with one another.

Both properties can beg the question in favor of a dimensional over a categorical understanding. Factor analysis asks "*If* there were dimensional unobserved factors, would the present data be most consistent with a single dimension or multiple dimensions?" It is not a test of whether the phenomena should best be thought of as dimensional or as categorical in the first place. Similarly, if indicators are being used to group individuals and not necessarily to measure a latent variable causing them, highly correlated indicators may be a nuisance rather than a virtue.[5] Recall our intuitive example of a taxometric test for gender as a category: the indicators that helped pick out the two groups worked well because their scores were *not* highly intercorrelated. Thus, for picking out categories, high internal consistency is not necessarily a virtue.

I will conclude this section with a further influential motivation for thinking of psychopathology as dimensional. Category schemes such as those of the *DSM* and screens based on them have lots of problems trying to shoehorn the various behaviors that clinicians see into a fixed set of yes or no groupings. Symptoms vary in severity. Screens have cutoff points for diagnosis but often seem arbitrary. The *DSM* uses a polythetic any-five-of-ten approach that allows two individuals with the same diagnosis to have different symptom sets. Such concerns were partly behind the considerable push to bring dimensional elements into *DSM*-5.

A number of points are worth making here because they will help considerably in fleshing out the view I am defending. The *DSM*'s shopping-list approach is not inherently flawed. It *could* be that the individuals who get picked out by such a list fall into objective classifications that ground prediction and explanation—whether that is true is an empirical question. The natural kinds I am defending are perhaps best thought of in terms of ideal types, prototypes, and family resemblances that allow for individuals not to share all the characteristic associated with the kind, so it may make dubious sense to add the characteristics together in some kind of score.

Of course the *DSM* represents a quite political process, and it is not my intention here to defend its specific categorizations. Moreover, the screens used to identify psychopathology also have their own history and often have a quite indirect connection to *DSM* categories (while still having "good psychometric properties"—here is one place where methods fetishes cause problems). Thus, I can defend the categorical status of depression (and will do so in section 3) without thinking that there is a score on the Beck Depression Inventory that fully captures the *DSM* concepts or even that those concepts are entirely well formed.

Finally, there are several ways to allow for dimensional aspects while defending mental kinds as natural kinds. The first way is to grant that existing screens and uses of the *DSM* in actual practice do group together a somewhat heterogeneous set of phenomena but to argue that there is good evidence that a smaller subset of those who get classified nonetheless make up a qualitatively distinct group that can ground objective predictions and explanations (as Ross et al. (2008) argue in regard to addiction). People have various kinds of problems with drugs, but perhaps there is a smaller hard core that have unfortunately predictable outcomes, neurobiological signatures, and behavioral patterns. Many people experience depression of some shade during their life, but perhaps there is a smaller hard core who also share a similar predictable life course. Thus, while those who get classified may vary along key dimensions, not everyone who is classified is only quantitatively different from all the rest.

We can also respond to heterogeneity by granting that variability exists and proposing ways to incorporate it into investigations premised on the existence of objective categorizations supporting predictions and explanations. One easy way to do that is to note that there can be clearly qualitatively distinct groups whose members nonetheless vary along some dimensions on some traits, even traits central to their group membership. For example, either you have Huntington's Disease or you don't, but the disease can vary in severity. The things in the universe that can have temperature and those that cannot are disjoint, but of course temperature varies among those that have it. Thus, in principle, categorical approaches do not rule out dimensional aspects.

The interesting question is how to incorporate those aspects. Earlier in the chapter I mentioned some attempts to do so that are not promising. Those approaches just add variability to regression equations containing variables for category membership and stewed. However, I showed in section 1 that working that way rests on implausible causal assumptions. Much more promising alternatives would build explicit causal models, like the one illustrated in figure 8.1, that incorporate and measure dimensional items along with category status. Testing a structural-equation model by maximum likelihood will produce estimates or path coefficients that will give a measure of the relative effects of dimensions over and above category status. However, such models are at this point only a promise—there is very little out there in the psychopathology literature that pursues them.

3   The Case of Major Depressive Disorder

In this section I turn from the general considerations discussed above to a specific psychopathology—major depressive disorder—that I believe instantiates my claim that some psychopathology can usefully be thought of as picking out natural kinds of a certain sort. I argue first for the claim that there is an objective categorization of individuals with depression, then for the claim that it grounds predictive explanations.

We have two kinds of evidence that there is a distinct group of depressed individuals: formal taxometric studies using various indicators (mostly survey questions or diagnostic interviews) and diverse results from neurobiology and experimental psychology that seem to converge on a distinct group among those diagnosed with major depressive disorder.

There have been several studies using the kind of formal taxometric methods mentioned in section 1. There is not complete agreement between studies—a majority find categorical results, but a significant minority find dimensional results. However, the dimensional results are suspect for several reasons. They rely heavily on the Beck Depression Inventory, which has little direct correlation to the *DSM* criteria and is perhaps best seen as a measure of general distress rather than major depression, thus naturally leading to dimensional interpretation. The dissenting studies also typically rely on patient samples rather than population or outpatient samples. Taxometric methods work best on samples with heterogeneous populations containing individuals with and without disorder (recall the height and baldness example) which patient samples do not provide. Patient samples may also contain many individuals with a chronic depressive disorder currently in remission and thus showing only subthreshhold characteristics, making the condition look dimensional.

More recent taxometric studies of depression use clinical interviews, self-reports directly tied to *DSM* criteria, and nonpatient samples. These provide support for a categorical account of depression. Ahmed et al. (2011), who worked with a large community sample using indicators directly tied to the *DSM* criteria, found evidence for a taxon group across three independent taxometric measures. Solomon et al. (2006), who worked with a large nonpatient sample (1,700) using MAXEIG—the most powerful (in the statistician's sense of getting positive findings when the condition is really present) of the taxometric methods—reached conclusions favoring a categorical over a dimensional interpretation of the data. Ruscio and Smith (2009), working with a large outpatient sample and using clinical interviews, found that a taxonic solution fit the data best.

These formal taxometric studies rely either on self-report questionnaires or interviews. However, there are a number of other indicators, perhaps more persuasive, that have not been used in formal taxometric analyses but which nonetheless seem to pick out a distinct set of individuals with major depressive disorder (MDD) and point to depression as a disorder of brain areas with antecedently fairly well-understood functions. In particular, these areas are ones known to be essentially involved in processing rewards, executive control, response to emotional stimuli and stress, especially fear. The prefrontal cortex, amygdala, anterior cingulate cortex, and the nucleus accumbens have well-described neurological circuits and behavioral responses in normal reward processing, emotion processing, fear recognition, and so on. On multiple indicators, individuals with MDD show abnormalities in these activities and brain areas. The measures include the following:

• Reinforcement-based studies find a bias toward reinforced stimuli in normal controls but fail to find such bias in individuals classified as MDD (Henriques et al. 1994; Pizzagalli 2005, 2008). This insensitivity to reward could be due to low motivation in depressed patients, but further studies seem to show that depressed patients do not experience positive emotional valence in anticipation of rewards. These studies are more concrete, measurable, and replicable instances of the "ahedonia" judgments made informally by clinicians.

• Intertemporal choice tasks show that patients with MDD discount future monetary gains and losses more deeply than normals (Takahashi et al. 2008).

• Patients with MDD have glucose metabolic abnormalities in the amygdala (Drevets 2008) and greater secretion of cortisol (which is associated with amygdala activity) under stress (Drevets 2002).

• Histopathological abnormalities are found in post-mortem studies of MDD individuals. Those abnormalities include reductions in gray-matter volume, thickness or wet weight in the sgACC, posterior orbital cortex, and accumbens (Drevets 2008).

• Depressed subjects exhibit increased hemodynamic responses of the amygdala to sad words, sad faces, and fearful faces. These elements seem to be trait-like characteristics since they also show up in remitted patients with MDD (Price and Drevets 2012).

• During reversal learning, MDD subjects show increased behavioral sensitivity to negative feedback relative to controls and decreased BOLD signal in PFC.

• MDD individuals are less able to generate autobiographical memories cued by positive words and show reduced activity in hippocampus during such tasks.

• Patients with MDD show increased baseline activation of amygdala. Antidepressant drugs produce decreased activation in the same region (Price and Drevets 2001).

Thus, there are results from a variety of different kind of indicators distinguishing a subset of individuals with MDD. They provide good evidence that an objective kind or grouping is being picked out, backing up the results of the taxometric studies.

Several other facts about these results are important. These results typically are most consistent and significant in patients with early onset and a familial history of MDD. Severe depression in the elderly without early onset show the signature of cardiovascular disease and ventral atrophy but not the full set of indicators typical of early-onset MDD, suggesting that the elderly subset constitute a distinct group. Similarly, normal subjects with induced sadness show on fMRI hyperactivation of amygdala but not the full set of regions involved in MDD. The full set of regions involved in MDD arguably involves a disruption of the normal homeostasis between these subsystems. Finally, the brain subsystems identified above are general ones that are also involved in addiction and in severe anxiety, potentially explaining why these disorders often coexist in individuals.

These facts are consistent with points made earlier. The *DSM* criteria and the screens based on them are far from perfect. However, they are consistent with a subset of individuals who get diagnosed as having a qualitatively distinct condition that makes for very serious and chronic problems. Of course, they overlap in symptoms with those falling outside the group and correspondingly in brain activation, but the evidence suggests the ongoing rupture of a hemostatic system rather than a continuous distribution of a latent trait "degree of depressed mood."

Providing predictive explanations based on an objective classification constitutes the other criterion for showing natural kinds in my sense. The evidence here in the case of depression is relatively strong: categorical classifications embedded in *explicit causal models* stand up well in tests against the data. Recall that we are looking for both predictors of depression and outcomes that depression predicts; we want explicit causal models rather than reported associations because we want to try to rule out spurious associations and because causal explanations in these cases are deeper explanations.

All the studies reported below involve structural-equation modeling (SEM), which turns a proposed model into a set of equations. Those equations imply a set of independence relations, both conditional and unconditional, that should be found in the model if true. Typically by means of maximum-likelihood estimation, the model's fit to the data is measured by means of the χ^2 distribution and the free parameters of the model estimated. A model with good fit statistics may not rule out other models that are also compatible with the data. However, bad models can often be ruled out, reducing worries about spurious causation, and competing good models may agree on some important subset of causal relations.[6]

Bronte-Tinkew et al. (2007) used data from a longitudinal study of a national US birth cohort that identified both causes and effects of depression. In their model, food insecurity causally influences depression, which in turn influences child health status. These causal relations are found while including other causes of health outcomes (e.g., parenting practices) and while allowing food insecurity to have its obvious direct effect, independent of depression, on outcomes. In short, they provide, as do all the studies cited here, a causal version of Meehl's "nomological net." The longitudinal nature of the data means that possible reverse-causality models (e.g., depression causes food insecurity) are ruled out. The model has good fit statistics, meaning that it is unlikely that the implications of the model could be found to the degree they are found in the data simply by chance.

Using a Latina sample, Hollist et al. (2007) confirmed previous results showing that martial discord significantly predicts depression status. Their study was longitudinal in nature, helping rule out reverse causality and confounding. In their final best-fitting model, depression at time 1 was not a statistically significant cause of depression at time 2, whereas marital discord was a statistically significant cause of depression at time 1.

Amagasa et al. (2012) looked at work-related causes of depression. Previous studies had used traditional regression approaches and had found inconsistent results on the role and importance of hours worked and "job demand" (meaning the demands of the job). Amagasa et al. identified a structural-equation model with good fit that made job demand an intervening mediating cause between hours worked and depression risk. Previous claims in the literature that job demand was a confounding variable produced models clearly rejected by the data.

The work of Amagasa et al. nicely illustrates the limits of ordinary least-squares multiple regression in trying to identify causes. Previous work on the topic that found inconsistent and inconclusive results used standard multiple regression in which job demand was treated as a control or a possible confounding variable—it was included in the final overall regression equation as an independent variable. However, if a mediating variable is conditioned on, it will eliminate the statistical association between the outcome and its distal cause if the distal cause has no independent direct effect on the outcome, and it will reduce the true statistical association if the distal cause does have an independent direct effect. There is good evidence that earlier studies were doing just this—missing the mediating role of job demand because it was being treated as a control variable.

The structural-equation model that best fit the data has the hours-worked variables asserting their influence indirectly by causing job demand levels that, in turn, affect depression occurrence. In the SEM tests of the model involved in the previous multiple-regression work there is not a statistically significant correlation between hours worked and depression; the χ^2 statistic reports there is no chance that the deviations of this model could happen by chance. The best-fitting SEM model has 0.001 probability of fitting by chance and finds significant correlations between hours worked and job demands and between job demands and depression.

The three pieces of SEM modeling described above all treat depression categorically; to that extent, they argue for categorical approaches to depression. However, none of them includes severity as an independent causal factor. In section 1, I indicated how that could be done intelligibly; in section 2, I argued that it was both compatible with categorical accounts of psychopathology and potentially useful. So there are many opportunities to provide more sophisticated accounts of kinds and traits in psychopathology still to be explored.

Acknowledgments

Thanks to Don Ross for helpful comments on an earlier draft and for many useful discussions.

Notes

1. Borsboom is thus mistaken in his claim that psychometrics cannot measure psychological traits because local independence is violated. The standard model with the assumption can certainly be tested against a more complex model where there is interaction. Both are structural-equation models and can be tested accordingly. The fact that they are not tested this way is consistent with a long tradition in psychology and psychometrics of trying to avoid messy causal concepts by sticking to formal tests of association.

2. The psychometric interpretation in terms of quantities and associations has itself been used to argue that, in an important sense, psychiatry does not have natural kinds—in that its categorical categorizations picking out mental disorders are unfounded because psychopathology is dimensional. That debate is the subject of the next section, in which I argue that those attacks are confused.

3. Thus, I am not sympathetic toward some parts of Wakefield's project, though I nonetheless think he has made valuable contributions pointing out that the term "disorder" is abused and overused in the study of psychopathology.

4. "Largely" because even in the case of constructs that are clearly motivated (consciously or unconsciously) by imposing order for practical ends such as insurance coverage, there are still some objective facets of the behavior that invoke the classification.

5. They may be a nuisance even if you are trying to measure latent variables. See Little et al. 1999.

6. Most of the research I discuss below comes from a perspective of public health and health behavior, so there is an understandable emphasis on the causes and the burden of disease. SEMs and explicit causal models are much rarer in the more purely academic research done in psychology departments, for example. Reporting uninterpreted and uninterpretable correlations may get you tenure in a university department but is much less impressive in a context of public health policy.

References

Ahmed, A., B. Green, C. Clark, K. Stahl, and M. McFarland. 2011. Latent structure of unipolar and bipolar mood symptoms. *Bipolar Disorders* 13 (5–6): 522–536.

Allison, D., M. Downey, R. Atkinson, C. Billington, G. Bray, R. Eckel, E. Finkelstein, M. Jensen, and A. Tremblay. 2008. Obesity as a disease: A white paper on evidence and arguments commissioned by the Council of The Obesity Society. *Obesity* 16 (6): 1161–1177.

Amagasa, T., and Nakayama, T. 2012. Relationship between long working hours and depression in two working populations: A structural equation model approach. *Journal of Occupational and Environmental Medicine* 54: 870–874.

Bailey, T. 1994. *Typologies and Taxonomies: An Introduction to Classification Techniques.* Sage.

Bernstein, A., T. Stickle, M. Zvolensky, S. Taylor, and S. Stewart. 2010. Dimensional, categorical, or dimensional-categories: Testing the latent structure of anxiety sensitivity among adults using factor-mixture modeling. *Behavior Therapy* 41: 515–529.

Borsboom, D. 2009. *Measuring the Mind: Conceptual Issues in Contemporary Psychometrics.* Cambridge University Press.

Bronte-Tinkew, J., M. Zaslow, M. Capps, A. Horowitz, and M. McNamara. 2007. Food insecurity works through depression, parenting, and infant feeding to influence overweight and health in toddlers. *Journal of Nutrition Community and International Nutrition* 137: 2160–2165.

Bryant, F. 2000.Assessing the validity of measurement. In *Reading and Understanding MORE Multivariate Statistics,* ed. G. Laurence and P. Yarnold. American Psychological Association.

Chang, H. 2004. *Inventing Temperature Measurement and Scientific Progress.* Oxford University Press.

Dennett, D. 1991. Real patterns. *Journal of Philosophy* 88: 27–51.

Douglas, H. 2004. The irreducible complexity of objectivity. *Synthese* 138: 453–473.

Drevets, W. 2001. Neuroimaging and neuropathological studies of depression: implications for the cognitive-emotional features of mood disorders. *Current Opinion in Neurobiology* 11: 240–249.

Drevets, W. 2002. Glucose metabolism in the amygdala in depression: relationship to diagnostic subtype and plasma cortisol levels. *Pharmacology, Biochemistry, and Behavior* 71: 431–447.

Drevets, W. 2008. Brain structural and functional abnormalities in mood disorders: implications for neurocircuitry models of depression. *Brain Structure & Function* 213: 93–118.

Henriques, J. B., et al. 1994. Reward fails to alter response bias in depression. *Journal of Abnormal Psychology* 103: 460–466.

Hollist, C., R. Miller, O. Falceto, and C. Fernandes. 2007. Marital satisfaction and depression: A replication of the Marital Discord Model in a Latino sample. *Family Process* 46: 485–498.

Horwitz, A., and J. Wakefield. 2007. *The Loss of Sadness: How Psychiatry Transformed Normal Sorrow into Depressive Disorder.* Oxford University Press.

Kincaid, H. 2004. Are there laws in the social sciences: Yes. In *Contemporary Debates in the Philosophy of Science*, ed. C. Hitchcock. Blackwell.

Kincaid, H. 2008. Do we need theory to study disease? Lessons from cancer research and their implications for mental illness. *Perspectives in Biology and Medicine* 51: 367–378.

Ladyman, J., and D. Ross. 2007. *Everything Must Go: Metaphysics Naturalized.* Oxford University Press.

Little, T., Lindenberger, U., and Nesselroade, J. 1999. On selecting indicators for multivariate measurement and modeling with latent variables: When "good" indicators are bad and "bad" indicators are good. *Psychological Methods* 4: 192–211.

Meehl, P. 2004. What's in a taxon? *Journal of Abnormal Psychology* 113: 39–43.

Meehl, P., and L. Yonce. 1994. Taxometric analysis: I. Detecting taxonicity with two quantitative indicators using means above and below a sliding cut (MAMBAC procedure). *Psychological Reports* 74: 1059–1274.

Meehl, P., and L. Yonce. 1996. Taxometric analysis: II. Detecting taxonicity using covariance of two quantitative indicators in successive intervals of a third indicator (MAXCOV procedure). *Psychological Reports* 78: 1091–1227.

Michell, J. 1999. *Measurement in Psychology: A Critical History of a Methodological Concept.* Cambridge University Press.

Moss, L. 2003. *What Genes Can't Do.* MIT Press.

Pizzagalli, D. 2005. Toward an objective characterization of an anhedonic phenotype: a signal-detection approach. *Biological Psychiatry* 57: 319–327.

Pizzagalli, D. 2008. Reduced hedonic capacity in major depressive disorder: evidence from a probabilistic reward task. *Journal of Psychiatric Research* 43: 76–87.

Price, J., and W. Drevets. 2012. Neural circuits underlying the pathophysiology of mood disorders. *Trends in Cognitive Sciences* 16 (1): 61–71.

Ross, D. 2000. Rainforest realism. In *Dennett's Philosophy*, ed. D. Ross, A. Brook, and D. Thompson. MIT Press.

Ross, D., C. Sharp, R. Vuchinich, and D. Spurrett. 2008. *Midbrain Mutiny: The Picoeconomics and Neuroeconomics of Disordered Gambling.* MIT Press.

Ruscio, J., N. Haslam, and A. Ruscio. 2006. *Introduction to the Taxometric Method: A Practical Guide*. Erlbaum.

Solomon, A., D. Haaga, and B. Arnow. 2001. Is clinical depression distinct from subthreshold depressive symptoms? A review of the continuity issue in depression research. *Journal of Nervous and Mental Disorders* 189: 498–506.

Strauss, M., and G. Smith. 2009. Construct validity: Advances in theory and methodology. *Annual Review of Clinical Psychology* 5: 1–25.

Takahashi, T., et al. 2008. Depressive patients are more impulsive and inconsistent in intertemporal choice behavior for monetary gain and loss than healthy subjects—An analysis based on Tsallis' statistics. *Neuroendocrinology Letters* 29 (3): 291–390.

Wilson, M. 2008. *Wandering Significance*. Oxford University Press.

9 Oppositional Defiant Disorder: Cultural Factors That Influence Interpretations of Defiant Behavior and Their Social and Scientific Consequences

Nancy Nyquist Potter

In this chapter I focus on school and prison as socializing mechanisms. Developmental pathways to socialization or to psychopathology and criminality are affected by school systems' assertions of authority when children are defiant and otherwise hard to manage. I identify cultural factors that affect how children's behavior is interpreted and responded to, looking particularly at racial and ethnic biases in diagnosis. I argue that the norms by which proper development are evaluated are those of the dominant group, and that they disadvantage other racial and ethnic groups. An examination of these factors gives us reason to question the disorder status of Oppositional Defiant Disorder (ODD) as it currently is conceptualized. I suggest that the decontextualized nature of the current classification system is flawed in that it doesn't take into account how norms function within stratified society. There is no question that the anxiety and crushing anguish of daily experiences of racism produce an unrelenting psychological strain (Hines and Boyd-Franklin 1996). Experiences of racial prejudice play a central role in problematic externalizing behaviors but, at the same time, racial stereotyping and dominant norms for behavior favor interpretations that African American boys are on a path toward mental illness or a life of crime or both. The results are potential harm done to children and the perpetuation of societal inequalities. In short, the current diagnostic category of ODD is an example of "bad science" or "science as usual" (Harding 1986).

Statement of the Problem

One of the most common reasons why children and adolescents in the United States are referred to mental-health clinics or treatment centers is that they show aggressive and antisocial behavior—a pattern associated with ODD and with conduct disorder (CD) (Frick and Ellis 1999, p. 149).

Frick and Ellis say that it is by far the kind of misbehavior that raises the greatest degree of social concern, because it can involve intentional and direct harm to others (ibid., p. 152). Not all aggressive and socially disruptive behavior signifies a developmental pathway toward mental disorder. But Antisocial Personality Disorder and psychopathy, including egocentricity, callousness, manipulativeness, impulsivity, irresponsibility, and antisocial behavior, are serious outcomes to be alerted to (ibid., p. 147). Again, not all disruptive and harmful early behavior results in later violent criminal behavior, but it's also true that violent adult offenders often have early childhood histories of antisocial and aggressive behavior (Frick 2006, p. 311). Thus, an understanding of these childhood disorders is both medically and socially important.

Yet in understanding developmental pathways to criminal and violent behavior, Frick and Ellis and some other researchers may be blurring the boundaries between medical and moral kinds that is so problematic in Cluster B personality disorders. (See also Zachar and Potter 2010; Charland 2006.) Teachers and other authority figures, even clinicians, may be conflating "mad" and "bad." As I will show, the place of black youth in American culture leaves them particularly vulnerable to the power of authority figures (teachers, law enforcement officers, clinicians) to project onto them a life of criminality and mental illness. Whether or not such projections are scientifically appropriate is the undergirding question of this chapter.

Furthermore, the nature of the *DSM*-5 (2013) classification and diagnostic system, with its complicated placement of social contexts into V codes while attempting to thread throughout Axis I and Axis II the many educational, economic, and social considerations that should go into making a diagnosis, renders many causal inferences weak. (A discussion of the *DSM*-5 changes and how context affects classification and diagnosis is beyond the scope of this chapter.) My worry is that the diagnoses of ODD and CD are called forth instead of grappling with many harder questions about how to socialize children while, at the same time, not squelch their ethnic, gendered, and idiosyncratic expressions. When we examine cultural norms for behavior, we see more clearly that appropriate behavior for children and youth is defined by a dominant white culture and that, when we neglect these matters, we do damage to ethnic minorities and to societal functioning overall.

I am not arguing that an overrepresentation exists among black boys in diagnosis of ODD; the evidence does not support that strong a claim. Furthermore, it is fair to say that the *DSM* classifications have been subjected to studies intended to detect and eliminate racial and other biases. Instead, I am arguing that something subtler is occurring—a systemic bias built on stereotypes and dominant cultural norms that penetrate more deeply into both classification and diagnosis of ODD. These institutionalized and systemic attitudes and beliefs (ontological-assumptive commitments, as I later refer to them) negatively affect black boys' development and socialization into mainstream society and therefore are detrimental to black males and are a social and ethical problem whether or not the data show an overrepresentation of this population with ODD. An additional factor that is often overlooked when assessing black boys who act out in schools is that their low socioeconomic status leaves them poorly prepared for school education and, instead of "feeling stupid" many young boys externalize their frustration and anxiety. Black boys, then, already disadvantaged, are vulnerable to more insidious racism in diagnosis and perhaps in the classificatory system. This chapter illustrates how important it is to disentangle racism as a factor in misinterpreting and misdiagnosing people from racism as a cause of dysfunctional behavior that may or may not indicate a mental disorder. Psychiatrists—historically and currently—face the challenge of discerning between dysfunctional behavior that may be a response to racism, and the hegemonic production of racial biases that can lead to misinterpretation and misdiagnosis of some minority people's behavior. And one of the nosological questions this chapter's analysis provokes is whether or not diagnoses such as ODD and CD are genuine mental disorders at all.

Racial bias and stereotyping have a long history in both taxonomy of medical diseases and nosology of psychiatric disorders. Sander Gilman (1985) presents a thorough and persuasive analysis of ways in which race, sexuality, and mental disorder are intertwined for African Americans and Jews. Harriet Washington (2008) carefully debunks the idea that African Americans' distrust of the American health-care system is due primarily to the famous Tuskegee case; in fact, Washington compellingly argues, abuses and ethical violations continue to persist in myriad ways, many of which she documents and exposes. Alisha Ali (2004) argues that the trauma and stress of being victims of racism is often decontextualized so that the cultural fabric of distress is lost as the patient's distress is pathologized. Jonathan Metzl (2009) shows how racism continues to have insidious influence on both medical theory and practice by his analysis of the long-standing equation of blacks with schizophrenia that results in misdiagnosis, stereotyping, and unscientific and unethical treatment of blacks.

Metzl began with a story about Cecil Peterson, a 29-year-old African American man who in 1966 was provoked by a white man into a confrontation that ultimately resulted in his being charged with and convicted of assault. No one else was charged. He was first incarcerated and then placed in a hospital for the criminally insane, ostensibly because he showed symptoms of paranoia and dangerousness. His declarations that his civil rights had been violated and that he was locked in a struggle with the white man, and his use of his native African language, all were read as signs of pathology rather than signifiers of his place within American culture in the 1960s.

Peterson's story is particularly alarming because he had never before been labeled or diagnosed with a mental disorder. Metzl showed that bias and stereotyping in the criminal and psychiatric domains can strike a black person at any age; they do not need to follow an early trajectory of being identified as troublemakers or diagnosed with childhood mental disorders. Metzl's example highlights difficulties that American science and culture have with African Americans who do not conform to white standards of behavior. I especially am concerned with ways in which defiant behavior is interpreted and responded to in school systems. My ultimate interest (beyond the scope of this chapter) is in the positive role of defiant behavior. To that end, I have argued elsewhere that defiance is sometimes a virtue (Potter 2011). In this chapter, I raise conceptual and practical concerns that defiance is almost uniformly treated as a vice or disorder when expressed by African American boys.

Characteristics

Oppositional Defiant Disordered behavior is characterized as "a frequent and persistent pattern of angry/irritable mood, argumentative/defiant behavior, or vindictiveness" (*DSM*-5 2013, p. 463). Children and youth who receive this diagnosis or one of CD are considered negative, defiant, disobedient, and hostile toward authority (Loeber et al. 2000, p. 1469). They disrupt social situations and victimize others, violating others' basic rights and defying social norms and rules (ibid., p. 1469). They are thought of as socially disruptive, highly impaired, and unlikely to get better.

The indignant but amusing children's exclamation "You're not the boss of me!" becomes less charming in children who see themselves as equals to adults or exhibit a drive to defeat adult authority. These children, according to Riley (1997), are grandiose, in that they think themselves smarter than adults, and use strategies such as guile, cunning, and lying to manipulate others, seeming not to feel an obligation to be fair. They also seem to lack insight, which makes it difficult to rehabilitate them.

In terms of developmental pathways, researchers have hypothesized that some children may have difficulty incorporating feedback from effects of their behavior on others and, hence, may be unable to bring about future modifications—a problem found in psychopathy. Frustration from authority can develop into more defiant and argumentative behavior, and an inability to pause and reflect leads to deficits in the development of empathy and guilt—providing, it is thought, a direct conceptual link to adult psychopathy.

Frick and Ellis identify several dimensions to behavioral problems associated with childhood onset, one of which is a dimension of types of aggression. Proactive childhood-onset disruptive and defiant behavior may be unprovoked, goal-oriented, and coercive, in which case it is considered premeditated. The reactive kind of disruptive and defiant behavior is provoked, retaliatory, and hostile. According to Frick and Ellis (1999), aggressive behavior is particularly salient to an understanding of childhood-onset ODD and the later development of CD. As I stated earlier, because aggression involves the intentional and direct harm to a victim, it carries the greatest societal concern regarding the development of antisocial (criminal and pathological) behavior in adulthood (ibid., p. 152). In one dimension of aggression, Frick argues in a later article (2006), we would expect to see personality traits of callousness and emotional detachment—characteristics that are found in childhood-onset CD and in adult psychopathy. Adolescent onset, on the other hand, is often the exaggerated defiance of a teenager attempting to separate and individuate from authority. Because it is an exaggeration of normal development, it may be maladaptive for a time but settle itself once the youth develops into maturity. Still, the consequences of maladaptive defiance may lead to impairments such as lack of success in school. This may be compounded when the adolescent is a youth of color, where experiences of racism and discrimination also contribute to difficulties in school, resulting in low self-esteem and sometimes developing into externalizing behaviors. The vast majority of black children live in low socioeconomic conditions, which conditions are correlated with a poorer quality of schoolwork. Poverty is a by-product of inequality that redirects blacks away from mainstream society (Western 2006, p. 87); poor education and poor preparedness for school advancement are consequences of systematic poverty. Frustrated by poor performance and lack of access to good nutrition and adequate health care, and by the continuing impact of historical violence against Africans and African Americans, children may develop a heightened sense of living in a hostile environment that holds little hope of success for them. (Also see chapter 4 of Western 2006.) Under such conditions, defiant behavior may in fact be maladaptive to success. But, as I will argue, defiance may also be complicated for black youth because racial discrimination, stereotyping, and cultural assumptions shape both the perception of adult authority figures and the behavior of the youth being subjected to unfair and biased treatment.

The childhood-onset subtype of callous-unemotional (CU) personality dimension is "characterized by a lack of guilt, lack of empathy, and lack of emotional expression" (Frick 2006, p. 315). Frick suggests that these CU traits are similar to those of psychopathic adults. Thus, developmentally, this research suggests a distinct temperamental style (ibid., p. 317). This style

leads to impulsive and overactive behaviors in early childhood that gradually develop into more defiant and argumentative behavior as a child becomes more verbal and his or her goal-directed behaviors are frequently frustrated by parents. Furthermore, the child's inability to pause and reflect on the consequences of his or her actions, and the inability to perceive the distress caused by his or her actions in others, leads to deficits in the development of empathy and guilt, providing a direct conceptual link to the psychopathic characteristics shown by adults. (Frick and Ellis 1999, p. 155)

Yet without a racial analysis such inferences are weak. For example, delinquent youth were tested for emotional reactions to words with negative emotional contact, and those with high levels of CU traits showed reduced emotional responses. But among the words chosen were "gun" and "blood" (Frick 2006, p. 318). Those words have a particular cultural currency and resonance: at a youth meeting with African Americans in Louisville last year, children described sleeping directly under their windows so as to avoid getting hit by bullets from drive-by shootings. Living with violence is an everyday occurrence for them and, as such, is normalized. This experience is reported anecdotally throughout the nation in poorer neighborhoods. It is, therefore, not surprising that young black boys would respond nonchalantly to "gun" and "blood," but a cultural analysis points to a need for a more complex explanation than just that such individuals are callous and unemotional.

Cultural Influences

Testing for callous and unemotional traits in African American boys without considering the environmental factors they bring to such psychological testing overlooks the social and cultural context in which many of them live and the survival skills necessary to endure racism and violence in their young lives. In reality, cultural conditioning and exposure to violence will desensitize children and youth. Furthermore, lack of empathy development may be a social defense against loss and/or ridicule (two different reasons to stifle automatic empathy). Disruptive and defiant behavior cannot be understood outside the context of racialization within a predominantly white population. As Coker et al. (2009) find, 90 percent of black adults report experiences of racial discrimination. This finding is important because racial discrimination is associated with mental illness. Coker et al. found that children who reported perceived racial discrimination were more likely to display symptoms of ODD and CD. The question is what those symptoms are indicative of. There are at least three possibilities. Some children and youth do respond to lives of racial discrimination by becoming violent and law-breaking. This behavior may be dysfunctional, and then the question for psychiatry is whether such responses—which pose a danger to others and, often, to themselves—are dysfunctional to the degree that they signify a mental disorder. For others, responses to racism tell us something about the context in which diagnoses are made: that psychiatry is not immune to bias and discrimination and that misinterpretation or misdiagnosis occur. In this case, I propose that some children and youth respond to racialized life by becoming rationally defiant—a response that leaves them open to misunderstood behavior and the medicalization of what may be, for them, reasonable defiance. Then again, I propose a third possibility—that isn't mutually exclusive of the second one: that problems exist in the status of the disorder itself.

With respect to the third possibility, John Sadler (2005) has developed the Moral Wrongfulness Test (MWT), a way to determine whether or to what degree a concept in a diagnosis contains substantive moral evaluations. Are the "bads" of the diagnosis (mostly) nonmoral, or are they moral? Sadler points out that in medical surgery the health values are almost universally nonmoral, whereas in psychiatry, the values in mental disorder are often ill-disguised moral ones. (Sadler analyzes the nosological history of homosexuality to illustrate the presence of moral values in a diagnostic category.) The MWT asks us to determine whether or not the "ontological-assumptive background belief system" (ibid., p. 218) has moral evaluation embedded in it to the degree that the concept is semantically and empirically dependent on those moral values (p. 222). The presence of moral values isn't, in itself, a reason to reject a diagnosis. (For a full discussion see Sadler 2005.) I do not apply specifically the MWT to ODD and CD, but in trying to understand what kind of things these diagnoses are I draw on Sadler's theoretical framework. My focus here is on the ontological-assumptive background belief system as it might function in the classificatory status of ODD and in evaluations of African American children's behavior.

The *DSM*-IV classification system set out symptoms that were meant to be treated independently of any particular causal explanation. (*DSM*-5 goes some way toward addressing this.) But even if we take symptoms of defiance and violation of social norms as socially caused, it is nevertheless a fact that experiences of racism can cause externalizing behaviors: racism and discrimination are correlated with elevated rates of deviant peer affiliation, violence, anger, and mental-health problems in black youth (Berkel et al. 2009, p. 2). This is why it is so important to distinguish between behaviors that are signs of genuine mental or criminal trouble and behaviors that are mistakenly read as such and should, instead, be considered as reasonable acts of defiance in the context of racist society. I'm not suggesting that unprovoked violence against others be excused but, instead, that interpreting the behavior of black children and youth in the context of racialized culture is far more complicated than either psychiatry or the school system admits. And part of the problem may be within the classification of ODD and CD themselves. What I do suggest is that the diagnosis cannot be sanitized of societal causes without running the risk of perpetuating a dominant white racial ideology in which the very fact of whiteness itself is privileged to be invisible to its possessors. (Cf. McIntosh 2000.)

Let me elaborate on the issue of bias. Highly stratified societies such as the United States make it difficult for people to perceive the racialized Other without confounding the culturally and socially situated individual with racial bias and stereotypes. A salient example is found in the association of African American males with higher rates of criminality. Blacks are eight times as likely to be imprisoned as whites (Western 2006, p. 3), and black males are much more likely than whites to be arrested for a drug offense—and to go to prison if arrested—even though they are no more likely to use drugs than whites (ibid., p. 50). Life milestones such as college graduation, military service, and marriage differ significantly from whites to blacks, but the greatest inequality is in racial differences in imprisonment (ibid., p. 28). In addition, especially within African American communities, youth would rather project a "bad" image than a "mad" one because a main barrier to treatment is that mental illness holds a stigma that going to prison does not. (Cf. Shelton 2004, p. 132.)

Furthermore, inequalities in how crimes are punished intersect with inequalities in health care. Decreases in health-care funding are especially detrimental to the most difficult-to-manage clients, who often do not have access to mental-health services. "Particularly evident in this current cycle of incarcerating the mentally ill are the significant disparities in mental health services for racial and ethnic minorities and for children," according to Shelton (2004, p. 129). Because I am skeptical of the classificatory status of ODD, I am not suggesting that better access to mental-health services for children who exhibit those diagnostic symptoms would decrease defiant and disruptive behavior; that would be to treat those symptoms as indicative of a good *DSM* classification. But *some* children could benefit from psychiatric interventions and thus more properly be hospitalized than imprisoned; the trick is in identifying between legitimate defiant behavior with illegitimate or mentally disordered behavior—and, of course, knowing which diagnoses to assign to children and which symptoms to associate with one diagnosis rather than another. Megan Kaden writes:

There is no question that the juvenile justice systems are overpopulated by Black boys: messages from the justice system, the media, the educational system, employers, and federal, state and local governments support the notion that African Americans are "inferior and troublemakers." Such harmful messages create racial anxiety and fearfulness among African Americans when they must function in mainstream society. The clash of the desire to succeed and the knowledge of the barriers one is up against make the internal psychological and emotional landscape a confusing and often tumultuous one for African American children and adults. (2009, p. 4)

American inequality thus produces a collective experience for young black men that is wholly different from the rest of American society—a "profound social exclusion that significantly rolls back the gains to citizenship hard won by the civil rights movement" (Western 2006, p. 6). The stigma of criminality, Western argues, forecloses upward mobility and deflates hope for an entire generation of young black men with little education (p. 7). For many, involvement in crime becomes a normal part of economic life (p. 23); black adulthood, identity, and masculinity are therefore defined and transformed by the rising risk of imprisonment (p. 25). Western states that "we should count prisons and jails among the key institutions that shape the life course of recent birth cohorts of African American men" (p. 31). (I am including schools as well.)

Black adulthood, identity, and masculinity are therefore defined and transformed by the rising risk of imprisonment (Western 2006, p. 25). This means that parents of African American children have a daunting task: they have to raise children who grasp the realities of racism, discrimination, and injustice while at the same time not fueling hatred and rage. They have to teach children how to succeed in a white-dominated world while not accepting the role society places them in. Researchers refer to this as "racial socialization": the task is for children both to learn to value their race and to alert them to the bias and discrimination they might encounter. In this sense, racial socialization is protective when it teaches youth to develop self-pride through racial identity and self-esteem without sugar-coating the inequalities they are likely to encounter (Berkel et al. 2009, p. 2). Berkel et al. report that when parents convey positive images about being African American, their children are more likely to reject negative stereotypes. That is, children need to be prepared for discrimination but in ways that allow them to still experience the world as (relatively) safe and trustworthy; adults (teachers included) need to show that they expect schoolchildren to do well in school and to do their best. The thinking is that children can learn to identify with the history of African Americans who have overcome odds to become successful and learn how to conduct themselves around the police when they are wrongfully targeted so they can avoid further persecution (ibid., p. 10). The parental goal is to foster pride in (aspects of) African Americans' history while, at the same time, teaching children how to be successful within the norms and practices of dominant white society.

From the perspective of black parents' ideal of racial socialization, antisocial behavior is that which reflects a "hostile view of the world, affiliation with deviant peers, and academic underperformance" (Berkel et al. 2009, p. 2). Parents aim to discourage attitudes and behaviors that could be construed as hostile to dominant white society. Yet in view of the life trajectory of African American males, it is difficult to see how a tendency to make hostile attributions can be avoided. Consider: In focus groups for black youth, African American male adolescents reported that "they were less likely to be engaged in the classroom or called on by their teachers and quickly noted that they were viewed as being subordinate to white students, as many underestimated their abilities and their intelligence" and that "their perceptions of being treated less well at school led the adolescents to feel undervalued" (ibid,, p. 8).

African American students routinely experience the classroom as a place where white students are granted more privileges, allowed more leniency in dress, given more credibility in how they address conflict, and disciplined less harshly if at all (Berkel et al. 2009, p. 8). A parents' ideal of racial socialization as instilling self-worth, capableness, and a moral right to fair and equal treatment, therefore, flies in the face of black children's experiences within racialized society. Assimilation into white society, therefore, clashes with students' experiences of unjust and prejudicial treatment, where hostility toward white society may fester but the expression of which endangers their flourishing as they develop.

Norms and Expectations

All children face the developmental task of building a knowledge base of necessary skills for navigating their way through the world. These skills include learning to read and write, being able to hold a conversation, being able to think critically, and to behave in ways that aren't harmful or annoying to others. These norms contain positive values in that they aim to help individuals compete, succeed, and flourish, and to provide "glue" for social groups. Thus, norms serve the function of encouraging education into reading and writing and of fostering basic civil behavior.

Civility, according to Joan McGregor (2004, p. 26), involves "treating others as if they matter." Yet, as Meir Dan-Cohen points out (1994, p. 35), civility also includes showing deference to authority and exhibiting courtesy to authority. It functions as a social lubricant but also as a socializing mechanism. Defiance can be understood as a response to authority, who call for deferential obedience but may overstep their bounds. It is especially difficult to treat others as if they matter when one is not being treated that way oneself, and to show deference to an authority who seems unjustly or prejudicially to use power and control.

In other words, acquiescence to authority is inculcated in African American boys (and students in general) and called "socialization." African American boys who seem to be defiant and/or hostile are punished for their seemingly disrespectful and open refusal to bow to authority.

As Loeber et al. report (2000), African Americans are misdiagnosed for ODD, CD, and APD. (They identify the problem as "misdiagnosis," and I leave open the possibility that some children may be symptomatic of some mental illness that is not ODD or CD. But my argument is that ODD may be inappropriately diagnosed in African Americans and that many of the problems we see of black boys within the school system are not due to individual pathology but appropriate responses to social and cultural factors that, in fact, call into question the classificatory status of ODD.)

The locus of concern is the intersection of the school setting, the prison industrial complex, poverty, and psychiatry. "The link between school environment and misdiagnosis is significant," Loeber et al. argue (2000, p. 11), "because adolescent behaviors are often first identified as problematic in the school setting." Let us look more closely at the school setting.

Ann Ferguson describes the authoritative power of the school system as follows:

In the classroom, teachers demand bodies be arranged in certain positions before work can begin: sit up straight, both feet on the floor, hands off the desk, eyes in front toward teacher, or down on the desk. Bodies must be properly arranged both individually and as a group before they can erupt from the classroom to play. They must organize themselves into neat lines before they can enter or exit from classrooms. (2001, p. 66)

The authority of teachers in the classroom is situated within complex relations that divide, exclude, classify, hierarchize, confine, and normalize (Best 1995, p. 92). These exclusions, confinements, and hierarchies are both gendered and racialized. Thus, character formation within American school systems creates people who are afraid to fight back (Tessman 2005, p. 38). In terms of racialization, we find that norms of civility are primarily norms of whiteliness. "Whiteliness" is a term coined by Marilyn Frye (1992) to refer to the complex behaviors that acculturated white people may (usually unconsciously) enact as an expression of their white privilege. "Acting whitely" is different from being white; one can be white and not reproduce attitudes of superiority toward African Americans.

As an example of norms for whiteliness I offer a family experience from a few years ago. At our daughter's high school graduation at a primarily white school, the master of ceremonies warned that there was to be no standing applause and cheering of graduates—that we were to sit circumspectly and hold our applause until all had received their diplomas. But that edict went against the style of local African American families, and so they disregarded the white norm. They were routinely removed from the auditorium by police, on the grounds that they were disruptive. Deviations from whitely norms are not tolerated; the conflict between norms is resolved not by weighing the value of one set of norms over the other but by the megaphone, police backing, and authority of a majority of the white community.

Yet when African Americans seem too acculturated to white society, they often are rejected by their own communities—taunted as "Uncle Toms" or "Oreos."

The dominant group with its cultural attributes of whiteness and middle-class home life are the standard by which the schoolchildren are evaluated and African Americans become Other. "To invest the dominant group's way of life with the stamp of 'ideal' or 'norm,'" Ferguson writes (2001, p. 202), "means that the subordinate group's family patterns, language, relational styles are constituted as deviant, pathological, deficient, inferior."

Thus, African American boys are praised by their teachers for being obedient and compliant in school even when their behavior does not facilitate flourishing particular to them. Though the pedagogical message is that all students will succeed according to merit, in truth the racial order of American society is reproduced. African American boys who want to be successful must adopt the mannerisms, behaviors, language, and values of their white peers but then accept accusations from their African American peers of "acting white"—or they can reject whitely ways but find the pathways to success closed off from them. One double bind, then, is between embracing the values of one's racial grouping or being ostracized for adopting white values.

But many African American boys are pushed into another, even more damaging, double-bind. As we have seen, African American boys are judged as defiant troublemakers who are expected to perform less well in academics and society. In this way, these boys' identities are subjugated, marginalized, and marked off as "mad" or "bad." The unconscious "choice" of either acquiescing to school rules, on the one hand, or risking the "mad or bad" signifiers, on the other, places them in a compromising no-win situation.

The point is that social norms reinforce a racial order where children and youth learn (or at least pretend to learn) the values of civility, cooperation, and so on and, as a result, may develop damaged characters. As Lisa Tessman (2005) says, having to develop virtues that are antithetical to flourishing is a real moral and social deprivation caused by oppressive systems. What is needed is the development of character traits that, at the very least, will enable black males to survive the dehumanization and humiliation of being oppressed (ibid.).

It is worth emphasizing the connection between individual development and social systems. Psychiatry errs when it downplays the role of racism, sexism, and other systematic oppressions. While not denying the individuality of people within groupings, I suggest that, in our highly individualistic American society, many of us tend to overlook the force of systematic oppression in development. Our individual character is, in part, up to us but also, in part, the product of group socializing factors such as ethnically motivated inequalities, refugee status, and gender discrimination. As Tessman argues (2005), we are categorized according to various group memberships, which categorizing results in our being subjected to different norms and expectations that we then, to some degree, internalize. This is why Claudia Card (1990) says that what is virtue for one group is a vice for another, and these socially derived moral discrepancies give rise to damaged characters that often parallel group memberships and not just individual flaws or pathologies.

Culturally Inflected Defiance

As we have seen, some children who are deemed "defiant" are eventually diagnosed with ODD or CD. Others are sent to juvenile detention centers. Defiance in the American school context is clearly viewed by those in authority as something to be stigmatized and stamped out—or treated as a pathology. Ann Ferguson's (2001) study shows that institutionalized discipline practices perpetuate the racial order through charging African American boys with defiance. African American boys are sent to disciplinary rooms for behaving in culturally specific ways that then become central to "bad boy" identity formation. Ferguson discusses "stylized sulking" as "a face-saving device" that "involved hands crossed at the chest, legs spread wide, head down, and gestures such as a desk pushed away" (p. 68). Similarly, Rebekah Denn (2002) discusses African American students' manner of speaking to teachers more as equals than as authority figures because that is how they are treated at home. Such behaviors are taken by teachers and principals to be indications of "bad attitudes" toward authority that warrant detention or placement in Punishing Rooms. Troublemakers, as these young boys come to be known, are "almost by definition characterized by school adults as defiant and disrespectful," and being defiant carries a strongly negative valuation (Ferguson 2001, p. 69). Both white and black teachers perceive these behaviors as threatening, expressions of a challenge to the demand that students conform to school standards. Teachers read this as a sign that defiant black students are aligning themselves with lower-class attitudes, and teachers re-assert their authority by sending those students to Punishing Rooms and by predicting criminality and pathology in their futures (ibid., p. 68). These are cases where it looks like behavior is being misinterpreted in ways that make diagnoses of ODD or CD more likely.

The argument, on the one hand, is that black boys are expressing different cultural norms—in which case socialization may be a stronger factor in their behavior than something like choice or will. On the other hand, they may be responding to subjugation in a reasonable, if hazardous, way—in which case choice and will may play a role in defiant behavior.

It's not clear which is a more accurate picture—and both explanations may hold—but I think it is unlikely that black boys mostly are just mad or bad. But if that isn't the explanation, what other one could there be for such behavior? If the suppressing, punishing, and diagnosing of young black boys who act defiantly is a probable outcome, would anyone ever deliberately be defiant? As we saw, appearing to be defiant runs the risk not only of being sent to punishing rooms but also of being diagnosed with a mental disorder. Why take the risk? In my essay on defiance as a virtue (Potter 2011), I offer three possible answers to this question. First, it affirms self-respect. Second, it expresses the claim that one's moral rights have not been given up. Third, it expresses the value that some ways of behaving are beneath one. That is, culturally inflected defiant behavior may not be a vice or pathology but an indication that a youth takes himself to be self-respecting and expects others to treat him that way, and that he holds at least some indefeasible commitments even under great pressure from predominantly white social norms. (See Potter 2011 for an expanded discussion.)

Conclusion

For young African American males, the cost of maintaining self-respect may be too high to bear. For psychiatrists, the difficulty remains that discriminating between internal dysfunction and reaction to social context is exacerbated by racialized norms that often go unrecognized. While (no doubt) genuinely troublesome behavior exists, some of it arises out of the messiness of cultural differences in hegemonic society. As Wakefield, Pottick, and Kirk (2002) point out, the *DSM*-IV diagnostic criteria for disruptive and disrespectful conduct (Conduct Disorder, that is) are purely behavioral and ignore the stated requirement that criteria must be met by internally driven behaviors instead of by reactions to social contexts. This qualifier does not apply currently to ODD, but it behooves clinicians carefully to attend to different cultural norms and to their own biases and assumptions hidden in the interpretation of, and responses to, black children's attitudes and behaviors.

Still, this critical consciousness will not address systemic biases and ontological-assumptive norms. Neither will it be sufficient if the classification itself is called into question—which questioning I am doing. Sandra Harding (1986) identified "bad science" as that which the dominant privileged group prejudicially considered the important problems to be addressed, what needed to be explained, and what that group viewed as puzzling. While Harding frames the issue in terms of gender, she also notes that racism, classism, and cultural imperialism may restrict life opportunities more than sexism does (ibid., p. 17). This chapter highlights ways in which racism and psychiatric science intersect to suggest that the diagnostic category of ODD is a form of bad science. Yet Harding argues that a distinction between "bad science" and "science as usual" may be a blurry one in that it may not be possible to correct for biases without overhauling the scientific paradigm (ibid., pp. 105–108). I suggest that the distinction between "bad science" and "science as usual" legitimizes the nosological status of ODD as a natural kind when, in fact, ODD is permeated with racialized cultural norms and assumptions. Referring to the looping effect of interactive kinds, Ian Hacking (1999, p. 104) rightly points out that we need to be concerned about "classifications that, when known by people or by those around them, and put to work in institutions, change the ways in which individuals experience themselves—and may even lead people to evolve their feelings and behavior in part because they are so classified."

On this view, if young black boys are being diagnosed with ODD and CD, they may begin to respond to their classification by exhibiting closer approximations to it. Even attempts to defy that classification serve to confirm it. The concern is that schools and other institutions are not merely identifying an existent mental disorder but are creating the conditions under which that disorder thrives. So the loopiness of human kinds is one problem that faces teachers who send their students to school psychologists for evaluation. To the extent that ODD is an interactive kind, then, it is a particularly worrisome one because the label gets attached to a multiply disadvantaged group.[1] In the nosology of psychiatry, the line between normal and pathological defiance is unclear. At the very least, the criteria for diagnosing ODD need to attend to socially mediated differences such as gender, race, and socioeconomic status in order for clinicians not to inadvertently perpetuate racial inequalities in society.

Acknowledgments

The author is grateful to Jay Englehardt, MD, to Mona Gupta, MD, PhD, to Dylan Brock, joint MD/MA-in-the-making, to Robert Kimball, to Peter Zachar, and to Harold Kincaid for their very helpful comments on drafts.

Note

1. A further difficulty in evaluating the merits of diagnosing children with ODD and CD is that the diagnosis may not only be marking an interactive kind but a kind not in the medical domain at all. Some of the personality disorders arguably are not medical kinds but instead are moral kinds. (Cf. Charland 2006. For an argument that some may be both, see Zachar and Potter 2010.)

References

Ali, A. 2004. The intersection of racism and sexism in psychiatric diagnosis. In *Bias in Psychiatric Diagnosis*, ed. P. Caplan and L. Cosgrove. Jason Aronson.

Berkel, C., V. Murry, T. Hurt, T., Y. Chen, G. Brody, R., Simons, C., Cutorna, and F. Gibbons. 2009. It takes a village: Protecting rural African American youth in the context of racism. *Journal of Youth and Adolescence* 38 (2): 175–188.

Best, S. 1995. *The Politics of Historical Vision: Marx, Foucault, Habermas*. Guilford.

Boxill, B. 1995. Self-respect and protest. In *Dignity, Character, and Self-Respect*, ed. R. Dillon. Routledge.

Card, C. 1990. Gender and moral luck. In *Identity, Character, Morality: Essays in Moral Psychology*, ed. O. Flanagan and A. Rorty. MIT Press.

Charland, L. 2006. Moral nature of the *DSM*-IV cluster B personality disorders. *Journal of Personality Disorders* 20 (2): 116–125.

Coker, T., et al. 2009. Perceived racial/ethnic discrimination among fifth-grade students and its association with mental health. *American Journal of Public Health* 99 (5): 878–884.

Dan-Cohen, M. 1994. In defense of defiance. *Philosophy & Public Affairs* 23 (1): 24–51.

Denn, R. 2002. Blacks are disciplined at far higher rates than other students. *Seattle Post-Intelligencer*, March 15.

DSM-IV-TR. 2000. *Diagnostic and Statistical Manual of Mental Disorders*, fourth edition, text revision. American Psychiatric Association.

DSM-5. 2013. *Diagnostic and Statistical Manual of Mental Disorders,* fifth edition. American Psychiatric Association.

Ferguson, A. 2001. *Bad Boys: Public Schools in the Making of Black Masculinity.* University of Michigan Press.

Frick, P. 2006. Developmental pathways to conduct disorder. *Child and Adolescent Psychiatric Clinics of North America* 15: 311–331.

Frick, P., and M. Ellis. 1999. Callous-unemotional traits and subtypes of conduct disorder. *Clinical Child and Family Psychology Review* 2 (3): 149–168.

Frye, M. 1992. White woman feminist. In *Willful Virgin: Essays in Feminism.* Crossing Press.

Gilman, S. 1985. *Difference and Pathology: Stereotypes of Sexuality, Race, and Madness.* Cornell University Press.

Hacking, I. 1999. *The Social Construction of What?* Harvard University Press.

Harding, S. 1986. *The Science Question in Feminism.* Cornell University Press.

Hill, T. 1995. Servility and self-respect. In *Dignity, Character, and Self-Respect,* ed. R. Dillon. Routledge.

Hines, P., and N. Boyd-Franklin. 1996. African American families In *Ethnicity and Family Therapy,* ed. M. McGoldrick, J. Giordano, and J. Pearce. Guilford.

Kaden, M. 2009. African American Adolescent Males and Conduct Disorder: An Examination of Diagnosis and Racial Bias. Dissertation, California Institute of Integral Studies, San Francisco.

Loeber, R., J. Burke, B. Lahey, A. Winders, and M. Zera. 2000. Oppositional Defiant and Conduct Disorder: A review of the past 10 years, part I. *Journal of the American Academy of Child and Adolescent Psychiatry* 39 (12): 1468–1484.

McGregor, J. 2004. Civility, civic virtue, and citizenship. In *Civility and Its Discontents: Essays on Civic Virtue, Toleration, and Cultural Fragmentation,* ed. C. Sistare. University of Kansas Press.

McIntosh, P. 2000. White privilege and male privilege. In *The Philosophical Quest: A Cross Cultural Reader,* second edition, ed. G. Presbey, K. Struhl, and R. Olsen. McGraw-Hill.

Metzl, J. 2009. *The Protest Psychosis: How Schizophrenia Became a Black Disease.* Beacon.

Potter, N. 2011. Mad, bad, or virtuous? The moral, cultural and pathologizing features of defiance. *Theory & Psychology* 22 (1): 23–45.

Riley, D. 1997. *The Defiant Child: A Parent's Guide to Oppositional Defiant Disorder.* Taylor.

Sadler, J. 2005. *Values and Psychiatric Diagnosis*. Oxford University Press.

Shelton, D. 2004. Experiences of detained young offenders in need of mental health care. *Journal of Nursing Scholarship*, second quarter: 129–133.

Tessman, L. 2005. *Burdened Virtues: Virtue Ethics for Liberatory Struggles*. Oxford University Press.

Wakefield, J., K. Pottick, and S. Kirk. 2002. Should the *DSM*-IV diagnostic criteria for CD consider social context? *American Journal of Psychiatry* 159: 380–386.

Washington, H. 2008. *Medical Apartheid: The Dark History of Medical Experimentation on Black Americans from Colonial Times to the Present*. Anchor.

Western, B. 2006. *Punishment and Inequality in America*. Russell Sage Foundation.

Zachar, P., and N. Potter. 2010. Personality disorders: moral or medical kinds—or both? *Philosophy, Psychiatry, & Psychology* 17 (2): 127–129.

10 Syndrome Stabilization in Psychiatry: Pathological Gambling as a Case Study

Don Ross

Systematic research into gambling behavior, especially problem and pathological gambling, has become a substantial academic industry. Several research centers and an annual conference draw investigators from psychiatry, psychology, neuroscience, and social sciences (particularly economics). Historical moments when interdisciplinary research matrices converge on norms that guide grant and journal reviewers are good opportunities for study by philosophers of science. They are also the occasions when philosophers of science can most usefully make contributions to science, since they are the junctures at which the relevant scientists will often agree that conceptual uncertainties merit self-conscious attention. The current state of research on gambling behavior exemplifies this situation, while also revealing features specific to conceptual stabilization at the intersection among psychiatry, neuroscience, and social science.

Murphy (2006) criticizes standard practice in psychiatric nosology as a philosopher of science. He argues that the model of pathology encapsulated in the fourth edition of the *Diagnostic and Statistical Manual of Mental Disorders* (American Psychiatric Association 2000) reflects a folk conception of the mental, and of malfunctioning, that is inadequately integrated with cognitive and behavioral neuroscience. The present chapter supports this view in the specific instance of pathological gambling.[1] The case does not rely on philosophical presuppositions of realism or empiricism, either of which, if dogmatically conventionalized in a science, would unduly constrain opportunism. However, realism and empiricism are useful constructs for describing particular trade-offs that scientists make between the motive to find unifying explanatory (causal) mechanisms (realism) and exploitation of statistical testing power provided by reduced-form models that are agnostic about constituents of model-independent reality (empiricism).

The *DSM* Operationalization of Pathological Gambling

From clinical lore gambling research inherited distinct constructs of "problem" and "pathological" gambling. This classification was motivated by reference to social criteria: some people's gambling is widely deemed to be *generally* socially catastrophic (to gamblers and usually their families), while other people's gambling wanders in and out of bounds set by norms regulating "appropriate" behavior. This construction of problem and pathological gambling has been based on an established popular distinction between "problem drinking" and "alcoholism."

Typically for research motivated by social concerns, the earliest research on problem and pathological gambling concentrated on establishing quantitative magnitudes—mainly, prevalence rates and aggregate social costs. This research has avoided mapping the distinction between problem gambling and pathological gambling onto any hypothesized distinction "internal to" the minds or brains of disordered gamblers. Researchers have instead relied on operationalizations referenced to social-behavioral consequences. Studies gather subject samples of suitable size and representativeness for estimating proportions of target populations that gamble never, "occasionally," "regularly," and "very frequently," and proportions that gamble more than the gamblers or their families wish they did. The first three categories refer to social norms, and the fourth category is not presupposed to be a strict subset of the third. What makes prevalence estimation scientific, along with sound analysis, is attention to cross-study comparability: similar methods are applied recurrently in different populations. We have evidence that prevalence estimates track a phenomenon stable enough for *accumulation* of knowledge just in case we discover similar category proportions in various populations after controlling for hypothetically relevant environmental conditions (e.g., availability of gambling opportunities).

Prevalence estimation is characteristic of a "phenomena counting" stage of science, preceding experimental and theoretical refinement. Policy, clinical practices, and diagnostic practices reliant on the problem/pathological distinction have not been able to wait for the science to mature. This does not mean that practice has *ignored* ongoing science pending its maturity. Clinicians and policy makers generally suppose that responsible policy at a given time t should reflect whatever scientists have agreed upon by time t. Furthermore, since funding for research on pathologies is mainly motivated by clinical imperatives, distinctions used in diagnosis condition the formulation of hypotheses. Thus, scientific and clinical conceptualizations interact, but clinical practices and principles dominate the interaction.

Let us idealize "scientific" isolation of a phenomenon as the identification of a causal regularity, relation or disposition that holds under a specified range of conditions.[2] Although clinical communities stabilize syndrome concepts in ways that depart further from this ideal than mature scientific research programs, clinicians' convergence on shared diagnostic criteria is not unsystematic. First, practitioners report symptoms they observe occurring together in their accidental patient samples. These reports are published in journals of patient observations, which are periodically reviewed by meta-analysts in search of co-morbidity patterns that significantly recur. Where such patterns can't be explained as consequences of the interactions of already established syndromes, they become the basis for new diagnoses. Once there is approximate consensus on a diagnosis and on the best treatment given current knowledge and technology, this is published in a diagnostic manual. Manual entries do more than summarize observations. They also refine diagnostic practice by supplying standard tests for confirmation. This allows clinicians to refer patients along through treatment networks using diagnostic labels that are interpreted in roughly the same way by everyone who consults the patient's file.

On the basis of this practice, *DSM*-IV[3] operationalizes "pathological gambling" as follows:

A chronic inability to refrain from gambling to an extent that causes serious disruption to core life aspects such as career, health and family. A person is diagnosed as a probable pathological gambler if they agree with five or more of the following statements:

1. You have often gambled longer than you had planned.
2. You have often gambled until your last dollar was gone.
3. Thoughts of gambling have caused you to lose sleep.
4. You have used your income or savings to gamble while letting bills go unpaid.
5. You have made repeated, unsuccessful attempts to stop gambling.
6. You have broken the law or considered breaking the law to finance your gambling.
7. You have borrowed money to finance your gambling.
8. You have felt depressed or suicidal because of your gambling losses.
9. You have been remorseful after gambling.
10. You have gambled to get money to meet your financial obligations.

As with other *DSM* entries, this is an operationalization in a precise sense, intended as the basis for constructing diagnostic screens for administration to reporting patients. The belief that most people with serious gambling disorders will agree with five or more of the statements above is not based on scientific research but on anecdotal clinical lore, and on a tradition brought over from more extensive psychiatric experience with patterns in alcohol dependence.

"Problem gambling" is not defined in *DSM*-IV. Nevertheless, the US Committee on the Social and Economic Impact of Pathological Gambling, composed mainly of scientists, operationalizes problem gambling as "gambling behavior that results in any harmful effects to the gambler, his or her family, significant others, friends, co-workers etc." (National Research Council 1999, p. 21). Though the committee endorsed the *DSM* operationalization of "pathological gambling" and explicitly defined "disordered gambling" as the union of pathological and problem gambling, its operationalization of the latter is unconnected to any screen. Taken literally, it is clinically unhelpful: losing $5 on a football bet and being late for lunch as a result of a queue at the betting window constitute "harmful effects" of gambling, however trivial. Since "problem gambling" is intended to denote a warning condition for vulnerability to pathological gambling, one might expect that operationalizations of the two ideas should have a common basis: an assessor should be able to use the same screen by which she identifies pathological gamblers to identify problem gamblers, applying a lower threshold for the latter. However, screens based on the *DSM* reflect no principled underlying scale robust under transformations to alternative threshold tests. Clinicians do not treat the statements in the *DSM* operationalization as equally diagnostic. Agreement with statement 5, statement 6, or statement 10 is taken to indicate a probable serious gambling problem, and likewise for statement 8 if "depressed" is interpreted clinically. This cannot be said of the other statements barring special interpretations. These asymmetries make it unclear what "lowering the threshold" on *DSM*-based screens might systematically mean.

Despite its unclarity, there are practical motivations for retaining the "problem gambling" construct. There is consensus in the gambling industry, in the treatment community and among regulators that large numbers of gamblers occasionally lose more money than they judge they can comfortably afford, while a much smaller proportion find their lives and welfare catastrophically impaired by relentless cravings to gamble. There is thus an acknowledged public-health interest in determining whether there is a scientific basis for hypothesizing a qualitative "jump" between typical consumers of gambling services with imperfect self-control, and truly addicted gamblers who should be treated according to precedents for Axis-I psychiatric disorders. Most casinos aim to identify and then exclude addicted gamblers, but not those who merely occasionally gamble more than they intended to. If there is *not* a qualitative jump between these types, and any frequency of self-control lapses has predictive significance for probability of developing a psychiatric disorder, then casino and lottery operators carry potentially dramatic levels of ethical responsibility. On the other hand, if pathological gambling is a distinctive and relatively *sui generis* condition, then operators might hope that their problem is no trickier in principle than aiming to keep people with tuberculosis off jetliners.

Conceptual questions about the relationship between minor and severe gambling problems have therefore been framed as questions about the ontogeny of the latter given rates of the former. Prevalence studies have proven largely uninformative here. They have generated consensus that, for any population, adolescent prevalence is *at least* three times higher than among adults. However, studies of alcohol use and drug use show that the majority of adolescents who consume at rates which in an adult would be regarded as reliable indicators of addiction endogenously reduce these rates by their late twenties. Thus, though it appears that most addicted adults were impulsively consuming adolescents, most impulsively consuming adolescents don't become addicted adults. Treatment community lore holds that pathological gamblers often enjoyed statistically deviant win frequencies in their first gambling experiences, which, it is conjectured, leads to over-estimation of expected payoffs that is for some reason difficult to un-learn (Collins 2003). However, this idea has never been tested in a longitudinal treatment.

This unsatisfactory conceptual impasse is not simply a function of the recentness of gambling behavior science. It reflects principled epistemological problems that arise when researchers rely on clinical screens.

Clinical Screens as Research Instruments

For conditions that can cause serious harm, the imperative to help suffering people has higher social priority than scientific knowledge. In screening to identify pathological gamblers, the treatment community prefers to err on the side of diagnosing risk in some people who aren't really in trouble, in order to avoid false negatives. Clinical screens are open to criticism if they do not build in this bias. This creates a dilemma for scientists choosing screens to select research samples. Use of clinical screens will over-estimate prevalence rates. If scientists instead develop customized research screens that aim to avoid bias, clinical and research samples will fail to match. This is problematic. Subject recruitment for studies of low-prevalence conditions, such as pathological gambling, is expensive. Practical considerations require frequent reliance on samples already assembled for treatment purposes, especially when an aspect of a research project is evaluation of a therapeutic approach. Ethical complications then arise because research cannot be concealed from its subjects. If we re-classify clinical populations to correct for screen bias, this sends patients confusing signals that may undermine their recovery. Thus most studies of pathological gambling have used samples that were sorted into treatment and control groups using clinical screens. This has had several important consequences.

First, it has created major uncertainties in prevalence estimation. One instrument, the South Oaks Gambling Screen (SOGS) (Lesieur and Blume 1987), had featured in 90 percent of published studies as of a survey by Dickerson and Baron (2000). The SOGS can be self-administered by respondents, which is cost-efficient in large samples because it avoids the need for reliance on qualified administrators of structured clinical interviews. However, its tendency to harvest false positives appears to be large even for clinical screens. Most textbooks and surveys cite estimates of 1–4 percent of adults as the "typical" prevalence of pathological gambling in jurisdictions with legal casinos. Robert Ladouceur, a leading pioneer of gambling research, anecdotally estimates the false positive rate produced by SOGS-based estimation at *at least* 1:1 (personal correspondence), and recent systematic evidence supports that estimate. New screens have been developed that, while still based on *DSM* criteria, better match the findings of structured clinical interviews than the SOGS. Using one of these instruments (Ferris and Wynne 2001), the British Gambling Prevalence Survey (Wardle et al. 2007) produced an estimate of 0.5 percent. This corresponds closely to the result of the most rigorous prevalence study ever conducted, the Gambling and Co-occurring Disorders component of the US National Comorbidity Survey (Kessler 2007). In that study, full structured clinical interviews administered to a random sample of more than 9,000 adults generated a prevalence estimate of 0.7 percent.

Second, in considering any inference of causal relationships from relative efficacies of therapies, one must know the average or marginal *severity* of pathology to which the screen used to recruit subjects was sensitive. Consider two hypothetical screens, A and B. Suppose that screen A consistently produces samples in which the median subject agrees with eight of the statements in the *DSM*-IV operationalization, while the median subject recruited by screen B agrees with six of them. One would then have reason to expect that research using screen B will be more likely to suggest that a given policy or therapy is effective than research on that same policy or therapy that recruits and pools subjects by means of screen A, because the A-screened samples will contain higher proportions of severe cases. On the other hand, as noted, not all the *DSM*-IV criteria are of equal diagnostic weight. Suppose, for example, that more of the B-screened subjects agree with statements 5 and 6.

Third, a major research question, indicated above, is whether there is a qualitative jump, revealed by some quantitative discontinuity on some measurable parameter, between sub-groups of disordered gamblers. However, as we saw, prevalence work based on clinical screens is ill suited to shedding light on this. Blaszczynski and Nower (2002) argue that there are three different kinds of pathological gambler, that each kind has a different etiology, and that people suffering from each kind respond best to different interventions. Where diagnostic screens are concerned, this suggests the possibility of different scales with discontinuities at different measurement points of magnitudes of different variables. So long as we are relying on operationalizations of folk concepts instead of functional relationships represented in exact models, we should therefore ideally run every test we think is important on several groups of subjects recruited using different screens, and run regressions. But then absence of a common underlying model would block attempts to estimate the contributions of different variable values to different group memberships.

Failure to apply a scientific model to identification of pathological gamblers also makes it difficult to integrate study of the phenomenon with investigations of mental health more generally. Considerable activity has aimed at estimating the tendency of pathological gamblers to manifest Axis-I comorbidities (substance dependence, depression, schizophrenia, and anti-social personality disorder). Discovering stable comorbidity rates across populations of pathological gamblers, if there are any, would be helpful for a number of reasons. First, it would help predict the likelihood that a given person is at risk for pathological gambling. Second, it would be relevant to design of treatments and interventions, possibly explaining some patterns of success and failure: interventions that work for pathological gamblers who lack certain comorbidities might fail for others who don't. (See, e.g., Ladd and Petry 2003.) Third, efforts to explain stable comorbidity patterns might lead us toward the explanation of pathological gambling itself if pathological gambling and comorbidities are sometimes or often consequences of common factors. Comorbidity data are what mainly motivate Blaszczynski and Nower's thesis concerning different kinds of pathological gamblers. They report that across studies with larger numbers of subjects, stable proportions of pathological gamblers show comorbidity with, respectively, nothing, depression and other mood disorders, and anti-social personality disorder. Subjects in these groups respond differentially to therapies. Blaszczynski and Nower then argue, more controversially, that the different comorbid factors causally contribute to pathological gambling in different ways.

Most recent gambling policy attends to scientific research on gambling out of interest in the extent to which availability of commercial gambling opportunities and regulated features of casino games *causally* impact on pathological gambling rates and severity. As the perspective of Blaszczynski and Nower reminds us, however, questions about causality are inherently bound up with whether pathological gambling is a *sui generis* disorder or a secondary expression of less specific problems. To the extent that we expect the latter, then gambling regulatory policy may be the wrong instrument for addressing the public-health issues.

Neuroscience and Molecular Genetics to the Rescue

If current prevalence studies of pathological gambling by themselves shed little light on causal relationships, how might we do better both for the sake of scientific knowledge and for the sake of improved treatment and policy? Brute-force methodology, such as running controlled behavioral experiments on random subject samples in which suspected causal factors are systematically manipulated, is impractical owing to the apparent low-frequency prevalence—much lower than formerly thought—of pathological gambling. The other way of inferring causes is to gather data by reference to an explicit causal model and then test the model using a tailored regression technique. To my knowledge this econometric approach has not yet been attempted in any pathological gambling prevalence study. There are two reasons for this. First, as has been noted, most pre-neuroscientific investigations of pathological gambling proceed on the basis of *no* underlying model. Second, the abstractness of the "pathological gambling" construct, along with its multifarious demonstrated comorbidities, gives rise to potentially vicious endogeneity problems for model estimation. It is likely that the dependent variable of ultimate interest—disposition to pathological gambling—is determined to different degrees by different observed independent variables and these in turn partly co-determine one another. This limitation forces most prevalence researchers (like most social psychologists) to be content with weak tests of significance (e.g., *T*-tests) on correlations, unable to employ stronger econometric tests that aim to isolate causal structure.

These problems are not insurmountable; on the cutting edge of gambling research they are indeed being gradually surmounted. As in cognitive and behavioral science generally, two disciplinary clusters are coming increasingly to the rescue: neuroscience and molecular genetics.

Recent combined neurochemical and neuroeconomic models of addiction, specifically including gambling addiction, are surveyed in Ross et al. 2008. It has been known for some time that addiction is correlated with abnormal levels of the neurotransmitter dopamine in ventral striatum. The dopamine circuit from midbrain to striatum has been more recently identified as responsible for predicting rewards, valuing potential rewards against alternatives, and preparing motor activity to procure rewards. New neuroimaging technologies yield sufficiently discriminating information about comparative neurotransmitter activity in addicts and non-addicts to test models of processes by which this circuit can capture the regulation of a person's or rat's molar behavior. All of these models share some general features. Essentially, they represent the mesolimbic dopamine reward system as gaining control of the organism's molar behavior by chemically attenuating feedback serotonin (and other) circuits from frontal and prefrontal cortex which normally bid for attention to, and for scheduling consumption of, longer-range sources of reward. Fear responses from emotional centers such as the amygdala are also suppressed. The reward system achieves this mutiny by exploiting the discovery that, through relentlessly searching for cues to the arrival of an addictive target, and then organizing consumption of that target, it can reliably produce floods of dopamine in striatum. This constitutes the reward the system is evolved to maximize, which simultaneously overwhelms the functioning of normally rival circuits.

People who report greatest behavioral disturbance with respect to gambling closely resemble drug addicts in having hyperactive striatal dopamine responses in the presence of cues for gambling (drugs), including their own fantasizing about gambling (drugs), and hypoactive opponent neurotransmitter responses. This explains why seriously afflicted pathological gamblers without comorbid substance abuse display behavioral tendencies familiar from drug addiction. It is hypothesized on this basis that some proportion of people diagnosed as pathological gamblers by the *DSM* criteria are neurochemically addicted to gambling. In view of the tendency of *DSM*-based screens to identify false positives, it is probable that the screens tend to capture mixes of addicts and neurochemically normal frequent gamblers. In this way they fail to cut nature at scientific joints, *whether by this idea we allude to a realist model of psychiatric natural kinds or only to an ambition to write down reduced-form models that permit isolation of asymmetrically co-dependent variables that will be robust under econometric tests.* In the interdisciplinary matrix of neuroeconomics, economists tend to emphasize empiricist virtues by pursuing the second aim. Neuroscientists tend to try to isolate real entities and mechanisms. This difference does not prevent them from jointly converging on a shared basis for dividing the normative concept of pathological gambling.

Discovering that at least a subset of what psychiatrists have called pathological gambling is a pathology in the balance of power among neurotransmitter circuits is directly relevant to progress in understanding the disorder's pathogenesis. There was already limited evidence from twin studies for a heritable aspect of pathological gambling. On the basis of examination of 3,359 pairs of twins, Eisen et al. (1998) conclude that inherited factors explain between 35 percent and 54 percent of reports of five *DSM* symptoms that could be estimated statistically, 56 percent of the report of three or more symptoms, and 62 percent of diagnoses. Potenza et al. (2005) find a matched genetic contribution with near-perfect overlap to pathological gambling and major depression. Slutske et al. (2000) report common genetic vulnerability to pathological gambling and alcohol dependence in male subjects.

All of this is at best suggestive. Tracing the phenomenon of severe pathological gambling to the dopamine circuit, however, enables molecular geneticists to hone in on the possible biological explainers of these data. Ibáñez et al. (2003) review seven association studies, all but one conducted by their group. An important property of their work is its motivation to provide separating evidence between conceptions of pathological gambling as an obsessive-compulsive disorder—the category in which *DSM*-IV places pathological gambling but *not* drug addiction—and the family of dopaminergic pathologies that clearly include the classic addictions. In light of the reward system mutiny model, as Ibáñez et al. say, "genes relevant to the function of serotonergic, dopaminergic and noradrenergic systems could be considered as candidate genes in pathological gambling" (p. 16). They find a promoter polymorphism sequence for expression of MOA-A protein, which has been associated with control of neurotransmitters found in the reward system, to be significantly increased in male pathological gamblers compared to controls. "Interestingly," Ibáñez et al.

comment, "although serotonin is a preferred substrate for MOA-A, MOA-A is expressed in the brain mainly in dopaminergic neurons, raising the question of whether these allele variants are more likely to result in changes in serotonergic or dopaminergic transmission" (p. 18). This comports suggestively with the mutiny model, according to which it is attenuation of serotonin circuits by dopamine activity that mediates suppressed frontal control in addicts. Perez de Castro et al. (1997) found the DRD4 7-repeat allele, which codes for less efficient receptors, to be significantly more frequent in female pathological gamblers than in controls. Finally, Ibáñez et al. cite a report, due to Comings et al. (1996), of "significant association between the Taq-A1 allele of the D2 dopamine receptor gene in pathological gamblers compared to controls," and note that the Taq-A1 allele "has also been found to be associated with other impulsive-addictive-compulsive behaviors, leading some researchers to propose a *Reward Deficiency Syndrome* as an underlying genetic foundation for these disorders" (Ibáñez et al. 2003, p. 18).

Conclusion

The philosophical interpretation I suggest is best motivated by these developments is as follows. There is good reason, independent of issues that divide realists and empiricists, for reconceptualizing the phenomenon that *DSM*-IV operationalizes as pathological gambling as a specific manifestation of disruption in frontal-cortical control of the mesolimbic dopamine system's influence on molar behavior. By this proposal I do not intend a baroque claim to the effect that the authors of *DSM*-IV always intended "pathological gambling" to refer to whatever unknown "constitutive essence" unites the stereotypical cases, which has since turned out to be dopamine floods in ventral striatum. To the extent that it makes sense in the first place to talk about "intentions" of "authors" of referential conventions that emerge from complex institutional politics and evolving diagnostic practice over many years, these "intentions" were highly unspecific, and should be inferred directly from the general function of the *DSM*. That function is to optimally facilitate and standardize clinical reference, diagnosis, and treatment of cases of patients with common symptoms, common etiologies of disturbances, and common response modalities to a common set of related interventions, with greater weight given to those whose suffering is most severe and chronic. Then, I claim, the empirical evidence suggests that the largest proportion of those "intended" (in this sense) to be diagnosed as pathological gamblers by the *DSM* operationalization, including almost all of those whose suffering is severe, chronic, and recalcitrant to low-intensity therapy, are afflicted with neu- roadapted hypoactivity of serotonergic circuits that normally inhibit impulsive behavior, and dopaminergic reward circuits that have learned to obsessively pursue and attend to predictors of gambling opportunities. Because of this common condition, almost all pathological gamblers are candidates for a common neuropharmacological treatment, identification of which should be (as it now is) a priority in applied research. A priority in basic research on pathological gambling should be (as it now is) the refinement and generalization of relevant dopamine learning models, so as to improve both predictive power and the depth of our explanation and integration of pathological gambling in the wider context of the behavioral and brain sciences.

This reduction of a social-behavioral syndrome to a relationship among neurotransmitter systems is not what philosophers often call "seamless." Some patients whom *DSM*-IV "intended" to class as pathological gamblers stand to be re-classified, though their social and behavioral problems remain as before. I believe that the case is typical in this respect, at least of all sciences that are partly regulated in their development by practical applications.

Notes

1. A caveat: I don't agree with Murphy that successful psychiatric science requires a *general* account of abnormal mental functioning—different disorders constitute disorders for different kinds of reasons.
2. This formulation is intended as neutral among philosophies of science; it might refer to Humean regularities, to nomological relations among "natural kinds," to Cartwright's (1992) "Aristotelian natures," or to functional dependencies among restricted parametric ranges of variables in models with specified domains of application.
3. This chapter was written before the outlines of *DSM*-5 were clear. Pathological gambling is called "gambling disorder" in the *DSM*-5 and falls under the category "Substance-related and addictive disorders." Nothing in this change contradicts the history presented here.

References

American Psychiatric Association. 2000. *Diagnostic and Statistical Manual of Mental Disorders*, fourth edition, textual revision.

Blaszczynski, A., and L. Nower. 2002. A pathways model of problem and pathological gambling. *Addiction* 97: 487–499.

Cartwright, N. 1992. Aristotelian natures and the modern experimental method. In *Inference, Explanation and Other Frustrations in the Philosophy of Science*, ed. J. Earman. University of California Press.

Collins, P. 2003. *Gambling and the Public Interest*. Praeger.

Comings, D., R. Rosenthal, and H. Lesieur. 1996. A study of the dopamine D2 receptor gene in pathological gambling. *Pharmacogenetics* 6: 223–234.

Dickerson, M., and E. Baron. 2000. Contemporary issues and future directions for research into pathological gambling. *Addiction* 95: 1145–1159.

Eisen, S., N. Lin, M. Lyons, J. Scherrer, K. Griffith, W. True, J. Goldberg, and M. Tsuang. 1998. Familial influences on gambling behavior: An analysis of 3359 twin pairs. *Addiction* 93: 1375–1384.

Ferris, J., and H. Wynne. 2001. The Canadian Problem Gambling Index draft user manual. www.ccsa.ca/pdf/ccsa-009381-2001.pdf.

Ibáñez, A., C. Blanco, I. Perez de Castro, J. Fernandez-Piqueras, and J. Sáiz-Ruiz. 2003. Genetics of pathological gambling. *Journal of Gambling Studies* 19: 11–22.

Kessler, R. 2007. Gambling and co-occurring disorders: Landmark research from the National Comorbidity Survey. Presentation at Eighth Annual NCRG Conference on Gambling and Addiction, Las Vegas.

Ladd, G., and N. Petry. 2003. A comparison of pathological gamblers with and without substance abuse treatment histories. *Experimental and Clinical Psychopharmacology* 11: 202–209.

Lesieur, H., and S. Blume. 1987. The South Oaks Gambling Screen (SOGS): A new instrument for the identification of problem gamblers. *American Journal of Psychiatry* 144: 1184–1188.

Murphy, D. 2006. *Psychiatry in the Scientific Image*. MIT Press.

National Research Council. 1999. *Pathological Gambling: A Critical Review*. National Academy Press.

Perez de Castro, I., A. Ibáñez, P. Torres, J. Sáiz-Ruiz, and J. Fernandez-Piqueras. 1997. Genetic association study between pathological gambling and a functional DNA polymorphism at the D4 receptor. *Pharmacogenetics* 7: 345–348.

Potenza, M., H. Xian, K. Shah, J. Scherrer, and S. Eisen. 2005. Shared genetic contributions to pathological gambling and major depression in men. *Archives of General Psychiatry* 62: 1015–1021.

Ross, D., C. Sharp, R. Vuchinich, and D. Spurrett. 2008. *Midbrain Mutiny: The Pico-economics and Neuroeconomics of Disordered Gambling.* MIT Press.

Slutske, W., S. Eisen, W. True, M. Lyons, J. Goldberg, and M. Tsuang. 2000. Common genetic vulnerability for pathological gambling and alcohol dependence in men. *Archives of General Psychiatry* 57: 666–673.

Wardle, H., K. Sproston, J. Orford, B. Erens, M. Griffiths, R. Constantine, and S. Pigott. 2007. *British Gambling Prevalence Survey 2007.* National Centre for Social Research.

11   The Social Functions of Natural Kinds: The Case of Major Depression

Allan V. Horwitz

The study of depression reveals a paradox about the view of mental disorder as a natural kind. On the one hand, until recently diagnosticians and practitioners held a fairly consistent view of depression. On the other hand, the concept and measurement of depression from 1980 to the present has been distinctly different from previous observations about this condition. In this chapter I use the continuities in depression across historical time to argue that current diagnostic criteria distort crucial aspects of this condition, in particular the distinction between natural sadness and depressive disorders. Historical analysis provides the best available basis for establishing the presence of a natural kind that can be used to critique the particular diagnostic criteria found in present classificatory manuals.

The current prominence of depression as a highly prevalent diagnosis and a well-known cultural condition is new. Until the 1970s, this condition was viewed as a relatively rare, but very serious, condition, mainly found among hospitalized patients. Outpatients were far more likely to receive diagnoses of some sort of anxiety condition than of depression (Herzberg 2009; Horwitz 2010). Likewise, anxiety was the major target of psychoactive medications at the time; anti-depressants were not widely used for commonly occurring mental-health problems.

The emergence of depression as the central mental-health condition resulted from the complete reformulation in 1980 of the official diagnostic criteria of the American Psychiatric Association that are found in the third edition of the *Diagnostic and Statistical Manual of Mental Disorders* (American Psychiatric Association 1980). Previous diagnostic manuals mainly associated depression with psychoses. Persons receiving this diagnosis showed "evidence of gross misinterpretation of reality, including, at times, delusions and hallucinations" (American Psychiatric Association 1952, p. 25). In contrast, these earlier manuals conceived of neurotic depression as an epiphenomenon of an underlying anxiety condition. *DSM*-III formulated depression in a radically new way.

The criteria for major depression in *DSM*-5 (issued in 2013) are virtually identical to the *DSM*-III criteria. They require that five symptoms out of the following nine be present during a two-week period (the five must include either depressed mood or diminished interest or pleasure): (1) depressed mood; (2) diminished interest or pleasure in activities; (3) weight gain or loss or change in appetite; (4) insomnia or hypersomnia (excessive sleep); (5) psychomotor agitation or retardation (slowing down); (6) fatigue or loss of energy; (7) feelings of worthlessness or excessive or inappropriate guilt; (8) diminished ability to think or concentrate or indecisiveness; (9) recurrent thoughts of death or suicidal ideation or suicide attempt (American Psychiatric Association 2013, p. 161). All patients who report five of these symptoms over a two-week period receive a diagnosis of major depression. In contrast to earlier manuals, however, the *DSM-5* no longer exempts symptoms arising from bereavement from a diagnosis.

These criteria have become the universal standard for diagnosing depression and are seen as reflecting an underlying natural kind. They are now used in all settings that require diagnoses, including general medical and specialty mental-health practices, in research studies, epidemiological investigations, and clinical trials of all forms of treatment. Its widespread acceptance notwithstanding, the diagnosis masks major flaws. Its utility does not stem from its ability to enhance understanding of the causes, prognoses, or treatment of depressive conditions but is the result of its enormous usefulness for a wide variety of interest groups that benefit from the formulation of depression as a natural kind.

The fact that the current definition of depression is socially shaped and maintained does not disprove the possibility that depression itself is a natural kind, that is, a non-arbitrary category that is present in nature rather than created by human minds. Indeed, a consistent and voluminous body of evidence indicates that depression is one of a very small number of mental disorders that has continuity across thousands of years of psychiatric history.

Depression as a Natural Kind

The earliest known definition of depression, then called "melancholia," is found in the writings of the ancient Greek physician Hippocrates from the fifth century BC. The symptoms Hippocrates associated with melancholia—"aversion to food, despondency, sleeplessness, irritability, restlessness"—

are remarkably similar to the current *DSM* criteria (Hippocrates 1923–1931, p. 185). Yet Hippocrates also emphasized that not symptoms themselves but only symptoms of unexpected duration indicated the existence of a disorder: "If fear or sadness last for a long time it is melancholia." (ibid., p. 263) Hippocrates' insistence about the prolonged nature of sadness or fear was a first attempt to capture the notion that disproportion to circumstances is an essential aspect of depressive disorder.

A century later, Aristotle (or his students) elaborated the distinction between normal mood states of sadness on the one hand and pathological disease states of melancholia on the other. Aristotle emphasized the idea that only sadness that is disproportionate to the context in which it arises is disordered. He noted that when black bile, the presumed cause of melancholia at the time, was "cold beyond due measure, it produces groundless despondency" (Jackson 1986, p. 32). Here "beyond due measure" refers to what is disproportionate to the circumstances, making the resultant sadness "groundless."

The distinction drawn in Aristotelian medicine between disordered melancholic states that were disproportionate to their contexts and those that were proportional reactions to external circumstances persisted for thousands of years. The English vicar Robert Burton's *Anatomy of Melancholy*, published in 1621, is perhaps the most renowned discussion of the condition. The affective, cognitive, and physical symptoms that Burton associated with melancholy are, akin to Hippocrates' description, very similar to the *DSM* criteria. Like Aristotle, Burton (1621/2001, p. 331) insisted that melancholic symptoms are not in themselves sufficient evidence of disorder; only those symptoms that are without cause provided such evidence. "*Without a cause,*" Burton noted, "is lastly inserted to specify it from all other ordinary passions of Fear and Sorrow."

Burton also eloquently described the natural proneness to melancholic states that are proportionate to their contexts, which can be symptomatically similar to disordered states of melancholy:

Melancholy (with cause) . . . is that transitory melancholy which goes and comes upon every small occasion of sorrow, need, sickness, trouble, fear, grief, passion, or perturbation of the mind, any manner of care, discontent, or thought, which causeth anguish, dullness, heaviness, and vexation of spirit. . . . And from these melancholy dispositions, no man living is free, no Stoic, none so wise, none so happy, none so patient, so generous, so godly, so divine, that can vindicate himself; so well composed, but more or less, some time or other, he feels the smart of it. Melancholy, in this sense is the character of mortality. (1621/2001, pp. 143–144)

The basic distinction between disproportionate (and therefore disordered) melancholic states and sadness that emerged from contexts of loss persisted into the twentieth century. Although Sigmund Freud rarely discussed depression, his essay "Mourning and Melancholia"—his sole notable contribution to the understanding of this condition—maintained the well-established distinction between normal and disordered sadness. In it, Freud focused on the difference between normal grief and disordered states of melancholia:

Although grief involves grave departures from the normal attitude to life, it never occurs to us to regard it as a morbid condition and hand the mourner over to medical treatment. We rest assured that after a lapse of time it will be overcome, and we look upon any interference with it as inadvisable or even harmful. (1917/1957, p. 242)

Freud, like the 2,500-year tradition that preceded him, accepted as self-evident the distinction between normal intense sadness that resulted from loss and symptomatically similar pathological depressive states that were disproportionate to loss.

Empirical research between the 1930s and the 1970s identified a distinct type of depression, which was a severe form of disproportionate melancholia. It featured vegetative symptoms, a despairing mood marked by preoccupation with death, and feelings of delusional guilt (Kuhn 1958; Mendels and Cochrane 1968; Paykel 1971). Likewise, melancholic depression seemed to be more responsive to electroconvulsive treatment and the anti-depressant drug imipramine than other depressed states (Klein 1974). The correspondence of melancholic and depressions that were "groundless" or "without cause," however, was not exact: stressful life events preceded the emergence of all forms of depression (Lewis 1934; Akiskal et al. 1978). Yet the isolation of a particularly severe type of depression, even when it was precipitated by stressors, was consistent with the centuries old tradition that associated melancholic depression with a disproportionate response to its context. *Psychotic*, *melancholic*, or *disproportionate* more accurately conveyed the nature of this form of depression than *without cause* or *endogenous*. It is one of a small number of mental disorders with a claim to reflect a natural kind.

The Confused State of Depression Research before *DSM*-III

Although theoreticians and researchers through the 1970s generally concurred that severe, disproportionate depressions represented a distinct type, they agreed on little else. One unresolved controversy was over whether the remaining types of depressive illnesses were continuous or categorical (Kendell and Gourlay 1970). Those who supported the former view argued that depressive illnesses ranged continuously from mild to severe, with no sharp cutting points (Eysenck 1970). Advocates of the latter perspective believed that distinct categories best captured the reality of depressive states (Kiloh and Garside 1963). Another controversy involved the number of discrete types of depression. Researchers posited the existence of a wide range of depressions, from a single type to as many as nine separate categories (Kendell 1976). A different debate concerned whether depression should best be viewed as a personality or temperament type rather than a disease condition (Eysenck 1970). On top of all of these issues was the issue of what principle ought to be used to classify depression in the first place: disputes abounded over whether depression should be classified according to its symptoms, etiology, or response to treatments (Ehrenberg 2010).

The definition of major depression in *DSM*-III (described above) was not the result of a grappling with the various debates over whether depression was continuous or categorical, how many types of depression existed, the relationship of depressive illness to depressive temperaments, or what principle ought to be used to organize classifications. Instead, it stemmed from the efforts of a tightly knit group of research psychiatrists to impose a medical model of disease on psychiatric diagnosis. This group (based in the Department of Psychiatry at Washington University in St. Louis) and its allies at Columbia University (including Robert Spitzer, the head of the *DSM*-III Task Force) dominated the construction of the new manual (Kirk and Kutchins 1992; Horwitz 2002). Their goals were to abandon psychodynamic etiology as a principle of classification and to ground diagnoses in the manifest symptoms of each condition.

As with the other diagnoses in *DSM*-III, the goal of the developers of the major depression diagnosis was to specify a defined group of symptoms that could be measured easily and reliably. In this way, diagnosis could become standardized. What was called "depression" in one site would become comparable to a case of depression in another site. This liberated cases from their particular contexts and created uniform and universal elements out of the messiness of actual clinical symptoms. Standardization was especially valuable for researchers who obtained a reliable system of measurement that allowed them to aggregate like cases, employ statistical procedures, and generalize beyond any particular patient, clinician, clinic, or research site (Kirk and Kutchins 1992).

The basis for the major depression category in *DSM*-III was found in the Feighner Criteria, which the Washington University group had developed for research purposes in the early 1970s (Feighner et al. 1972). These criteria were purely symptom-based and established discrete categories of 14 diagnoses including depression. Before they became the foundation of *DSM*-III, the Feighner Criteria had no special standing as being more adequate than other possible diagnoses. One prominent review of twelve different classifications of depression that was published shortly before *DSM*-III did not find them superior in any way to the eleven alternatives (Kendell 1976). The developers of *DSM*-III did not compare them to other ways of conceptualizing depression, assess their validity, or use them to predict responses to various treatments. Instead, their selection resulted from the shared social bonds and ideological commitments between Robert Spitzer and the Washington University group that developed the Feighner Criteria.

The Feighner Criteria for depression and the resulting *DSM*-III category of major depression did encompass the major elements of the classical tradition of melancholic depression. They included symptoms of recurrent thoughts of death and feelings of worthlessness that were associated with melancholy. Patients who had melancholic forms of depression would also be likely to display the non-melancholic symptoms in the criteria for a two-week period. Thus, the criteria would accurately diagnose patients with melancholic or psychotic depression as having major depression. (The *DSM*-III criteria also included subcategories of psychotic and melancholic depression but these categories were only applicable to patients who already met the full criteria for major depression.) Accordingly, the major depression category did capture the disproportionate conditions of patients who the classical tradition would have called "groundless" or "without cause."

However, patients could also meet the diagnostic criteria without displaying any melancholic symptoms at all. Those who simply were sad, had a poor appetite, couldn't sleep, had low energy, and got little pleasure from their usual activities would also receive a diagnosis of major depression. Moreover, in sharp contrast to Hippocrates' notion that depressive disorders must last "a long time," the *DSM*-III criteria stipulated just two-week duration of symptoms. In addition, all patients—with the exception of the bereaved—who displayed these symptoms regardless of the context in which they developed would meet the criteria. People who had two-week periods of sadness after losses of interpersonal relationships, jobs, aspirations, or physical health among many others, so even transient responses to stressors could be diagnosed as major depression. Major depression thus encompassed the very different loss responses that the classical tradition clearly distinguished from those that were "without cause." The diagnosis was extraordinarily heterogeneous, capturing not only severe and disproportionate depressions but also short-lived responses to losses other than bereavement.

The major depression diagnosis included a wide range of conditions within a single representation of a presumed natural kind. Conditions that had been distinct for thousands of years of psychiatric history became indistinguishable: the capacious major depression criteria encompassed conditions that were mild and severe, transitory and long-standing, and proportionate and disproportionate to their contexts. This conflation of brief stress reactions with a serious disease condition where both could be viewed as aspects of a "natural kind" of depressive disorder proved to be enormously helpful to the mental-health community. Short-lived stress responses could be equated with the most severe conditions because both met the criteria for major depression. Both could therefore be presented as discrete, serious, and genuine disease conditions. This feature of the diagnosis was to have major consequences that extended far beyond the psychiatric profession itself.

The Social Functions of a Natural Kind

The ability of the major depression diagnosis to link stress responses and severe melancholic conditions within a single category made it an especially valuable vehicle for a variety of interest groups including clinicians, epidemiologists, mental-health advocates, and pharmaceutical companies.

The drug industry was one major beneficiary of the major depression diagnosis. During the 1960s, benzodiazepine drugs such as Valium and Librium had become wildly popular. They were widely viewed as medications that relieved states of "stress," or "tension" that were linked to anxiety rather than depression (Herzberg 2009; Tone 2009). In the 1970s, however, prescriptions for the tranquilizers plummeted when they were linked to addiction, suicide, and a broad range of negative side effects (Gabe 1990). Sales remained slow until a new class of medication, the selective serotonin reuptake inhibitors (SSRIs), came on the market toward the end of the 1980s.

The SSRIs did not have specific effects but were used to treat a wide range of conditions encompassing anxiety and depression as well as eating disorders, substance abuse, and numerous physical symptoms among many others. The Food and Drug Administration, however, required that psychoactive drugs could only be approved and marketed after clinical trials showed that they effectively treated some specific *DSM* diagnosis. Given the stigma attached to the anti-anxiety drugs at the time, it was undesirable to associate the SSRIs with the treatment of anxiety. Major depression, however, featured many of the hallmarks of stress responses, including fatigue, loss of appetite, insomnia, restlessness, and sadness. It therefore presented a highly desirable target for the promotion of the SSRIs because its symptoms potentially captured the same market as the discredited tranquilizers. More than any other single diagnosis in the *DSM*, major depression provided a gateway into a huge consumer market.

Advertisements for the SSRIs presented them as targeting the specific condition of depression, which they emphasized was a real illness with genuine biological causes. They associated the condition with such common stressors as poor familial relationships, troubles at work, and poor motivation. These life difficulties, however, were presented as the *results*, not the causes, of depression. The cause of the illness was portrayed as a chemical imbalance related to deficiencies of serotonin, which the use of the SSRIs would remedy. In this way, depression was at the same time linked to a brain-based disease and associated with the kinds of problems of living that could command the largest possible consumer market. Widespread stress responses could be equated with genuine disease conditions that required medication therapies.

The marketing of the SSRIs as treatments for depression was a tremendous success. From 1996 to 2001 the number of users of SSRIs increased rapidly, from 7.9 million to 15.4 million. By 2000, the SSRIs were the best-selling category of drugs of any sort in the United States; fully 10 percent of the US population was using an anti-depressant (Mojtabai 2008). Prescriptions for the SSRIs continued to grow in the new century, and by 2006 Americans received over 227 million anti-depressant prescriptions, an increase of more than 30 million since 2002 (IMS Health 2006).

In fact, these drugs treated a huge variety of symptoms including not just those associated with depression but also with nerves, anxiety, physical pain, and general psychological distress (Mojtabai and Olfson 2008). Nevertheless, prescriptions required some specific diagnosis, and depression was the most suitable available category. The ability of major depression to link such a wide range of commonly occurring symptoms to a natural kind was an enormously profitable gift to the pharmaceutical industry.

Drug manufacturers were far from the only interest group that benefited from the ability of the depression diagnosis to formulate extremely widespread forms of distress as biologically grounded disease conditions. The marketing of major depression as a serious and specific disease also enhanced the credibility of the psychiatric profession. During the 1970s, psychiatry desperately needed to acquire the specific and sharply bounded disease entities that any respected medical specialty needed to treat. "This modern history of diagnosis," the historian Charles Rosenberg notes, "is inextricably related to disease specificity, to the notion that diseases can and should be thought of as entities existing outside the unique manifestations of illness in particular men and women." "During the past century especially," Rosenberg continues, "diagnosis, prognosis, and treatment have been linked ever more tightly to specific, agreed-upon disease categories" (2008, p. 13). Legitimate medical specialties required delineated natural kinds as the objects of their treatment in order to have professional credibility.

Through the 1970s, the profession's extant manual, *DSM*-II, provided only cursory definitions informed by psychodynamic conceptions of etiology. The definition of reactive depression in this manual, for example, read, in its entirety, as follows: "This disorder is manifested by an excessive reaction of depression due to an internal conflict or to an identifiable event such as the loss of a love object or cherished possession." (American Psychiatric Association 1968, p. 40) Such definitions not only could not reliably measure depression but also embodied psychosocial assumptions of causality that were incompatible with brain-based notions of diseases that a medical model of psychiatry required.

Major depression provided psychiatry with the kind of diagnosis that could bolster the profession's legitimacy. It was highly specific, easily measurable, free from assumptions of psychodynamic causality, and compatible with the tenets of the newly emergent biological psychiatrists who were beginning to dominate the profession. Its clear delineation and easily measurable symptom criteria seemed to invalidate complaints that psychiatry could not even define and quantify its most central conditions. Depression was presented as the sort of natural-kind that could enhance the notion that psychiatry was a medical specialty that dealt with real diseases.

Clinicians also found great value in the depressive diagnosis. Although psychodynamically oriented therapists initially opposed the creation of major depression in the *DSM*-III (Bayer and Spitzer 1985), their opposition waned after the manual was published. During the 1960s and the 1970s the economic basis of the therapeutic relationship had been transformed as private and public insurers came to fund most mental-health treatment. Third parties would pay only for the treatment of discrete diseases, not for problems of living or other difficult to define conditions. A wide range of patients who had problems in dealing with stress, identity, lack of personal fulfillment and the like displayed symptoms such as sadness, lack of pleasure, sleep and appetite difficulties, and fatigue that met the criteria of the major depression diagnosis. This allowed clinicians to maintain their base of clients whose problems of living could be named and treated as a distinct, reimbursable disease.

Depression became by far the most popular mental-health diagnosis and since 1980 has been the most common diagnosis of the psychiatric profession (Olfson et al. 2002). About 40 percent of outpatients receive a diagnosis of depression, far more than any other condition (ibid.). In the period between 1987 and 1997, the proportion of the population receiving outpatient treatment for conditions that were called "depression" increased by more than 300 percent. In the early 1980s about 2.1 percent of American adults were treated for depression; the proportion grew to 2.7 percent in the early 1990s and then to 3.7 percent in the early 2000s (Kessler et al. 2003). Thus, at the beginning of the twenty-first century several million more people were being treated for depression than were being treated for it 20 years earlier. In addition, community studies show that nearly 20 percent of Americans will suffer from major depression at some point in their life (ibid.). The World Health Organization estimates that depression is the leading worldwide cause of disability for middle-aged people and for women of all ages (Murray and Lopez 1996).

The National Institute of Mental Health, the major sponsor of psychiatric research, was also both the benefactor and the recipient of the advantages of the major depression diagnosis. For most of its history, the NIMH had featured a broad portfolio of research that spanned psychosocial and developmental as well as biological influences on mental illness (Grob 1991). However, beginning in the late 1960s, the studies it sponsored about social problems such as poverty, racism, and crime became a lightening rod for criticisms that the agency promoted an ideological, rather than a scientific, research agenda. As a result, funding for the agency began to sharply decline around this time (Baldessarini 2000).

The NIMH was the major underwriter of the development of the disease categories in *DSM*-III (Robins 1986). The resulting classificatory manual sharply transformed perceptions of the agency's activities. It now was viewed as funding research on conditions that were comparable to those studied by other agencies that dealt with cancer, heart or lung disease, and the like. The makeover of its perceived subject matter from social problems to diseases muted criticisms that the agency had an ideological mission. The highest priority of the NIMH during subsequent decades became the study of presumably brain-based conditions that had no political liabilities.

Depression became the brightest star in the firmament of the new disease conditions. The epidemiological studies the NIMH sponsored to measure the prevalence of the *DSM* categories in community populations showed that the amount of major depression was far higher than previously suspected. Estimates, which ranged from 3 percent to 6 percent in the initial studies, rose to 17 percent by the early 1990s (Robins et al. 1984; Kessler et al. 1994). Depression was the single most common mental disorder found in the community (Kessler et al. 2005).

The conflation of common reactions to stress with a serious disease in the major depression diagnostic criteria generated these extraordinarily high prevalence estimates. Low mood, poor appetite, insomnia, fatigue, lack of concentration, and the like can be common responses to ubiquitous stressful experiences such as the loss of valued relationships, jobs, or goals. When diagnoses require just two-week duration they can include many short-lived responses to stressors. Moreover, the lack of exclusion criteria other than bereavement virtually ensured that the criteria could not separate natural symptoms of sadness from dysfunctional depressive disorders. The result is that epidemiological studies produce many false positive diagnoses (Wakefield et al. 2007). Moreover, these studies make it appear as if a high proportion of people who actually have depression do not receive treatment for it.

The result was that the major depression criteria, when applied in the community, produced estimates that made the condition seem to be a huge public-health problem. This greatly enhanced the size and the importance of the problems that concerned the NIMH and the epidemiologists and researchers that it supported. Depression could be promoted as a genuine disease that required growing resources to study and treat an enormous problem. Funding for the NIMH began to steadily rise in the 1980s and has continued at a high level since that time.

The successful marketing of depression as a natural kind reached its apogee when the World Health Organization declared that by 2020 depression would be the number-two cause of worldwide disability, behind only heart disease (Murray and Lopez 1996). According to this agency, depression is already the largest source of impairment among women and people in mid life. The WHO estimates stem from taking the estimates of prevalence from epidemiological studies and assuming that each case is comparable in severity to conditions such as paraplegia and blindness. Such claims can create a moral urgency to deal with a widespread and seriously impairing condition. (See, e.g., Kramer 2008.) Yet they result from criteria that equate transient responses to losses with truly severe and disabling conditions and call both "major depression."

The portrayal of depression as a natural kind also allows for the defeasibility of moral responsibility. Before *DSM*-III, psychiatric theories focused on how patterns of parental socialization in early childhood laid the foundation for the development of mental illnesses such as depression later in life. During the 1970s a social movement composed primarily of parents whose children had developed severe mental illnesses became influential with Congress and the NIMH. At the heart of this movement's ideology was the belief that mental illness was a brain-based disease comparable in all respects to diabetes or cancer (McLean 1990). This conception of mental illness as a natural kind deflected parental responsibility for the emergence of their child's illness. Depression became a problem of chemistry, not of character, and therefore not subject to the stigma attached to motivated behaviors.

Many patients came to portray themselves as victims of a real disease. Peter Kramer's 1993 book *Listening to Prozac* cemented the coupling of depression with a wide range of identity and psychosocial problems. "Depression" became the label associating numerous experiences with a biology-based disease. A flood of autobiographies connected depression to the development of drug addictions, suicide attempts, failed aspirations, loneliness, romantic breakups, and general unhappiness as well as to its treatment through SSRIs as the way to free oneself from these difficulties (Cronkite 1995; Wurtzel 1995; Slater 1999). Depression was a non-stigmatized identity category that seemed to reflect a natural kind that led to a wide range of suffering and unhappiness.

Creating depression as a natural kind thus served a variety of constituencies. It helped the drug industry to sell its products, clinicians to be reimbursed for their services, psychiatrists to gain professional credibility, government agencies to confront public-health problems rather than political problems, parental interest groups to deflect moral responsibility for creating their children's problems, and patients to get a non-stigmatizing explanation of their problems. Combining distressing, short-lived symptoms with a serious and disabling condition under the single label of "major depression" was one of the greatest achievements in the history of psychiatry.

Natural Kinds as a Critique of Psychiatric Classification

Just because the current diagnostic criteria for major depression have little relationship to a single natural kind does not mean that such a natural kind doesn't exist. Indeed, some concept of a natural underlying condition is necessary for developing a critique of the current *DSM* classification. Such a critique strives to bring diagnostic criteria more in line with a natural kind that resembles the condition portrayed in thousands of years of psychiatric history.

The most basic change the current criteria require would expand the bereavement exclusion so that the diagnosis would accurately separate symptoms of natural sadness that arise in response to some loss from depressive disorders that are disproportionate to their contexts (Horwitz and Wakefield 2007). As psychiatry recognized before 1980, depressive disorder is either without sufficient cause or is disproportionate to actual loss. Stressors other than bereavement often lead to natural sadness so that the same reasons for the bereavement exclusion hold for these stressors. Extending this exclusion would more clearly separate depressive disorder from normal sadness and so more accurately reflect a natural kind. Nevertheless, the *DSM-5* eliminated the bereavement exclusion on the grounds that "evidence does not support separation of loss of loved one from other stressors." The criteria for depression in the new manual actually represent a regression from the flawed definition in *DSM*-III. Clearly, the argument that diagnostic criteria ought to reflect natural kinds is far from constituting sufficient grounds for settling a highly political issue.

A second change that would improve the major depression diagnosis would extend the duration requirement from its current two-week period. Though it is sometimes clear within two weeks of onset that someone has a depressive disorder, it is also the case that much natural sadness after loss might only persist for a brief period and dissipate soon afterwards. Indeed, one of the hallmarks of depressive disorders, as Hippocrates realized, is their disproportionate length relative to the context of loss. A more reasonable duration criteria could be two months (as was the case for bereavement), or even six months (as the current criteria for generalized anxiety disorder specify). Criteria that would make the diagnosis more closely resemble a natural kind would extend the duration standards to exclude short-lived symptoms and to reflect a more enduring condition.

Another change that might make the depression criteria better reflect a natural kind has to do with whether the condition should be viewed as continuous or discrete. The current criteria are categorical so that there is a sharp distinction between people with four depressive symptoms who are not considered to be depressed and those with five symptoms who are. Yet it does not seem as if any sharp dividing line exists between four and five symptoms or at any other point in nature. "Our current *DSM*-IV diagnostic conventions," the geneticists Kenneth Kendler and Charles Gardner write, "may be arbitrary and not reflective of a natural discontinuity in depressive symptoms as experienced in the general population" (1998, p. 177).

Advocates of viewing depression as dimensional rather than categorical correctly see that depressive symptoms naturally lie on a continuum. In addition, they rightly note that the presence of a small number of symptoms can indicate the early stages in the development of a more serious disorder. Moreover, studies of genetic, biological, and personality susceptibilities show that the same vulnerabilities are likely to be present in both mild and severe forms of depression.

Despite this evidence, implementing continuous criteria for depression involves tremendous difficulties. In particular, any dimensionalization that does not separate symptoms of natural sadness from depressive disorder could result in a vast pathologization of normal emotions. The existence of a small number of symptoms often results from transitory distressing situations as opposed to mental disorders (Horwitz and Wakefield 2007). In addition, the fewer the number of symptoms that are required for a depressive diagnosis, the more likely they are to indicate natural sadness rather than depressive disorder. Moreover, as various writers have recognized since Aristotle's time, a small number of persistent depressive symptoms can represent a melancholic, but natural, personality disposition as well as a normal response to loss. Any movement to dimensionalize depression, therefore, could lead to even more confounding of ordinary distress, melancholic temperament, and pathological depression. If continuous diagnostic criteria make a clear initial separation of natural sadness and personality dispositions from depressive disorder, however, they might better represent a natural kind of depression that varies from a small to a larger number of symptoms.

Conclusion

Creating a more homogeneous category of depression—perhaps a continuous category that excludes normal sadness, transient stress responses, and melancholic temperaments—ought to reproduce more closely a natural kind or kinds. If this change were to come about, the diagnostic criteria could more adequately perform the functions of all good scientific classifications. They should be better able to explain who develops a depressive disorder, as opposed to who becomes naturally sad after some loss. In addition, they should better predict the course of symptoms and the probability of their recurrence. Finally, and perhaps most important, they might discriminate between treatment responses. The current criteria for major depression do not perform these functions well, most likely because they do not reproduce any natural kind.

Diagnostic criteria that more accurately represent a natural kind must ensure that symptoms are disproportionate responses to given contexts. Better criteria would expand the bereavement exemption to symptoms that develop after other kinds of losses, extend the duration requirement to exclude transient stress responses, and ensure that symptoms are severe enough to be truly impairing. They would target depressive disorders that are severe and prolonged responses, which are disproportionate to their contexts. These changes would be only the initial steps toward developing criteria that would specify the varieties of depressive disorder and distinguish them from normal sadness and melancholic personality dispositions.

It is unlikely that the major depression diagnosis will come to embody such standards. Too many interest groups have strong stakes in maintaining and even expanding the scope of this diagnosis. The social functions that portrayals of depression as a natural kind serve seem to outweigh the scientific advantages that could stem from more accurate diagnostic criteria. It is perhaps naïve to believe that diagnoses should strive to reflect underlying natural kinds as accurately as possible. Nevertheless, the effort to produce better mirrors of nature has a powerful moral imperative of its own that perhaps might eventually override the many social functions that natural kinds serve.

References

Akiskal, H., A. Bitar, V. Puzantian, T. Rosenthal, and P. Walker. 1978. The nosological status of neurotic depression. *Archives of General Psychiatry* 35: 756–766.

American Psychiatric Association. 1952. *Diagnostic and Statistical Manual of Mental Disorders.*

American Psychiatric Association. 1968. *Diagnostic and Statistical Manual of Mental Disorders*, second edition.

American Psychiatric Association. 1980. *Diagnostic and Statistical Manual of Mental Disorders*, third edition.

American Psychiatric Association. 2013. *Diagnostic and Statistical Manual of Mental Disorders*, fifth edition.

Baldessarini, R. 2000. American biological psychiatry and psychopharmacology, 1944–1994. In *American Psychiatry After World War II: 1944–1994*, ed. R. Menninger and J. Nemiah. American Psychiatric Association.

Bayer, R., and R. Spitzer. 1985. Neurosis, psychodynamics, and *DSM*-III: History of the controversy. *Archives of General Psychiatry* 42: 187–196.

Burton, R. [1621] 2001. *The Anatomy of Melancholy.* New York Review of Books.

Cronkite, K. 1995. *On the Edge of Darkness: America's Most Celebrated Actors, Journalists, and Politicians Chronicle Their Most Arduous Journey.* Delta.

Ehrenberg, A. 2010. *The Weariness of the Self: Diagnosing the History of Depression in the Contemporary Age.* McGill–Queen's University Press.

Eysenck, H. 1970. The classification of depressive illness. *British Journal of Psychiatry* 117: 241–250.

Feighner, J., E. Robins, S. Guze, R. Woodruff, G. Winokur, and R. Munoz. 1972. Diagnostic criteria for use in psychiatric research. *Archives of General Psychiatry* 26: 57–63.

Freud, S. [1917] 1957. Mourning and melancholia. In *Standard Edition of the Complete Works of Sigmund Freud*, volume 14, ed. J. Strachey. Hogarth.

Gabe, J. 1990. Towards a sociology of tranquillizer prescribing. *British Journal of Addiction* 85: 41–48.

Grob, G. 1991. *From Asylum to Community: Mental Health Policy in Modern America.* Princeton University Press.

Herzberg, D. 2009. *Happy Pills in America: From Miltown to Prozac.* Johns Hopkins University Press.

Hippocrates. In *Works of Hippocrates*, volumes 1–4. Harvard University Press, 1923–1931.

Horwitz, A. 2002. *Creating Mental Illness.* University of Chicago Press.

Horwitz, A. 2010. How an age of anxiety became an age of depression. *Milbank Quarterly* 88: 112–138.

Horwitz, A., and J. Wakefield. 2007. *The Loss of Sadness: How Psychiatry Transformed Normal Misery into Depressive Disorder*. Oxford University Press.

IMS Health. 2006. Top 10 therapeutic classes by U.S. dispensed prescriptions. At http://www.imshealth.com.

Jackson, S. 1986. *Melancholia and Depression: From Hippocratic Times to Modern Times*. Yale University Press.

Kendell, R. 1976. The classification of depressions: A review of contemporary confusion. *British Journal of Psychiatry* 129: 15–28.

Kendell, R., and J. Gourlay. 1970. The clinical distinction between psychotic and neurotic depressions. *British Journal of Psychiatry* 117: 257–260.

Kendler, K, and C. Gardner. 1998. Boundaries of major depression: An evaluation of *DSM*-IV criteria. *American Journal of Psychiatry* 155: 172–177.

Kessler, R., P. Beglund, O. Demler, R. Jin, D. Koretz, K. Merikangas, et al. 2003. The epidemiology of major depressive disorder: Results from the National Comorbidity Survey replication. *Journal of the American Medical Association* 289: 3095–3105.

Kessler, R., W. Chiu, O. Demler, and E. Walters. 2005. Prevalence, severity, and comorbidity of 12-month *DSM*-IV disorders in the National Comorbidity Survey Replication. *Archives of General Psychiatry* 62: 617–627.

Kessler, R., K. McGonagle., S. Zhao, C. Nelson, M. Hughes, S. Eshelman, et al. 1994. Lifetime and 12-month prevalence of *DSM*-III-R psychiatric disorders in the United States. *Archives of General Psychiatry* 51: 8–19.

Kiloh, L., and R. Garside. 1963. The independence of neurotic depression and endogenous depression. *British Journal of Psychiatry* 109: 451–463.

Kirk, S., and H. Kutchins. 1992. *The Selling of DSM: The Rhetoric of Science in Psychiatry*. Aldine de Gruyter.

Klein, D. 1974. Endogenomorphic depression: A conceptual and terminological revision. *Archives of General Psychiatry* 31: 447–454.

Kramer, P. 1993. *Listening to Prozac: A Psychiatrist Explores Antidepressant Drugs and the Remaking of the Self*. Viking.

Kuhn, R. 1958. The treatment of depressive states with G22355 (imipramine hydrochloride). *American Journal of Psychiatry* 115: 459–464.

Kramer, P. 2008. *Against Depression*. Viking.

Lewis, A. 1934. Melancholia: A clinical survey of depressive states. *Journal of Mental Science* 80: 1–43.

McLean, A. 1990. Contradictions in the social production of clinical knowledge: The case of schizophrenia. *Social Science & Medicine* 30: 969–985.

Mendels, J., and C. Cochrane. 1968. The nosology of depression: The endogenous-reactive concept. *American Journal of Psychiatry* 124: 1–11.

Mojtabai, R. 2008. Increase in antidepressant medication in the US adult population between 1990 and 2003. *Psychotherapy and Psychosomatics* 77: 83–92.

Mojtabai, R., and M. Olfson. 2008. National patterns in antidepressant treatment by psychiatrists and general medical providers: Results from the National Comorbidity Survey Replication. *Journal of Clinical Psychiatry* 69: 1064–1074.

Murray, C., and A. Lopez, eds. 1996. *The Global Burden of Disease.* World Health Organization.

Olfson, M., S. Marcus, B. Druss, L. Elinson, T. Tanielian, and H. Pincus. 2002. National trends in the outpatient treatment of depression. *Journal of the American Medical Association* 287: 203–209.

Paykel, E. 1971. Classification of depressed patients: A cluster analysis derived grouping. *British Journal of Psychiatry* 118: 275–288.

Robins, L. 1986. The development and characteristics of the NIMH diagnostic interview schedule. In *Community Surveys of Psychiatric Disorders*, ed. M. Weissman, J. Myers, and C. Ross. Rutgers University Press.

Robins, L., J. Helzer, M. Weissman, H. Orvaschel, E. Gruenberg, J. Burke, et al. 1984. Lifetime prevalence of specific psychiatric disorders in three sites. *Archives of General Psychiatry* 41: 949–956.

Rosenberg, C. 2008. *Our Present Complaint.* Johns Hopkins University Press.

Slater, L. 1999. *Prozac Diary.* Penguin.

Tone, A. 2009. *The Age of Anxiety: A History of America's Turbulent Affair with Tranquilizers.* Basic Books.

Wakefield, J., M. Schmitz, M. First, and A. Horwitz. 2007. Extending the bereavement exclusion for major depression to other losses: Evidence from the National Comorbidity Survey. *Archives of General Psychiatry* 64: 433–440.

Wurtzel, E. 1995. *Prozac Nation: Young and Depressed in America: A Memoir.* Riverhead.

12 The Missing Self in Hacking's Looping Effects

Şerife Tekin

A significant philosophical discourse has been dedicated to the ontological status of mental disorders. (See, for example, Hacking 1986, 1995a,b, 2007a,b; Cooper 2004a,b, 2007; Samuels 2009; Graham 2010; Zachar 2001.) The primary focus has been on whether mental disorders are natural kinds—that is, whether they are similar to the kinds found in the non-human natural world, such as gold.[1] Ian Hacking argues that mental disorders are human kinds, differing from natural kinds insofar as they are subject to the looping effects of scientific classifications.[2] The precise reason why mental disorders cannot be natural kinds is that being classified as having a mental disorder can bring on changes in the self-concept and the behavior of individuals so classified. Such changes, in turn, can lead to revisions in the initial descriptions of mental disorders. Members of natural kinds, however, are not subject to such looping effects.

The phenomenon of looping effects is considered a compelling challenge to the claim that mental disorders are natural kinds, and thus is discussed widely by both Hacking's followers and his critics. It is also widely resorted to by social scientists, especially those in critical disabilities studies, sociology, and anthropology. (See, e.g., Carlson 2010; Stets and Burke 2003.) Yet the inherent complexity of the phenomenon has not been addressed, even by Hacking himself. In particular, the causal trajectory in which looping effects are generated and the way in which the subject responds to being classified remain unclear. Nor it is clearly understood how looping effects come about in the context of psychopathology. In this chapter, with a view to filling in some of these gaps, I note two connected shortcomings in Hacking's analysis of looping effects. First, his framework lacks an empirically and philosophically plausible account of the self to substantiate the complex causal structure of looping effects. Second, he fails to engage with the complexity of mental disorder in the consideration of this phenomenon in the realm of psychopathology. Once the complexity of selfhood and the complexity of the encounter with mental disorders are considered, it becomes clear that the causal trajectory of looping effects is more complex than hitherto envisioned.

Hacking uses the phenomenon of looping effects to articulate a dynamic nominalism, according to which the scientific classifications of human phenomena interact with those phenomena, leading to mutual changes. In other words, there is an interactive causal trajectory between scientific classifications and the subjects classified. Instead of describing what looping effects are, in reference to the features of the subject classified and the features of scientific classifications, Hacking uses examples to illustrate them. He includes not only mental disorders but also other human phenomena that are subject to scientific research, such as obesity, child abuse, and refugee status. With these examples, Hacking shows how scientific classifications may generate changes in a subject's self-conceptions and behavior. However, a full discussion of looping effects requires both an account of the way in which scientific classifications influence the subjects and an account of how and why the subject responds to being classified in the way she does. Such scrutiny requires recognition of what the self is, of how self-concepts are formed, and of how behavioral changes are motivated. In addition, when the phenomenon of looping effects is considered in the context of psychopathology, this scrutiny requires recognizing the complexity of the ways in which mental disorder influences the subject. The encounter with mental disorder changes an individual's self-concept and behavior, and it is not easy—if indeed possible—to discriminate the influence of diagnosis of mental disorder on self-concepts and behavior from that of the mental disorder itself. The fact that the diagnosed subject changes her self-concepts and behavior not only in response to being classified but also in response to her encounter with mental disorder reveals that the causal net of looping effects is much more complex than Hacking envisions. To the extent that he discusses the self (he seems to be using self/person/subject/soul interchangeably—see, e.g., Hacking 2004), he is informed by a simplified account of personhood that situates the subject somewhere between genetic and neurobiological dispositions and freedom of choice. Hacking neither offers an account of mental disorders nor embraces the complex ways in which they shape people's self-concepts and behavior. Owing to his superficial treatment of the self and mental disorder, he fails to make explicit the necessary and sufficient conditions for looping effects to be generated. This caveat makes his account the target of several partially successful criticisms (e.g., Cooper 2004a,b; Khalidi 2010).

In this chapter, I offer a close reading of Hacking's work on looping effects, evaluating his early and later works. Focusing primarily on the first arc of looping effects (that is, on how scientific classifications influence the subject classified), I show how Hacking overlooks the complexities of the self and mental disorder. I then offer a model of the multitudinous self that substantiates the phenomenon of looping effects. In section 1, I expand on Hacking's work on looping effects and emphasize his dynamic nominalism—the key to understanding the features of looping effects. In section 2, I focus on Hacking's application of looping effects to mental disorders. In section 3, I zoom in on Hacking's discussion of the self and discuss its superficiality. In section 4, I posit the multitudinous self, a philosophically and empirically plausible model of the self that substantiates the complexity of looping effects in the context of psychopathology. This model of the self, I point out, can help scientific research programs to taxonomize mental disorders and can facilitate successful interventions in the lives of those with mental disorders, allowing them to flourish (Tekin 2010, 2011). Thus, with the multitudinous self, I advocate a new style of reasoning about mental disorders in philosophy of psychiatry.

1   Dynamic Nominalism and Looping Effects

The phenomenon of looping effects is the linchpin of a series of works on what Hacking calls "making up people"—works that point to the way in which a new classification made by human sciences may bring a new kind of person into being (e.g., Hacking 1986, 1995a,b, 1999, 2004, 2007a,b). Looping effects have two arcs. The first arc is constituted by the influence of classifications on those so classified; the second comprise the ways in which some of those who are classified—and altered—modify the systems of classification. Some people with mental disorders (e.g., multiple personality and schizophrenia) are subject to the looping effects of psychiatric classifications; but looping effects are not restricted to the domain of mental disorders. Hacking also uses as examples women refugees, pregnant teenagers, child abusers, the obese, and the genius. (See, e.g., Hacking 1986, 1995a,b, 2007a,b.)

Hacking's dynamic nominalism is the metaphysical scaffolding for the phenomenon of looping effects; he explores "making-up people" by applying the realism versus nominalism debate to human phenomena.[3] The fundamental question in this debate is whether there is anything in reality that corresponds to universals, or whether there are only particulars.

Realists accept universals into their ontology as mind-independent objects; that is, they believe that universals are given by nature and that they exist independent of any perceiving human mind. Nominalists, on the other hand, argue that there are no universals, and that they are not to be included in our ontology. Only particulars exist, and it is human convention that individuates particulars according to human interests. Hacking applies this query to what he labels "human kinds"—kinds of human beings, their embodiment, their character, their emotions, and so on (1995b). He asks whether human kinds are given by nature, sorted and categorized independent of human intellect, or whether they are artifacts of human conventions. Does our naming, conceptualizing, and classifying individuate phenomena in the human world, or are human kinds determined by nature prior to our ordering them? Hacking's traditional "static nominalist" would deny the existence of a mind-independent world sorted into neat categories (1986, 1995b), holding that all classifications, taxonomies, and classes are imposed by human conventions, not by nature. Over time, these categories become fixed. The traditional realist, in contrast, is committed to the idea of a naturally ordered world; as science progresses, we come to recognize and name pre-given categories. These categories are independent from humans; we discover them through science (Hacking 1986, p. 228).

Hacking's dynamic nominalism is situated somewhere between traditional realism and static nominalism. He believes that "many categories come from nature, not from the human mind" (1986, p. 228). However, these categories are not static, because the acts of sorting out, naming, and classifying influence the individuals classified in those categories:

The claim of dynamic nominalism is not that there was a kind of person who came increasingly to be recognized by bureaucrats or by students of human nature, but rather that a kind of person who came into being at the same time as the kind itself was being invented. In some cases, that is, our classifications and our classes conspire to emerge hand in hand, each egging the other on. (p. 228)

Dynamic nominalism, situated as it is between traditional nominalism and realism, tracks interactions over time between the phenomena of the human world studied by the human sciences and the classifications of these phenomena. It is, for Hacking, "realism in action," because "real classes of people" are sorted in new and specific ways; "making and moulding people as the events were enacted" (2004, p. 280). Another way of making sense of dynamic nominalism, Hacking points out, is thinking of it as "dialectical realism." Kinds of individuals come into being as a result of the dialectic between classifications and the classified. The naming of individuals as an outcome of scientific inquiry "has real effects on people," and such changes in people have "real effects on subsequent classifications." For Hacking, this phenomenon, can be captured neither by "an arid logical nominalism" nor by a "dogmatic realism" (p. 280).

Hacking appeals to dynamic nominalism not only to elaborate on how sciences carve out human phenomena but also to consider the implications of the study of human phenomena on the "possibilities of personhood" (1986, p. 230). Descriptions of human kinds influence the self-reflection of those human beings being described. Put otherwise, creating new ways of classifying people changes the subjects' epistemic and moral relations with themselves, including their self-concepts and self-worth. New ways of classifying even changes how these subjects remember their own pasts (Hacking 1995b, p. 369). Hence, for Hacking, whenever philosophers think about persons as particulars, they "must reflect on this strange idea, of making up people" (1986, p. 230).

It is important to emphasize that even though dynamic nominalism provides the metaphysical scaffolding, there is no "uniform tale" or "general story to be told about making up people" (Hacking 1986, p. 233).

If we wish to present a partial framework in which to describe such events, we might think of two vectors. One is the vector of labeling from above, from a community of experts who create a "reality" that some people make their own. Different from this is the vector of autonomous behavior of the person so labeled, which presses from below, creating a reality every expert must face (ibid., p. 234).

Although Hacking acknowledges the need to attend to both the scientific labeling from above and individual's response from below in making sense of looping effects, I argue that his primary focus is on how human sciences influence and change the subjects they study. This is evident in his strategy to explain the phenomenon of looping effects: in accordance with his dynamic nominalism, he provides a plethora of examples to illustrate how human sciences generate changes in the individuals they study. However, as I show in section 2, his analysis of how the self—the subject of scientific study—responds to being classified remains superficial.

Let me turn to Hacking's understanding of how human sciences induce changes in the subjects they study. The goal of these sciences is to acquire systematic, general, and accurate knowledge about puzzling and idiosyncratic phenomena pertaining to human beings in "industrialized bureaucracies"—for example, suicide, child abuse, multiple personality, obesity, and refugee status. They seek to attain "generalizations sufficiently

strong that they seem like laws about people, their actions, or their sentiments," so that helpful interventions can be made (Hacking 1995b, p. 352).
Unlike the objects of inquiry in natural sciences, the subjects of human
sciences—i.e., human kinds—respond to how they are classified. Hacking
distinguishes between human and natural kinds by noting that human
kinds are subject to looping effects due to the "self-awareness" of at least
some of those classified[4]:

Responses of people to attempts to be understood or altered are different from the
responses of things. This trite fact is at the core of one difference between the natural
and human sciences, and it works at the level of kinds. There is a looping or feedback
effect involving the introduction to classifications of people. New sorting and theorizing induces changes in *self-conception* and in *behaviour* of the people classified.
Those changes demand revisions of the classifications and theories, the causal connections, and the expectations. Kinds are modified, revised classifications are
formed, and the classified change again, loop upon a loop. (ibid., p. 370, emphasis
added)

Hacking's best-known example of looping effects is multiple personality.
Through this example, elaborated on in the next section, the discussion
of looping effects enters philosophical discussions of psychopathology,
challenging the view that mental disorders are natural kinds.

2   Mental Disorders and Looping Effects

Hacking (1995a, p. 5) uses multiple personality as a "microcosm of think-
ing-and-talking about making-up people." He wants to understand how
"the sciences of the soul," in their attempts to make the soul an object of
scientific query, make up people (1986, 1995a,b). Thus, he is interested in
the soul/subject/self/person[5] insofar as the soul is the *object* of scientific
study; he does not consider the soul as a *subject*—that is, he does not delve
into what it is about the self that is prone to being made up (Tekin 2010,
p. 2011). This poses a problem concerning the details of the mechanism
of the first arc of the looping effects, namely, what it is about the subject
that makes her amenable to changing her self-concepts and behavior after
being classified.

In Hacking's view, the popularity of the phenomenon of multiple personality among philosophers in the late 1980s and the 1990s stemmed
from the challenges it posed to widely accepted conceptions of the self.
Simply stated, it "refute[d] the dogmatic transcendental unity of appercep-
tion that made the self prior to all knowledge" (Hacking 1986, p. 224).
Hacking observes that the symptoms that characterize multiple personality

disorder changed as knowledge of the illness entered popular culture under the combined influence of curious psychiatrists, television-show producers, and alliances of patients. As Hacking sees it, those diagnosed with multiple personality start displaying different symptoms as they learn more about the illness and its manifestations in different individuals through popular culture. In other words, the symptoms that individuals display fit the popular descriptions of this condition. The changes in the symptoms they display, in turn, alter the classification of multiple personality. The following is a formulation of how looping effects are manifest in those with multiple personality:

PM1 Psychiatry (as a human science) acquires systematic knowledge (K1) about human subjects (S1) who exhibit alternating personalities that are amnesic to one another. K1 picks out the perceived law-like regularities about S1 (e.g., alternating personalities).

PM2 On the basis of K1, psychiatry forms classifications (CL1) of S1, labeling S1 "persons with multiple personality."

PM3 At least some individuals with multiple personality become aware of their categories as K1 is disseminated in popular culture through the combined impact of psychiatrists, television-show producers, alliances of S1a and so on (Hacking 1999, p. 106). (S1a), informed by K1, change their (b) behavior and (c) self-concepts.

PM4 The awareness of being classified, the changes in the behavior and the changes in the self-concepts of those classified (S1a) amount to changes in the perceived regularities about these people. S1a, different from S1, starts to feature new symptoms; e.g., they exhibit animal personalities.

PM5 Changes in the perceived regularities of S1a lead to changes in knowledge (K1) about their classifications (CL1), because S1a no longer fits the criteria for CL1.

CM Thus, classification of some people as "people with multiple personality" results in the creation of new knowledge (K1a), new classifications (CL1a) and new kinds of people (S1a) (e.g., according to K1a, people with multiple personality may exhibit animal personalities).

Hacking's claim that looping effects are not manifest in natural kinds is challenged by those who advance what I call the Parity Argument (PA), according to which there are looping effects in natural kinds comparable to those observed in human kinds and the interaction between classifications and individuals is not exclusive to the human or social realm. (See Bogen 1988; Khalidi 2010; Cooper 2004a,b.) Proponents of PA suggest that our classificatory practices result in looping effects that alter some natural kinds. As examples, they note the influence of being classified as harmful on microbes, the influence of legal bans on the shape of the marijuana plant, the influence of selective breeding on animals, and the influence of training on the domestication of dogs (Bogen 1988, Cooper 2004a,b; Khalidi 2010; Douglas 1986). A corollary to PA is the failure of Hacking's claim that mental disorders are not natural kinds; if looping effects are not exclusive to human kinds but also are exhibited by natural kinds, it would be plausible to argue that those with mental disorders who exhibit looping effects can also be considered natural kinds (Cooper 2004a,b).

In his early writings, apparently foreseeing such objections, Hacking attempts to clarify precisely what is unique about the looping effects in human kinds. He emphasizes, through different examples, that in the case of human kinds, because subjects are "aware" of "what we are doing to them," they are influenced by our "descriptions," and they change their self-concepts and their behavior accordingly (1999, p. 106). However, he is not consistent in his emphasis on the changes that occur in a subject after classification. In particular, in some examples he postulates "being aware of being classified," "changes in self-concepts," and "changes in behavior" as individually sufficient changes that have to occur in the subject to generate looping effects (e.g., women refugees), while in other examples all three are construed as jointly necessary changes for the looping effects (e.g., multiple personality). This inconsistency obscures his discussion of looping effects; it remains unclear whether these three variables are individually sufficient or jointly necessary for the looping effects to be generated. In his later writings Hacking adds new elements to the causal trajectory of the looping effects, but it remains unclear how and why the subject responds to being classified in the way she does.

In his early work, Hacking takes into account that the scientific classification of certain microbes as harmful and the resulting interventions influence these microbes. Such influence, however, is different from the influence of being classified on people:

Elaborating on this difference between people and things: what camels, mountains, and microbes are doing does not depend on our words. What happens to tuberculosis bacilli depends on whether or not we poison them with BCG vaccine, but it does not depend on how we *describe* them. Of course we poison them with a certain vaccine in part because we describe them in certain ways, *but it is the vaccine that kills, not our words.* Human action is more closely linked to human description than bacterial action is. (1986, p. 230, emphasis added)

Hacking emphasizes here that, in addition to the "intervention" facilitated by the classifications of human sciences, our "descriptions" guide subjects' self-directed feelings, concerns, and actions, generating changes in their self-concepts and in their behavior. Natural kinds, on the other hand, are not subject to such looping effects: our words do not lead to changes in the self-interpretations of natural kinds; it is our interventions, *qua* classifications, that change them.

Elsewhere, Hacking develops this idea when he argues that naming and classifying, in and of themselves, do not make a difference in natural kinds: "the mere formation of the class, as separable in the mind, and in language, our continuing use of the classification, our talk about it, our speculation using the classification, does not 'of itself' have the consequences" (1992, pp. 189–190). To this, he adds (in a later work) the following:

If N is a natural kind, and Z is N, it makes no direct difference to Z, if it is called N. It makes no direct difference to either mud or a mud puddle to call it 'mud.' It makes no direct difference to thyrotropin releasing hormone or to a bottle of TRH to call it TRH. Of course seeing that the Z is N, *we may do something to it* in order to melt it or mould it, or drown it, breed it, barter it. . . . *But calling Z, N, or seeing that Z is N, does not, in itself make any difference to Z.* If H is a human kind and A is a person, then calling A H may make us *treat* A differently, just as calling Z N may make us do something to Z. We may reward or jail, instruct or abduct. But it also makes a difference to know that A is an H, precisely because there is so often a *moral connotation to a human kind.* Perhaps A does not want to be H! *Thinking of me as an H changes how I think of me.* Well, perhaps I could do things differently from now on. Not just to escape opprobrium (I have survived unscathed so far) but because I do not want to be that kind of person. *Even if it does not make a difference to A it makes a difference to how people feel about A—how they relate to A—so that A's social ambiance changes.* (1995b, pp. 367–368, emphasis added)

Note that in the passages quoted above Hacking emphasizes how the classification (or naming) changes the subject's epistemic and moral relations with herself. In other words, the category (the outcome of scientific query) into which the subject is placed leads her to reflect on and judge herself differently. Being classified as A changes how she "thinks" about herself and her "self-worth." Such self-related epistemic and moral changes are generated through the scientific knowledge of the categories and are mediated *qua* self and *qua* others (who share the same cultural and linguistic community). Thus, in human kinds, naming and classifying *qua*-self and *qua*-others change the person. But natural kinds change only when naming and classifying lead to interventions.

Consider Hacking's (1986, pp. 100–102) response to Mary Douglas, a proponent of the Parity Argument. Douglas, arguing for looping effects in microbes, suggests that microbes adapt themselves to the attempts to eradicate them (based on our classifying them as harmful) by mutating to resist antibacterial medications. This, in turn, eventually results in the modification of the classification scheme. Hacking responds as follows:

My simple-minded reply is that microbes do not do all these things because, either individually or collectively, *they are aware of what we are doing to them*. The classification microbe is indifferent, not interactive. (1999, p. 106)

Hence, emphasizing the subjects' "awareness" of "what we are doing to them" and the change in their self-concepts and behavior is Hacking's way of distinguishing human kinds from natural kinds. However, he is not consistent in his emphasis on the "awareness" of being classified as a necessary condition for the generation of looping effects. Consider the following point about women refugees:

A woman refugee may learn that she is a certain kind of person and act accordingly. Quarks do not learn that they are a certain kind of entity and act accordingly. But I don't want to overemphasize the awareness of an individual. Women refugees, who do not speak one word of English, may still, as part of a group, acquire the characteristics of women refugees precisely because they are so classified. (Hacking 1999, p. 32)

Hacking presents women refugees' inability to speak English as a detriment to the degree to which they are "aware" of their labels and to the extent of the knowledge they acquire about their categorizations. Yet lack of awareness or limited access to knowledge about their labels does not prevent them from "acquiring the characteristics" associated with their category. How refugee women acquire these characteristics is not clearly articulated by Hacking, but it appears to be closely connected to their social cognition. A plausible explanation may go as follows: A refugee woman's interactions with others, who treat her as such, may lead her to change how she operates in the world and shape her behavior in a way that fits the label "women refugee."[6]

Proponents of PA, in developing the claim that natural kinds may be subject to the looping effects that Hacking attributes to human kinds, point out the ambiguity in Hacking's notion of "awareness" and discuss whether it is a necessary condition for looping effects to be generated. For instance, Muhammad Ali Khalidi (2010), a PA proponent, looks at Hacking's discussion of women refugees. For Khalidi, this example is a testament to the idea that awareness is not a necessary causal variable in the trajectory of looping effects. Thus, "awareness of being classified" does not demarcate human kinds from natural kinds. Rachel Cooper, another PA proponent, also considers Hacking's emphasis on awareness. She suggests that, in itself, awareness of being classified does not show that human kinds cannot be natural kinds, because Hacking's discussion, as it stands, merely shows that "human kinds are affected by a mechanism to which other kinds of entity are immune" (Cooper 2004a, p. 79). Although this indicates a difference between human kinds and other kinds, Cooper does not take it to be fundamentally significant, because "many other types of entity can be affected by mechanisms to which only entities of that type are vulnerable (ibid.). In other words, PA proponents conclude that awareness of being classified is not necessary for generating looping effects; thus, natural kinds can exhibit looping effects.

In my view, PA proponents are seeking to deflate Hacking's emphasis on the subject's awareness of classification and the changes in her self-concepts upon being diagnosed. In particular, PA proponents neglect "the changes in self-concept" in Hacking's premises PM3 and PM4, taking the classification-induced changes in the subject to be primarily changes in behavior and interpreting these as culminating in "alterations in the kind." But Hacking doesn't offer a clear account of what a self-concept is, of how self-concepts are formed, or of exactly how being labeled in a certain way changes a subject's self-concepts. In addition, as the PA proponents rightly point out, Hacking is ambiguous as to whether awareness of being classified is a necessary variable in looping effects. Though I agree with the claim that natural kinds are subject to some feedback effects, I contend that the types of causal loops exhibited in natural and human kinds, especially in the case of psychopathology, are significantly different from one another owing to the complexity of selfhood and the complexity of the encounter with mental disorders. Once the shortcomings of Hacking's account are remedied by adding an empirically and philosophically plausible model of the self to the looping effects (see section 4), the types of differences between causal loops in natural kinds and those with psychopathology are explicit.

Figure 12.1 summarizes the causal web of looping effects in Hacking's early work. Scientific classifications influence and alter the self-concepts and behavior of those classified; this, in turn, influences and alters the initial classifications.

My main concern with this framework is Hacking's reduction of the subject/soul/person/self to "classified person." Even when he considers the subject's awareness of her label and the alterations in self-concept and behavior, he does not offer a detailed scrutiny of the self—the subject of classification. He does not explain what is involved in subjects' being "aware of what we are doing to them," or how people are influenced by

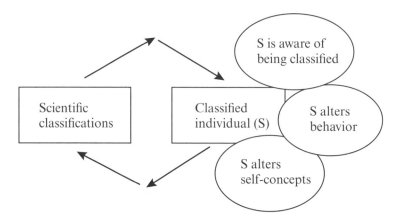

Figure 12.1
Looping effects in early Hacking.

"our descriptions of them" and change their self-concept and behavior accordingly. Is it a rudimentary level of awareness, or is it reflective and more elaborate? What motivates changes in self-concepts and behavior?[7]

In fact, Hacking's treatment of the "classified person" is superficial. This superficiality is problematic, especially when the phenomenon of looping effects is used in the context of psychopathology, as the subject of classification (or the clinical diagnosis) is also the subject of the mental disorder. In particular, the following three questions remain unanswered:

How much of the change in the subject's self-concepts and behavior is connected to the knowledge she receives about the diagnosis?

How much is connected to the particular mental disorder to which she is subject? For instance, if the mental disorder is disruptive of her "awareness" and connected capacities for self-reflection, we need to take that into account. Anosognosia in schizophrenia is a good example.

How much of the change in the subject's self-concepts and behavior is connected to the clinical "treatment" she receives from mental-health professionals upon diagnosis?

It is hard to isolate these questions, as changes in the subject can be connected to a few factors, to none, or to all of them. Answers require a detailed scrutiny of the self and a close examination of the mental disorder. Although Hacking fails to consider these questions, they have important implications to understanding what looping effects actually are.

In his later work, Hacking—partially responding to PA—advocates the abandonment of the notion of "natural kind" altogether and offers a framework within which to understand looping effects. In this latter discussion of looping effects, the causal net is wider; it includes not only the classifications and the individuals classified, but also experts, institutions, and knowledge as the core generators of looping effects.

Consider first Hacking's abandonment of the concept of natural kind (2007a,b). He argues that there are now so many radically incompatible theories of natural kinds that the concept has destroyed itself. Some classifications, he suggests, are "more natural than others," but "there is no such thing as a natural kind" (2007b). This is not to say that there are not kinds in the world, but the idea of a well-defined class of natural kinds is obsolete (ibid., p. 205). For Hacking, the sheer heterogeneity of the paradigms for natural kinds invites skepticism (ibid., p. 207). Calling something a natural kind no longer adds new knowledge; rather, it leads to confusion:

Take any discussion that helps advance our understanding of nature or any science. Delete every mention of natural kinds. I conjecture that as a result the work will be simplified, clarified, and be a greater contribution to understanding or knowledge. Try it. (ibid., p. 229).

Corollary to this change, Hacking no longer employs the term "human kind" when referring to human phenomena studied by the human sciences. Instead, he writes exclusively about the causal net of looping effects and instances of making up people, continuing to illustrate the phenomenon with examples (2007a). He proposes a "framework for analysis" to understand the kinds of people studied by human sciences. In this new framework, the looping effects no longer occur on the two axes previously noted: *classifications made by human sciences* and *people so classified*. Rather, they emerge from the interaction of five "axes," including the *experts* who classify, study, and help people classified, and the *institutions* within which the experts and their subjects interact. Additionally, there is an evolving body of *knowledge*[8] about the people in question, as well as *experts* who generate the knowledge and apply it in their practice. The interaction between these axes leads to changes in individuals' self-concepts and behavior, as well as to changes in each component of this causal network, which, in turn, change the classifications.

Thus, whereas in his earlier writings Hacking focuses on how classifications lead to the alterations in self-concept and behavior of persons, in the new and more complex framework the other three axes are equally responsible. Hacking points to the experts involved in the research on human phenomena, and to the connected interventions, arguing that the experts, through their engagement in these activities, influence the subjects they study. Similarly, the institutional framework within which these subjects are studied or helped also influence the subjects' self-concepts and behavior. Finally, the knowledge generated in this process is a mediator of change.[9] Thus, the causal net of looping effects, according to this new framework, is much wider. See figure 12.2 for an illustration.

Hacking's later framework is more responsive to how human sciences may generate changes in people's self-conception and behavior, with the inclusion of the instruments though which these changes are mediated. However, Hacking still does not explain what it is that about the individual that makes her respond to being studied in the way she does. He continues to overlook the complexities of the "classified people" and the complexities of mental disorders they are subject to. The three questions raised above remain unanswered. How much of the changes in the subject's self-concepts and behavior are connected to the knowledge she receives about the diagnosis, how much of such changes are connected to her particular mental disorder, and how much of the changes in her self-concepts and behavior are connected to the clinical treatment she receives upon diagnosis still aren't explicit. In other words, the course of illness and the influence of treatment remain excluded from the causal net of looping effects.

Let me illustrate with an example why these three questions are important. This case, depicting the complexity of looping effects, exemplifies why we need to know the complexities of selfhood and the complexities of mental disorders to understand how, why, and when looping effects occur.[10]

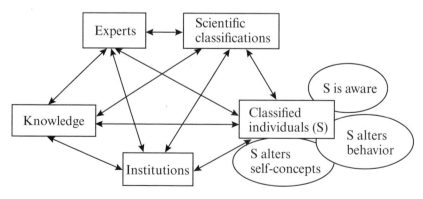

Figure 12.2
Looping effects in later Hacking.

Karl is a 26-year-old student working on a doctorate in music. He is known as a nice and respectful person. Although he is usually quiet, he opens up when he gets to know people. In his spare time, he teaches piano to children. He has two roommates. His dog has been with him since Karl was his early twenties. While studying for his PhD comprehensive exams, Karl begins to hear voices and see horrifying images. The voices are loud, and they order him to do things he does not want to do, such as hitting the walls of his bedroom. He sees flames burning in his surroundings. He is unable to sleep. He talks to himself in an attempt to quiet the voices in his head. He is confused. Owing to these orientational obstacles connected to his condition, he behaves differently at home and at school: he does not talk to his roommates, and he ignores the walking hours of his dog. Karl sees a specialist. After a few visits, the specialist decides that his symptoms are best individuated with the diagnosis of schizophrenia; she prescribes a kind of medication that, in her experience, is effective in reducing or removing hallucinatory symptoms.

Interrelated sets of conceptual and behavioral changes happen in Karl upon the diagnosis—the starting point of Hacking's looping effects. As Karl's illness unfolds, he continues to hear voices and talk to himself, but the visual hallucinations diminish with the help of the medication. The immediate changes are mediated by his illness; his treatment influences how he behaves and how he conceives himself. For instance, after noticing people's questioning looks when he is caught talking to himself, he spends less time in public spaces. For similar reasons, he stops giving piano lessons. His medication has side effects, which lead to more changes in his behavior: he sleeps too much, and he keeps his hands in his pockets to prevent them from shaking. The course of his illness and the treatment he receives also lead to alterations in his self-concepts. He used to consider himself a healthy person, fairly social, and a good dog owner; now he considers himself ill and socially isolated, and contemplates giving his dog away, as he is unable to care for him.

The knowledge Karl gains about his mental disorder, as well as the stereotypes associated with it, motivates changes in his self-concepts and in his behavior. He surfs the Internet, he consults books, and he reads the blogs and personal writings of other patients. He learns about aspects of his illness to which he was previously blind. After learning, for instance, that some schizophrenics have poor hygiene, he over-attends to his personal hygiene, to the extent that he annoys his roommates. Having encountered stereotypical representations in the media of the inability of people with schizophrenia to hold a job, he begins to doubt his ability to finish graduate school.[11] He considers leaving graduate school, fearing that he is not well suited to becoming an academic. Yet at times he wants to continue. He is confused.

Note that the changes Karl undergoes upon diagnosis are associated with (i) the knowledge he gains about his illness (including professional and cultural conceptions, as well as stereotypes), (ii) the course of his illness, and (iii) the clinical treatment he receives. Hacking's looping effects, applied to psychopathology, primarily target (i). As cited above, Hacking suggests that changes occur in the subjects due to their awareness of being classified, and that "new sorting and theorizing induces changes in *self-conception* and in *behavior* of the people classified." In so suggesting, he takes knowledge about categories to be fundamental to the subject's changes. However, in the example above, the changes in Karl's self-concepts and behavior after diagnosis are not just mediated by (i), the knowledge Karl receives about his illness, but also by (ii), the course of his illness, and (iii), the psychiatric treatment he receives. It is difficult, therefore, to discriminate the influence of (i), (ii), and (iii) on Karl's self-concepts and behavior. If changes in the subject, i.e., "awareness of being classified," "changing self-concepts," and "changing behavior" are the fundamental generators of looping effects, Hacking must explain what leads to these changes. The course of the mental disorder and the treatment the subject receives are as influential as Karl's knowledge of his illness.

Nor does Hacking's addition of new elements to the complex causal structure of the looping effects in his more recent work answer these questions. Although the explicit articulation of the interaction of institutions, experts, and knowledge, and their separate and combined influence on the subject's self-concepts and behavior, show that the causal net of looping effects is wider and more complex than originally envisioned, it remains unclear how and why the subject responds to these factors in the way he does. Hacking continues to consider the subject of human sciences as the "classified individual," and overlooks the complexity of the self that is subject to a mental disorder. To account for precisely how and why self-concepts and behavior may change upon diagnosis, he must take into account (ii), the course of the illness, and (iii), the subject's clinical treatment, not just (i), the knowledge the subject acquires about the illness.

These three questions can be answered by including the complexity of the self in the causal net of looping effects because the self is the *subject* of mental disorder, diagnosis, and treatment. The self is the agent of "awareness," as well as the agent of the changes in self-concept and behavior—the three causal variables of looping effects. It is also necessary to acknowledge the complexity of the subject's mental disorder. In section 4, I flesh out these contentions by including an empirically and philosophically plausible model of the self in its causal trajectory.

3   The Self/Soul/Subject/Person in Hacking

Arguably, I am overstating my case; Hacking did, in fact, write about self-hood, though not frequently. Be that as it may, my claim that Hacking's "classified individual" does not depict the complexity of selfhood is supported by his own work (Hacking 2004). In "Between Michel Foucault and Erving Goffman: Between Discourse in the Abstract and Face-to Face Interaction" Hacking discusses his view of "making up people." He clarifies his notion of "personhood," while developing his view that human sciences, in their classifications of people, their actions, and their sentiments, generate looping effects and make up new people:

I must repeat my caution that there is not, and never will be any universally applicable theory of making up people. Just because dynamic nominalism is grounded in the intricacies of everyday and institutional life it will not lead to a general philosophical structure, system or theory. There is, nevertheless, a rather plausible general question in the offing. If we talk about making up people, we can sensibly be asked: 'What is your idea of a person, who can be thus made up?' I believe my own view was unwittingly formed in one of the heroic episodes of philosophy. Philosophy is heroic (in my version of events) when it tries to paint a picture of the *whole* human nature—and of the place of human beings in nature. Kant was heroic. Aquinas was heroic. Aristotle was heroic. I am the very opposite of heroic, not cowardly but proudly *particularist*. I think there is no fixed whole of human nature to discuss. (2004, p. 281, emphasis added)

This particularist stance is shaped by Sartrean existentialism. Hacking states that he relies on Sartre's conception of a person as a free individual, with no essential features, who makes choices and creates his own destiny:

We are born with a great many essential characteristics that we cannot change. Most of us can change how fat or thin, how trim or flabby our bodies are. But we can make only the most miniscule alterations to our height. A very great many physical characteristics appear to be fixed at the moment of conception, and many more are determined before the fetus sees the light. We do not yet have the genetic technology to change that, even if it were desirable. Neurologists and cognitive scientists teach us the same about the brain—that a great many of our potential thoughts and thought processes are innate, and that many more mental traits are part of our biological constitution. Many of the possibilities available to us, and many of the constraints imposed upon us, were dealt us at birth. At most we can choose what to do with what is there, although we know little except the most obvious facts about what is 'in our genes' and what is the result of other develop-mental processes. The chances of birth, of family, of war, of hunger, of social station, of the supports and the oppression that can result from religion or caste—the chances of wanton cruelty or high rates of unemployment—once you start listing everything there does not seem to be much room for choice at all. But of course there is. All that stuff is the framework within which we can decide who to be. (2004, p. 283)

It seems to me that Hacking places persons somewhere between "facticities" (Sartre's term)—that is, one's biological, genetic, neurological dispositions, and limitations, as well as social and cultural realities—and the "freedom" to choose whoever one wants to be in the face of these facticities, but he does not take into account the complexities involved in such placement. In other words, it is not straightforward to make choices in the face of facts; human decision-making capacities work in complex ways and do not allow one to "freely" make choices in the face of facticities. Consider, for instance, how Hacking takes the existentialist motto "Existence precedes essence." Despite "constraints" to freedom, one can still choose:

I favour an almost existentialist vision of the human condition over an essentialist one. But that vision is wholly consistent with good sense about what choices are open to us. We take for granted that each of us is precluded from a lot of choices for the most mundane of physiological or social reasons. Social: as a young man growing up in Vancouver, I could not have chosen to be an officer in the Soviet Navy. Physiological: my father thought I should spend my first two university years at a college that trains officers for the Royal Canadian Navy, because tuition was free, I would get free room and board, and it would make a man of me. Happily my vision was not good enough for me to be accepted. So I had the moral luck not to have to make a choice between a fight with my family and enrolling in the naval college. (2004, p. 286)

But while trying to avoid an essentialistic account of the self, an attitude consistent with his dynamic nominalism, Hacking stumbles on a simplistic account of the self that is not responsive to the complexities of real experi-ence, the features of selfhood that make us responsive to our social and cultural environments and to scientific classifications.[12] This rather simpli-fied account is not responsive to how selves actually experience the world, how they interact with others, how they develop self-related concerns and change their self-concepts, or what motivates behavioral change and how individuals make choices. Empirical evidence in cognitive sciences supports these intuitions about the complexity of human cognition. They offer perspectives on how the self interacts with the social world, how self-concepts are developed, what factors motivate behavior and behavioral changes, how the self experiences mental disorder, and how mental disorders shape behavior and self-concepts. (See, e.g., Neisser 1988; Flanagan 1991; Nisbett and Wilson 1977; Pennebaker 1993; Miller, Potts, Fung, Hoogstra, and Mintz 1990; Marin, Bohanek, and Fivush 2008; Jopling 2000.) They point to the limitations of our computational capacities and to those aspects of our reasoning processes that are driven by short-sighted reasoning strategies, cognitive biases, and opportunistic oversimplifications (Gilbert 2006; Kosslyn 2006; Wilson 2002). Such findings exhibit the complexity of selfhood and show that a Sartrean account is too simplistic. Most important, this simplistic account of the self does not enable us to answer the three questions raised above in the context of looping effects in psychopathology, i.e., how the subject's self-concepts and behavior change in response to knowledge about the illness, the course of the illness, and the clinical treatment.

4   The Multitudinous Self and Looping Effects

In what follows, I substantiate the complexity of looping effects in the context of psychopathology by including what I call the multitudinous self in its causal trajectory.[13] The multitudinous self is an empirically and philosophically plausible model of the self that captures the complexities of mental disorders and the process in which alterations occur in self-concepts and behavior. The multitudinous self is a dynamic, complex, relational, multi-aspectual, and more or less integrated configuration of capacities, processes, states, and traits that support a degree of agential capacity subject to various psychopathologies. To develop the multitudinous self, I build on Ulric Neisser's (1988) account of the self as a complex configuration specified by various kinds of information originating from the subject and its social and physical environment. Neisser argues that the forms of information that individuate the self are so different from one another that it is plausible to suggest that each establishes a different "self." Therefore, he distinguishes five separate selves: the ecological self, or the self who perceives and who is situated in the physical world; the interpersonal self, or the self embedded in the social world who develops through intersubjectivity; the extended self, or the self in time grounded on memory and anticipation; the private self, or the self exposed to private experiences not available to others; and the conceptual self, or the self that represents the self to the self by drawing on the properties of the self and the social and cultural context to which she belongs. All five selves are empirically traced by research in cognitive sciences, including developmental psychology, social psychology, cognitive psychology, and neuroscience.[14]

Instead of construing these five as distinct selves, I take them to be five aspects of the self, forming the multitudinous self. Each aspect is identifiable from the first-person and third-person points of view. These aspects are instrumental in connecting the subject to her self and to the physical and social environment in which she is situated (Neisser 1988). The multitudinous self can be construed as a self-organizing system of these five aspects, a locus of agency that remains more or less integrated through time. The ecological and intersubjective aspects of the self are based on perception and action and are present at the earliest stages of human development. Meanwhile, the temporally extended, private, and conceptual aspects of the self are often grounded upon memory, reasoning capacities, representational skills, and language. These aspects of the self develop as the cognitive mechanisms mature. (See Neisser 1988; Jopling 1997; Pickering 1999; Gibson 1993.) The ecological aspect of the self is embodied: it perceives the immediate physical environment and acts on it. It is specified by the physical conditions of a particular environment and the active perceptual exploration of these conditions by the subject (Neisser 1988).[15] It is continuous over time and across varying physical and social conditions (Jopling 1997, 2000). The intersubjective aspect is individuated by "species-specific signals of emotional rapport and communication" between the self and others (Neisser 1988, p. 387). It appears from earliest infancy, as the infant engages in social exchange through interaction with caregivers. (See Trevarthen 1980; Neisser 1988; Fogel 1993; Murray and Trevarthen 1985; Bowlby 1969; Stern 1993.)

The temporally extended aspect of the self emerges through memory: it is based on what the self remembers and anticipates. It relies on autobiographical memory or other stored information.[16] What the subject recalls depends on what she now believes, as well as what she once stored. The private aspect of the multitudinous self contains the subject's felt experiences that are not phenomenologically available to anyone else (such as pain); it appears when children first notice that some of their experiences are unique to them.[17]

What is most important for the purposes of this chapter is the conceptual aspect of the multitudinous self, because it hosts self-concepts, which are influential in guiding behavior. Self-concepts selectively represent the self to the self. They are the products of the dynamic interaction between the aspects of the self and the features of the social and cultural environment. In turn, self-concepts inform and shape the aspects of the self as well as some features of the social and cultural environment. Self-concepts are thus informed by the features of the four aspects of the multitudinous self and by the subject's embodied experiences in the world (such as illness) (Neisser 1988; Jopling 1997; Tekin 2011). Let me consider them in turn.

Self-concepts include ideas about our physical bodies (ecological aspect), interpersonal experiences (intersubjective aspect), the kinds of things we have done in the past and are likely to do in the future (temporally extended aspect), and the quality and meaning of our thoughts and feelings (private aspect). (See Jopling 1997, 2000; Neisser 1988.) For instance, my self-concept as a "friendly person" is a product of the intersubjective aspect of my selfhood and of the norms of friendliness in the culture of which I am a part.

Self-concepts are informed by the pathologies to which the person is subject. This influence is mediated by the changes that occur in the ecological, intersubjective, temporally extended, and private aspects of the self owing to illness, by the scientifically based or folk-psychological knowledge available to the person about her illness, and by the person's self-narratives in making sense of her condition (Tekin 2010, 2011). For example, my having lung cancer affects my ecological self by, say, making it difficult for me to breathe, and this may lead to alterations in how I conceive myself and may cause me to limit my actions. (I may decide to stop running outside.) This, in turn, affects my self-concept about my body, something tied to my ecological layer. (I may form a self-concept as a person who has difficulty breathing.) Or consider Karl. Because he hears voices, he talks to himself. To avoid being seen talking to himself, he stops taking public transit. His self-concept as a responsible person caring for the environment by using public transit may shift in the light of his altered behavior.[18]

Self-concepts are shaped by folk and scientific knowledge available to the subject about his or her illness. For instance, what Karl learns about the course of his illness from various scientific and folk media may lead him to alter his self-concepts. Before his illness he considered himself someone who wanted to pursue a career in academia, but upon learning the scientific accounts of the course of his illness he revises his self-concepts. In addition, the narratives Karl tells himself about his illness may alter his self-concepts.

Self-concepts are action-guiding; our ideas about ourselves inform how we behave. My self-concept of my physical strength affects my physical activities. (I may or may not reach out to lift a suitcase, depending on how strong I feel and how heavy I perceive the suitcase to be.) Similarly, my self-concept of my intelligence and my ability to learn new philosophical material influences what I can actually learn or how well I do in a job interview. Similarly, in the context of mental disorders, the self-concepts formed or altered in this vein influence a subject's actions. For instance, Karl's concept of himself as a person with schizophrenia who will not be able to finish graduate school may in fact influence his decision to quit the graduate program in which he is enrolled. Similarly, his self-concepts may constrain or expand his resources in responding to his illness (Tekin 2010, 2011). Perceiving himself as someone who needs help, he may reach out to the communities of other individuals with schizophrenia who experience a similar condition. Thus, self-concepts motivate the subject to think, act, and behave in certain ways, restricting or expanding his or her possibilities for action (Tekin 2010, 2011, in press; Jopling 1997).

Note that the multitudinous self incorporates psychopathology in its structure, taking it as a possible feature of the self. Mental disorder is broadly construed in this model of the self by considering how well the subject functions with respect to the layers that connect her to her self, her social world, and the physical world; it takes the complexity of selfhood as the norm. Because the multitudinous self embraces the complexity of being subject to psychopathology, we can use it to make sense of how self-concepts change after the subject receives a diagnosis of mental disorder. Self-concepts and behavior change as a result of the subject's knowledge of the illness (as Hacking emphasizes in his discussion of looping effects), as a result of the course of illness, and as a result of the psychiatric treatment the subject receives.

The multitudinous self illuminates the case study cited above. Karl's experience with schizophrenia can be traced through the five aspects of the multitudinous self. The symptoms of schizophrenia, such as hearing voices and encountering hallucinations, are encountered by the private aspect of the self. These can also be traced through the ecological aspect, insofar as some neurochemical changes are associated with such experiences. Schizophrenia compromises Karl's interpersonal relationships; he does not talk to his roommates and ignores the walking hours of his dog, phenomena linked to the intersubjective aspect of his selfhood. Schizophrenia may also compromise Karl's plans for the future and his feelings about the past, thereby affecting the temporally extended aspect. All these alterations in the way Karl experiences himself and the world change how he conceives himself and how he behaves. The diagnosis he receives, the psychiatric treatment that accompanies the diagnosis, the onset of schizophrenia, the social treatment he receives from his community, and the knowledge he acquires about his illness lead to interrelated changes in his self-concepts and behavior. As was discussed above, some symptoms may diminish while others remain: although he may continue to hear voices and talk to himself, the visual hallucinations may diminish with the help of the medication. But other experiences may present themselves; he may begin sleeping excessively, for instance, or he may become more socially isolated. His former conception of himself as a healthy person, as fairly social, and as a good dog owner may be replaced by the idea that he is ill and socially isolated. Knowledge he gains about his schizophrenia, the cultural stereotypes and prejudices associated with it, and the self-narratives he creates will all influence his self-concepts and behavior.

Thus, the changes in Karl stem not only from (i) the knowledge he gains about his illness (including professional and cultural conceptions as well as stereotypes), as Hacking emphasizes, but also from (ii) the illness itself and (iii) the clinical treatment he receives. Thus, Hacking's discussion of looping effects (see figure 12.2), insofar as it emphasizes (i), is only the tip of the iceberg; the changes in those receiving a psychiatric diagnosis are more complex, in view of the dynamic and multilayered nature of selfhood and the complexity of the encounter with mental disorder.

The multitudinous self bolsters our understanding of looping effects by explaining how and why the self responds to being studied in the way it does. Three features of the multitudinous self framework permit such scrutiny: the multitudinous self explains the reflective influence of psychiatric diagnosis on people, it considers the illness experience as a part of the self-experience of the subject, and it explains how the clinical and intersubjective treatment the subject receives changes her self-concepts and behavior.

In short, the multitudinous self is an empirically and philosophically plausible model of the self; the aspects of the self are responsive to experiences of actual people as we encounter them in daily life and can be scrutinized by multiple, interdisciplinary scientific analyses.[19] Because unexplainable phenomena will remain despite the multiple approaches offered by various sciences and first-person accounts of selfhood, it is important to work with a model of the "self" rather than with the particular properties of the self, say, "genetic make-up" or "moral luck" (as Hacking

Multitudinous Self

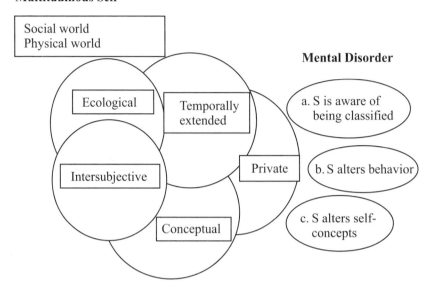

Figure 12.3

does). Doing so prevents the reduction of a complex set of questions per-taining to the self and mental disorders. Without the multitudinous model of the self, in other words, we will lose important information about actual persons. Figure 12.3 illustrates the multitudinous self.

Conclusion

In this chapter I have filled in some gaps in Hacking's account of looping effects by introducing the multitudinous self in its causal trajectory. In particular, I have argued that there are two connected gaps in Hacking's analysis of looping effects. First, the causal structure of looping effects lacks an empirically and philosophically plausible account of the self. Second, Hacking fails to engage with the complexity of mental disorder in the consideration of this phenomenon in the realm of psychopathology. Because of these shortcomings, exactly how classifications of mental dis-orders change the self-concepts and behavior of those diagnosed with these conditions is not explicit in Hacking's looping effects. I have offered the multitudinous self, an empirically and philosophically plausible model of the self that fills these gaps. The multitudinous self, capturing the complex-ity of selfhood and the encounter with mental disorder, makes explicit how self-concepts are formed, how they evolve, and how they motivate behavioral changes in the subjects. Grounded as it is in the sciences of the mind and responsive to the experiences of those living with mental disorders, the multitudinous self better explains the causal trajectory of looping effects. The multitudinous self, I have further suggested, is a fruitful schema for both the scientific research programs in their investigation of mental disorders and the clinical and ethical contexts in facilitating successful interventions in the lives of those with mental disorders, allowing them to flourish (Tekin 2010, 2011). Thus, with the multitudinous self, I advocate a new style of reasoning about mental disorders in philosophy of psychiatry.

Acknowledgments

I owe special thanks to Jackie Sullivan, Owen Flanagan, Muhammad Ali Khalidi, Harold Kincaid, George Graham, Peter Zachar, David Jopling, Francoise Baylis, and Nathan Brett for helpful feedback. An earlier version of this chapter was presented at a weekly colloquium at Dalhousie University's Philosophy Department. I am grateful to the audience for their comments. I acknowledge Canadian Institutes of Health Research grant NNF 80045, Canadian Institutes of Health Research, States of Mind: Emerging Issues in Neuroethics.

Notes

1. There is no uncontroversial definition of natural kinds (Cooper 2004a,b). Philosophers who discuss whether mental disorders are natural kinds mostly work with specific examples from the natural-kind family—water, gold, animals, and so on. (See, e.g., Hacking 1986; Cooper 2004a,b; Khalidi 2010.) I follow their lead in this chapter.
2. "Feedback effects" and "looping effects" are used synonymously by both Hacking and his critics. Throughout this chapter, I use the latter.
3. Although it is crucial to understanding the notion of looping effects, Hacking's critics have not discussed this metaphysical framework. (See, e.g., Cooper 2004a,b; Khalidi 2010.)
4. Two other traits distinguish human kinds from natural kinds. First, human kinds pertain to certain individuals and behaviors at a particular time and in a particular social setting, whereas natural kinds refer to the same kinds at all times. Second, human kinds are laden with social values (e.g., schizophrenia is a mental condition that is "bad" and is to be "healed"), whereas natural kinds are value neutral (e.g., mud is not intrinsically good or bad) (Hacking 1995b, p. 367).

5. As I noted above, he uses the "self," "soul," "person," and "subject" interchange-ably. I follow his lead.

6. Changes in behavior are explainable as outcomes of "socialization," a concept used in social psychology and sociology that is broadly defined as the way in which individuals are guided in becoming members of a social group. During their socialization, individuals conceptualize cultural knowledge as they do any other social information; they acquire, maintain, and apply these cognitive conceptual-izations in their cognition and behavior (Kesebir, Uttal, and Gardner 2010). The effects need not be conscious; indeed, they are often automatic. Women refugees may go through such socialization and unconsciously and automatically adapt to their labels.

7. Some of these challenges are raised by proponents of PA, as was discussed above. For an overview, see Khalidi 2010.

8. By "knowledge," he does not have in mind traditional epistemology's "justified true belief" but rather a Popperian conjectural knowledge.

9. The influence of knowledge is discussed in Hacking's early work, but in his later work he makes this influence more explicit.

10. The example of Karl is informed by various memoirs of schizophrenia (e.g., Saks 2007) in a bid to show the complexity of mental disorder experience, something neglected by Hacking.

11. There is considerable evidence that stigma robs people with mental disorders of work, independent living, and important life opportunities (Corrigan, Edwards, Green, Diwan, and Penn 2001; Farina 1998; Phelan, Link, Stueve, and Pescosolido 2000). Further, self-stigma may lead to impoverished self-esteem and self-efficacy (Corrigan and Holzman 2001; Corrigan and Lundin 2001; Wahl 1999).

12. Feminist philosophers have criticized Hacking's neglect of the complexity of subjectivity and its inherent relationality, saying that, especially in his discussion of women's experience of multiple personality, he neglects the importance of oppression on the way women remember their past. In particular, Susan Campbell challenges Hacking's claim that the cultural acceptance of traumatic forgetting has allowed women to become suggestible to re-narrating their past as having encoun-tered and forgotten being abused as a child. Campbell (2003, p. 192) criticizes Hacking's failure to consider social and relational influences on how women remem-ber their past, and to politically analyze women's oppression.

13. The inspiration for this model of the self is the poem "Song of Myself" by Walt Whitman, in which he proclaims "Do I contradict myself? Very well, then, I contradict myself; (I am large—I contain multitudes.)" Special thanks to Owen Flanagan, who steered me in the direction of these lines; hence the word "multitudinous."

14. Neisser investigates each of these selves by appealing to a wide range of research in developmental, social and cognitive psychology. He edited and co-edited several volumes on the different selves. See, e.g., Neisser 1993; Neisser and Fivush 1994; Neisser and Jopling 1997.

15. Eleanor Gibson (1993, p. 41) calls this the "rock-bottom self" that collects information about the world and interacts with it.

16. See Bartlett 1932.

17. It is difficult to determine when introspective reference to private experiences develops, but many studies show that children are aware of the privacy of their mental life before the age of five years.

18. Of course, not every illness experience leads to alterations in self-concepts. People with delusional disorder (once known as paranoia) and schizophrenia commonly suffer from anosognosia—that is, a lack of awareness of their disorder, its symptoms, and its severity (Amador and Seckinger 1997; Amador, Strauss, Yale, and Gorman 1991). Such psychiatric patients may not change their self-concepts in response to the illness experience.

19. Flanagan, natural method.

References

Amador, X., and R. Seckinger. 1997. The assessment of insight: A methodological review. *Psychiatric Annals* 27: 798–805.

Amador, X., D. Strauss, S. Yale, and J. Gorman. 1991. Awareness of illness in schizophrenia. *Schizophrenia Bulletin* 17: 113–132.

Bartlett, F. 1932. *Remembering*. Cambridge University Press.

Bogen, J. 1988. Comments. *Noûs* 22: 65–66.

Bowlby, J. 1969. *Attachment and Loss*. Hogarth.

Campbell, S. 2003. *Relational Remembering: Rethinking the Memory Wars*. Rowman and Littlefield.

Carlson, L. 2010. *The Faces of Intellectual Disability: Philosophical Reflections*. Indiana University Press.

Cooper, R. 2004a. Why Hacking is wrong about human kinds. *British Journal for the Philosophy of Science* 55: 73–85.

Cooper, R. 2004b. What is wrong with the *DSM*? *History of Psychiatry* 15 (1): 5–25.

Corrigan, P., and Holzman, K. 2001. Do stereotype threats influence social cognitive deficits in schizophrenia? In *Social Cognition and Schizophrenia*, ed. P. Corrigan and D. Penn. American Psychological Association.

Corrigan, P., and Lundin, R. 2001. *Don't Call Me Nuts! Coping with the Stigma of Mental Illness*. Recovery Press.

Corrigan, P., and Nelson, D. 1998. Factors that affect social cue recognition in schizophrenia. *Psychiatry Research* 78: 189–196.

Corrigan, P., A. Edwards, A. Green, S. Diwan, and D. Penn. 2001. Prejudice, social distance, and familiarity with mental illness. *Schizophrenia Bulletin* 27: 219–225.

Douglas, M. 1986. *How Institutions Think*. Syracuse University Press.

Farina, A. 1998. Stigma. In *Handbook of Social Functioning in Schizophrenia*, ed. K. Mueser and N. Tarrier. Allyn & Bacon.

Flanagan, O. 1991. *Varieties of Moral Personality*. Harvard University Press.

Fogel, A. 1993. *Developing through Relationships: Origins of Communication, Self, and Culture*. Harvester Wheatsheaf.

Gibson, E. 1993. Ontogenesis of the perceived self. In *The Perceived Self*, ed. U. Neisser. Cambridge University Press.

Gilbert, D. 2006. *Stumbling on Happiness*. Vintage Books.

Graham, G. 2010. *The Disordered Mind*. Routledge.

Hacking, I. 1986. Making up people. In *Reconstructing Individualism*, ed. T. Heller, M. Sosna, and D. Wellberry. Stanford University Press.

Hacking, I. 1992. World-making by kind-making: Child abuse for example. In *How Classification Works*, ed. M. Douglas and D. Hull. Edinburgh University Press.

Hacking, I. 1995a. *Rewriting the Soul: Multiple Personality and the Science of Memory*. Princeton University Press.

Hacking, I. 1995b. The looping effects of human kinds. In *Causal Cognition*, ed. D. Sperber and J. Premack. Oxford University Press.

Hacking, I. 1999. Kind making: The case of child abuse. In *The Social Construction of What?* Harvard University Press.

Hacking, I. 2000. *The Social Construction of What?* Harvard University Press.

Hacking, I. 2002. *Mad Travelers: Reflections on the Reality of Transient Mental Illnesses*. Harvard University Press.

Hacking, I. 2004. Between Michel Foucault and Erving Goffman: Between discourse in the abstract and face-to-face interaction. *Economy and Society* 33 (3): 277–302.

Hacking, I. 2007a. Natural kinds: Rosy dawn, scholastic twilight. *Royal Institute of Philosophy* 61 (Supplement): 203–239.

Hacking, I. 2007b. Kinds of people: Moving targets. *Proceedings of the British Academy* 151: 285–318.

Jopling, D. 1997. A 'self of selves. In *The Conceptual Self in Context*, ed. U. Neisser and D. Jopling. Cambridge University Press.

Jopling, D. 2000. *Self-Knowledge and the Self*. Routledge.

Kesebir, S., D. Uttal, and W. Gardner. 2010. Socialization: Insights from social cognition. *Social and Personality Psychology Compass* 4 (2): 93–106.

Khalidi, M. 2010. Interactive Kinds. *British Journal for the Philosophy of Science* 61: 335–360.

Kosslyn, S. 2006. On the evolution of human motivation: The role of social prosthetic systems. In *Evolutionary Cognitive Science*, ed. T. Shackelford and J. Keenan. MIT Press.

Marin, K., J. Bohanek, and R. Fivush. 2008. Positive effects of talking about the negative: Family narratives of negative experiences and preadolescents' perceived competence. *Journal of Research on Adolescence* 18 (3): 573–593.

Miller, P., R. Potts, H. Fung, L. Hoogstra, and J. Mintz. 1990. Narrative practices and the social construction of self in childhood. *American Ethnologist* 17: 292–311.

Murray, L., and C. Trevarthen. 1985. The infant in mother-infant communication. *Journal of Child Language* 13: 15–29.

Neisser, U. 1988. Five kinds of self-knowledge. *Philosophical Psychology* 1: 35–59.

Neisser, U. 1993. *The Perceived Self: Ecological and Interpersonal Sources of Self- Knowledge*. Cambridge University Press.

Neisser, U., and R. Fivush. 1994. *The Remembering Self: Construction and Accuracy in the Self-Narrative*. Cambridge University Press.

Neisser, U., and D. Jopling. 1997. *The Conceptual Self in Context: Culture, Experience, Self-Understanding*. Cambridge University Press.

Nisbett, R., and T. Wilson. 1977. Telling more than we can know: Verbal reports on mental processes. *Psychological Review* 84: 231–259.

Pennebaker, J. 1993. Putting stress into words: Health, linguistic, and therapeutic implications. *Behaviour Research and Therapy* 31 (6): 539–548.

Phelan, J., B. Link, A. Stueve, and B. Pescosolido. 2000. Public conceptions of mental illness in 1950 and 1996: What is mental illness and is it to be feared? *Journal of Health and Social Behavior* 41: 188–207.

Pickering, J. 1999. The self is a semiotic process. In *Models of the Self*, ed. S. Gallagher and J. Shear. Imprint Academic.

Saks, E. 2007. *The Center Cannot Hold: My Journey through Madness*. Hyperion.

Samuels, R. 2009. Delusion as a natural kind. In *Psychiatry as Cognitive Neuroscience: Philosophical Perspectives*, ed. M. Broome and L. Bortolotti. Oxford University Press.

Stern, D. 1993. The role of feeling for an interpersonal self. In *The Perceived Self*, ed. U. Neisser. Cambridge University Press.

Stets, J., and Burke, P. 2003. A Sociological Approach to Self and Identity. In *Handbook of Self and Identity*, ed. M. Leary and J. Tangney. Guilford.

Tekin, Ş. 2010. Mad Narratives: Self-Constitutions Through the Diagnostic Looking Glass. PhD dissertation, York University.

Tekin, Ş. 2011. Self-concepts through the diagnostic looking glass: Narratives and mental disorder. *Philosophical Psychology* 24 (3): 357–380.

Tekin, Ş. Forthcoming. Self-insight in the time of mood disorders: After the diagnosis, beyond treatment. *Philosophy, Psychiatry, & Psychology*.

Trevarthen, C. 1980. The foundations of intersubjectivity: Development of interpersonal and cooperative understanding in infants. In *The Social Foundations of Language and Thought*, ed. D. Olson. Norton.

Wahl, O. 1999. Mental health consumers' experience of stigma. *Schizophrenia Bulletin* 25: 467–478.

Wilson, T. 2002. *Strangers to Ourselves*. Harvard University Press.

Zachar, P. 2001. Psychiatric disorders are not natural kinds. *Philosophy, Psychiatry, & Psychology* 7 (3): 167–182.

13 Stabilizing Mental Disorders: Prospects and Problems

Jacqueline Sullivan

A primary focus of the debates in philosophy of psychiatry addressed in each of the chapters in this volume is whether mental disorders are natural kinds. The question subdivides into several interrelated questions: Are mental disorders real and stable regularities in nature that exist independent of our systems of classifying them? Do the sets of necessary and sufficient conditions that constitute the categories of mental disorders put forward in the *Diagnostic and Statistical Manual of Mental Disorders* and in the *International Classification of Diseases* track these regularities? Are those groups of phenomena individuated by the categories suitable for discovering their causes and identifying viable targets for therapeutic intervention?

The vast majority of philosophers of psychiatry are realists about mental disorders. The consensus, however, is that current mental disorder categories do not pick out stable regularities in nature that are subject to the same causal-mechanical explanations. (See, e.g., Craver 2009; Kendler, Zachar, and Craver 2011; Haslam 2000, 2002, and this volume; Insel 2013; see also the chapters in this volume by Kincaid and Murphy.) Yet if the categories do not track real divisions in nature—if research into mental disorders begins with indefinite and poorly circumscribed explanatory targets—it is likely that the projects of identifying their causes and developing successful therapeutic interventions to treat them will also fail. That scientific explanation requires well-delineated explanatory targets, and mental disorders do not seem to qualify, is one of the primary reasons why philosophers of psychiatry have been reluctant to abandon the natural kinds ideal for psychiatric classification and why debates about whether or not mental disorders are natural kinds persist in the philosophical literature.

Some of the chapters in this volume (those by Kincaid, Horwitz, Murphy, and Ross) focus on how to revise current categories of mental disorders so that the disorders they individuate correspond to bona fide regularities in nature or something close enough. In this chapter, I take a slightly different approach. Specifically, I consider the instability to which psychiatric kinds may be subject when they become explanatory targets of areas of science that are not "mature" (see, e.g., Hacking 1988, 1992) and are in the early stages of discovering the mechanisms of cognitive phenomena (see, e.g., Bechtel and Richardson 1993; Bechtel 2008; Craver 2007). I focus primarily on two such areas of science that have been independently involved in the investigation of the mechanisms of mental disorders: cognitive neuroscience (which has as its task the localization of cognitive functions in the brain) and cognitive neurobiology (which aims to discover the cellular and molecular mechanisms of learning and memory).

There is a growing consensus among research scientists that mental disorders are simply disorders of cognition. (See, e.g., Carter et al. 2009; Insel 2013; Nuechterlein et al. 2012.) This has led to the emergence of intra-disciplinary and inter-disciplinary research initiatives to identify the cognitive functions and the underlying synaptic, cellular, and molecular mechanisms that are disrupted in mental disorders, the ultimate aim being the development of effective therapeutic interventions. In this chapter, I evaluate one such research initiative: the Cognitive Neuroscience Treatment Research to Improve Cognition in Schizophrenia (CNTRICS) initiative. I use this case study as a basis to show that such research does not begin with "stable phenomena" (see, e.g., Hacking 1988, 1992) that track mechanisms; neither the mental disorders nor the cognitive functions under study qualify as such. The reason for this instability is that the methods used to individuate these explanatory targets are not standardized either within or across disciplinary boundaries. Thus, for inter-disciplinary interactions to be effective, specific measures must be taken across different contexts of experimentation to ensure the stability of the phenomena under study. What is interesting about the CNTRICS initiative is that investigators have sought to impose intra-disciplinary and inter-disciplinary "strategies of stabilization" (see, e.g., Hacking 1983, 1988, 1992) to operationally fix the cognitive functions that are disrupted in schizophrenia across investigators and levels of analysis. I assess the potential for these strategies to succeed at the goal of stabilizing mental disorders as scientific kinds.

Mental Disorders and Stability

Ian Hacking has discussed the stability of scientific kinds in two separate contexts. First, he has used historical case studies to demonstrate that categories of mental disorders and the phenomena to which they refer are unstable. (See, e.g., Hacking 1995a,b, 2007.) Such instability originates in the context of psychiatric diagnosis when an individual is informed that he or she has a mental disorder, and that he or she may thus be classified as a specific kind of person. Second, he has shown that the stability of the kinds under study in laboratory sciences is very much tied to how established a particular laboratory science is. (See, e.g., Hacking 1983, 1988, 1989, 1992.) In mature areas of science we often encounter stable kinds of phenomena under study, whereas in immature laboratory sciences the kinds have a tendency to oscillate wildly. The source of stability or instability in this case arises in the context of the laboratory and has to do in part with investigators experimentally harnessing a phenomenon. Although in this chapter I am primarily interested in this latter kind of stability, I want to say something about Hacking's worry that psychiatric diagnosis may be a source of the instability of psychiatric kinds because it has featured prominently in philosophical debates about whether mental disorders are natural kinds. (See, e.g., Bogen 1988; Cooper 2004; Khalidi 2010; Tekin, this volume.)

Hacking characterizes mental disorders as paradigmatic examples of kinds that lack stability because they are subject to what he dubs "looping effects." (See, e.g., Hacking 1995a,b, 2007.) Specifically, classifying a human subject as a kind of thing (e.g., a "manic depressive") or diagnosing that subject with a mental disorder may prompt changes in that individual such that the criteria that constitute the mental-disorder category are no longer applicable and require revision. Such revisions, if they are made at all, are only stopgap measures; they do not guarantee the stability of psychiatric kinds since future looping effects are always possible. Categories of mental disorders, thus, can never be stable, because the kinds they pick out are "moving targets." (See, e.g., Hacking 2007.)

Hacking's "looping effects" argument is convincing in part because the effects are so plausible—human beings do adjust their behaviors in response to being categorized. Furthermore, in the cases of multiple personality disorder (1995b) and dissociative fugue (1998) Hacking puts forward two convincing examples of looping effects in action that make it seem plausible that other mental disorders may be subject to similar types of effects. However, if psychiatric kinds are indeed unstable in the way Hacking suggests, this has negative implications not only for psychiatry and psychiatric diagnosis but also for any area of science that is in the business of investigating the mechanisms of mental disorders and developing successful therapeutic interventions for treating them, for truly explaining a phenomenon seems to require a stable and fixed explanatory target. (See, e.g., Bechtel 2008; Bechtel and Richardson 1993; Craver 2007; Sullivan 2010.) If Hacking is correct and categories of mental disorders have moveable rather than fixed referents, then we will not be able to explain and treat mental disorders.

The response in the philosophical literature to Hacking's claim about mental disorders' being subject to looping effects has been mixed. (See, e.g., the chapter by Tekin in this volume.) However, philosophers of psychiatry have, for the most part, dismissed looping effects as real obstacles to discovering the causes of mental disorders, for two reasons. First, although it is plausible that individuals may change in detectable (and undetectable) ways in response to a diagnosis of a mental disorder, no evidence exists to establish that the process actually happens for all categories of mental disorders and all individuals or to what extent. This leaves open the possibility that at least some mental disorders are kinds that track relatively stable regularities in nature that do not change radically in response to classification. (See, e.g., the chapters by Haslam, Kincaid, Murphy, Ross, and Zachar).

Another strategy for responding to Hacking's worry about looping effects is to demonstrate that a lot of important causal discoveries are made in science in the absence of stable or "natural" kinds. For example, Kincaid (2008, p. 373) argues that we have "piecemeal causal explanations of cancer," and that we have learned how to intervene in various forms of it and treat patients with it even though what "constitutes a cancerous cell" cannot be specified "in terms of necessary and sufficient conditions." He claims that the kinds of causal explanations we have of mental disorders are similarly fragmentary. He points to the example of depression, for which we have "piecemeal causal explanations" (e.g., low levels of the neurotransmitter serotonin at serotonergic synapses in the brain) and treatments (e.g., selective serotonin reuptake inhibitors) even though it is not a natural kind. Though Kincaid does not regard such piecemeal causal explanations of mental disorders as ultimately satisfactory, his primary aim is to demonstrate that science often proceeds quite successfully in the absence of natural kinds and well-developed theories of those kinds.

Such piecemeal explanations of mental disorders arise in part from the fact that mental disorders are complex phenomena: the biological systems that exhibit them are ontologically complex, consisting of physical parts and processes that span multiple levels of organization, from genes to neurons to behavior. Because each constitutive level may be probed in order to identify the causes of a mental disorder, the sciences directed at investigating these causes are many and diverse, spanning multiple levels of analysis from molecular genetics to behavior and incorporating a wide range of techniques—from functional imaging studies on human subjects to pharmacological intervention techniques in animal models. Thus, when we look at the scientific literature on mental disorders we encounter what William Wimsatt says we find with respect to the scientific study of complex phenomena more generally: "a plurality of incompletely articulated and partially contradictory, partially supplementary theories and models," each taken in isolation having "individually, [an] impoverished view[] of [its] objects" (2007, p. 180). Such pluralism is an important contributing factor to the instability of mental disorders as kinds of phenomena insofar as each area of science has different assumptions about the best way to operationalize mental disorders (e.g., which measurement techniques to use), where to look for the mechanisms (i.e., where in the brain or world and at what level of organization), how to look for them (i.e., different methodological strategies), and where to intervene so as to determine causal relationships (e.g., which neurotransmitter system, which receptors).

However, inter-disciplinary pluralism is not the only obstacle to stabilizing mental disorders as scientific kinds. As I have argued previously (e.g., in Sullivan 2009), intra-disciplinary methodological pluralism is also an obstacle to relating explanations of phenomena across multiple levels of analysis. Often researchers working in the same area of science but in different laboratories vary the methods used for studying a phenomenon, which leaves open the possibility that they are not all investigating the same phenomenon. (See Sullivan 2009.) This kind of local inter-disciplinary pluralism is characteristic of what Hacking refers to as "immature laboratory sciences" (1992, p. 57). The phenomena under study in such sciences are unstable "in part because [they] are produced by fundamentally different techniques, and different theories answer to different phenomena that are only loosely connected" (ibid.).

Whereas in mature areas of science the "theories and laboratory equipment [have] evolve[d] in such a way that they match each other and are self-vindicating" (Hacking 1992, p. 56), as I show later in the chapter, in those laboratory sciences (e.g., cognitive neuroscience and cognitive neurobiology) that have come to direct their attention to investigating the mechanisms of mental disorders, the requisite symbiosis between what phenomena investigators take their investigative strategies to measure and what phenomena are actually being measured is absent. These areas of science fail to be "self-vindicating" on Hacking's understanding of the term, insofar as there is a lack of coordination among investigators with respect to how to produce, measure, and detect what they refer to as the same phenomenon. Investigators in both areas of neuroscience may be described as sharing a set of background assumptions, basic methods, investigative strategies, and explanatory goals (even a "Kuhnian paradigm"), but both areas afford investigators the flexibility to modify specific aspects of standard tasks or experimental paradigms in ways that affect, for example, what cognitive functions, areas of the brain, and cellular and molecular activities are involved in a given experiment. Such flexibility actually promotes the development of a plurality of explanations of mental disorder phenomena rather than the discovery of single unified explanations for such phenomena.

Scientists do not regard such piecemeal causal explanations as an adequate stopping point for research into the causes of mental disorders. For example, in a recent blog post the director of the US National Institutes for Mental Health, Thomas Insel, encouraged research scientists to develop "a new nosology of mental disorders" that understands them as "biological disorders involving brain circuits that implicate specific domains of cognition, emotion, or behavior," the study of which requires that "each level of analysis . . . be understood across a dimension of function" (Insel 2013). However, achieving this aim requires that the phenomena in question be stable or that investigators reach consensus that the term used to refer to a particular function or a particular mental disorder had the "same" referent.

However, such translatability doesn't simply emerge. Scientists have to impose both inter-disciplinary and intra-disciplinary standards in order to achieve it. Recent work to discover the mechanisms that mediate cognitive dysfunction in schizophrenia indicates that scientists must actively structure practice in such a way so as to ensure the stability of their explanatory targets, because the goals they aim to achieve are not thought to be attainable by any other means. Even though ensuring the stability of scientific kinds appears attractive with respect to specific explanatory and therapeutic goals, it may not be attainable, and if realized it may lead to undesirable consequences.

Schizophrenia Research

Schizophrenia is classified as a psychotic disorder that, on "the narrowest definition," involves "distortions or exaggerations in inferential thinking" (i.e., delusions) and "in perception" (i.e., hallucinations) (American Psychiatric Association 1994, p. 274). On the *DSM*-IV definition, a set of necessary and sufficient conditions must be satisfied in order for a person to be diagnosed as having schizophrenia. First, the individual must exhibit at least two of the following characteristic symptoms, which must be present for at least a month: "delusions, hallucinations, disorganized speech, grossly disorganized or catatonic behavior, and negative symptoms, i.e., affective flattening, alogia, or avolition" (ibid., p. 285). The symptoms must result in social and/or occupational dysfunction, and the "continuous signs of the disturbance" must "persist for at least 6 months" (ibid., p. 285). In addition, the diagnosis must rule out that the symptoms are due to substance use or a general medical condition and must exclude that the person suffers from Schizoaffective Disorder, Mood Disorder, or Pervasive Developmental Disorder. Insofar as many persons with schizophrenia have symptoms that are differentially manifest, some symptoms (e.g., paranoia or disorganized thoughts) being more prominent than others, the disorder has five identified subtypes to accommodate these differences: paranoid, disorganized, catatonic, undifferentiated, and residual.

The primary symptoms of schizophrenia are characterized as "cognitive and emotional dysfunctions" and are divided into two classes: positive symptoms, so called because they involve "an excess or distortion of normal functions," and negative symptoms, which "appear to reflect a diminution or loss of normal function" (American Psychiatric Association 1994, p. 274). Although anti-psychotics and neuroleptics, when taken regularly, eliminate or mask the delusions and the hallucinations associated with schizophrenia, no reliable treatments exist for the negative symptoms (e.g., disorganization in speech and behavior and affective flattening). Some experts regard these negative symptoms, considered independent of side effects from anti-psychotics, as constituting a set of "core cognitive deficits," which they regard as primary obstacles to persons diagnosed with schizophrenia maintaining steady employment and meaningful interpersonal relationships (Green, Lee, and Kern 2009, p. 158). Such failures to "achieve adequate community functioning, including finding a job, forming a network of friends or living independently" (ibid., p. 160) are taken to be responsible for "up to 40% of the excess premature mortality" in schizophrenics that "may be attributed to suicide and unnatural deaths" (Hor and Taylor 2010, p. 81).

The "cognitive deficits [that] have been demonstrated at multiple levels in schizophrenia" are said to "range from early sensory processing deficits" in both auditory and visual processing to "higher order information-processing deficits" in "attention, executive function, working and episodic memory, and affective processing" (Belger and Barch 2009, p. 303). Cognitive neuroscientists have been careful to differentiate these cognitive deficits from the negative clinical symptoms identified in the *DSM* as indicative of schizophrenia. In fact, research scientists on the whole have been critical of the lack of validity of the categories of mental disorders identified in the *DSM*. Cameron Carter and colleagues express this sentiment best in claiming that, although the *DSM* and similar manuals "segregate mental disorders into distinct categories,"

in actuality these disorders may reflect a complex combination of disturbances in more fundamental processes, or dimensions of function, that do not necessarily align with currently identified categories of disorder. For example, schizophrenia and depression may ultimately be better understood as particular changes in the functioning of underlying cognitive and emotional systems (such as executive control and reinforcement learning) with different combinations of deficits in these underlying systems producing different behavior deficits that are categorized clinically as two distinct illnesses. If this is so, then it suggests that a more powerful way of characterizing and understanding these illnesses is to draw on the conceptual and experimental framework provided by cognitive psychology by developing behavioral paradigms that can sensitively and specifically measure the critical functions of interest. This also promises a more direct path toward relating clinical disturbance to underlying neurobiological pathology, insofar as fundamental cognitive processes are more likely to map onto specific identifiable neurobiological mechanisms. (Carter et al. 2009, p. 169)

Carter and other cognitive neuroscientists are advocating for an inter-disciplinary initiative to revise current categories of mental disorders, with the ultimate aim of "understanding the neurobiological underpinning of . . . cognitive deficits" in mental disorders like schizophrenia by "linking [them] to selected cortical and subcortical neural circuits" (Belger and Barch 2009, p. 303). Such discoveries would then pave the way for cognitive neurobiologists who study the synapses, cells, and molecules that constitute these neural circuits to investigate the cellular and molecular mechanisms that underlie cognitive dysfunctions in schizophrenia in animal models and to test pharmacological interventions. This might lead to translational work from animal models to clinical trials to test experimental drugs in human schizophrenics.

I think the vast majority of researchers who are interested in understanding, explaining, and treating mental disorders agree that the current crisis in mental health will be resolved only by means of inter-disciplinary initiatives and that we must move beyond what everyone regards as the inadequacy of current categories of mental disorders for tracking mental-disorder mechanisms. However, initiating and sustaining collaborative and coordinated efforts among investigators working in two radically different areas of neuroscience that are both immature and lack stable and potentially valid explanatory targets in their own right is an extremely difficult task. Before considering the structure of one inter-disciplinary initiative that has these aims in mind, and in order to be able to evaluate its potential for achieving these aims, I want to consider some of the differences between the two areas of neuroscience that may be regarded as obstacles to achieving these aims.

Cognitive neuroscientists generally assume that "mental function is composed of distinguishable fundamental processes and that these processes can be selectively engaged by properly designed experimental task manipulations" and localized, via functional imaging techniques (e.g., fMRI, EEG), to specific areas of the brain (Carter et al. 2009, p. 169). In designing such task manipulations, cognitive neuroscientists engage in task analysis; they aim to provide "a clear specification of the [cognitive] processes thought to be engaged by the experimental task" and to determine "how these processes will be influenced by the variables to be manipulated in the experiment" (ibid.). For example, if an investigator is interested in creating a task to discriminate recognition memory from familiarity memory, in the process of designing the task she will consult previously published studies in the research literature, textbook understandings of each cognitive function, what is known about the temporal ordering of these processes in relationship to other processes, and which areas are thought to subserve those other processes (e.g., attention, working memory). Designing tasks that successfully individuate a cognitive function and simultaneously localizing that function in the brain requires a great deal of ingenuity. Cognitive neuroscientists have substantial freedom to produce, detect, and measure cognitive functions using the experimental paradigm or task that they take to be most reliable for achieving their investigative aims.

Not all cognitive neuroscientists will agree that a particular experimental task or paradigm is subject to only one unique task analysis. In fact, disagreements about the potential functions that play a role in the execution of a given task may prompt revisions to that task and/or the development of new tasks. Such disagreements have arisen in the cognitive neuroscience literature with respect to the Stroop task, which has been widely used to understand cognitive deficits in schizophrenia. (See, e.g.,

Perlstein et al. 1998; Barch et al. 1999a,b, 2004; Cohen et al. 1999.) In the standard version of the Stroop task, subjects are presented across trials variously with the word "red," the word "green," and a color-neutral word (such as "dog") in red or green type. The trials typically include congruent, incongruent, and neutral stimulus presentations. In the congruent condition the color of the text of the word matches the color word (e.g., "red" is presented in red-faced type); in the incongruent condition the color of the text differs from the color word (e.g., "red" is presented in green-faced type); in the neutral condition a color-neutral word is presented in either red or green type. The subject's reaction time from the point of presentation of the stimulus on a given trial to the point of responding with the correct word for the color seen (but not read) is measured, and errors in identifying the correct color word are recorded. On the non-computerized card version of the task, "patients [with schizophrenia] exhibit overall slowing of reaction times estimated across an entire card or . . . complete fewer items across all conditions" (Perlstein et al. 1998, p. 414). On the computerized version of the task, "normal" subjects have been shown to exhibit increased reaction-time (RT) interference (measured as difference between reaction time on neutral and incongruent trials) on the incongruent condition but exhibit few errors. Schizophrenics do not exhibit increased reaction time interference but may make more errors on the incongruent trials than controls and may also show increased RT facilitation (measured as the difference in neutral-congruent reaction time). Many investigators have interpreted the data as indicating that schizophrenics have a deficit in selective attention, insofar as they cannot "attend to a single dimension of a stimulus while simultaneously ignoring other task-irrelevant dimensions" (Perlstein et al. 1998, p. 414). Other investigators suggest that schizophrenics have a deficit in inhibition because they are unable to ignore the word in the incongruent condition, or because they "have difficulty suppressing the intrusive effects of the words" (ibid., p. 414). Another explanation is that schizophrenics have a deficit in "context processing" insofar as they cannot actively use information about context or what they are required to do in a task in order "to mediate task appropriate behavior" (Cohen et al. 1999). Thus, precisely what cognitive function the Stroop task individuates remains a subject of debate. (See also Barch et al. 2004.)

Such disagreements stem from several sources. First, there are different versions of the Stroop task. The computerized and non-computerized versions should not be classified as identical tasks, because the subject-stimulus interaction and the task demands placed on the subject (e.g., requiring a subject to press a button or provide a verbal response) differ. However, even if we concede that these two versions of the same task are really different tasks, we still encounter, with respect to each version of the task on its own, differences in the number and ordering of stimuli presented and in the duration of inter-stimulus and inter-trial intervals. Such differences again prompt us to wonder if these tasks may be classified as the same and whether they can be said to involve the same cognitive processes and in the same ways.

The proliferation of competing hypotheses as to what cognitive function is disrupted in schizophrenia on the basis of Stroop-task data also makes sense in view of the fact that that different investigators put forward different task analyses to understand why schizophrenics exhibit the errors they do. Since these task analyses are likely to vary as a function of the version of the task that is being analyzed, we can anticipate that there will never be one single analysis of the Stroop task.

The Stroop task is also a complex task insofar as it places demands on a variety of what historically have been regarded as separable cognitive processes, including attention, working memory, language processing, visual processing, and implicit memory. For this reason, there is increasing consensus among cognitive neuroscientists that the Stroop task is not effective for individuating a single cognitive function and that Stroop-task data may not be used to adjudicate between competing interpretations of the cognitive functions it involves and the precise functions that are disrupted in schizophrenia.

Which areas of the brain are involved in Stroop-task performance has also been a focus of debate, different versions of the task being accompanied by different activation profiles for prefrontal cortex and anterior cingulate. (See, e.g., Adams and David 2007.) The fact that the behavioral data and the imaging data are subject to multiple distinct interpretations suggests that the Stroop task, which historically has been one of the better tasks for studying cognitive dysfunction in schizophrenia, does not individuate a single stable cognitive function or allow localization of a function in the brain in a way that could direct investigations into the cellular and molecular mechanisms that mediate such functions.

Such differences may be attributable to differences in task design across different computerized version of the task, but they may also be attributable to differences across research studies in the criteria used to recruit schizophrenic subjects. For example, the diagnostic screening and interview instruments or rating scales (see, e.g., Rush, First, and Blacker 2008) used to recruit schizophrenic subjects are not standardized across laboratories. Some investigators take satisfaction of the *DSM*-IV definition alone to be sufficient; others require subjects to have a specific score on the Schizophrenia Rating Scale. And whereas some investigators exclude subjects on the basis of comorbidity of schizophrenia with another mental disorder (e.g., depression), a history of substance abuse, or a low IQ, other investigators use some of these criteria or none of them.[1]

Overcoming obstacles such as the ones identified above is a primary aim of the CNTRICS initiative. In fact, progress in cognitive neuroscience more generally is thought to be attainable by refining experimental tasks and correspondingly the taxonomy of kinds of functional processes as well as by standardizing fundamental features of experimental tasks and protocols. (See, e.g., Carter et al. 2009.) If such measures are successful, functional localization claims could become ever more fine grained, increasing the possibility of discovering the cellular and molecular mechanisms of these functions. Thus, cognitive neuroscience may be regarded as a field aiming towards stabilizing its kinds.

However, stabilizing the kinds of cognitive processes under study in cognitive neuroscience brings neuroscience only part of the way toward identifying the mechanisms that give rise to cognitive functions. Though it tells us where in the brain to look for cellular and molecular mechanisms, it does not tell us what those mechanisms are. Inter-disciplinary initiatives such as CNTRICS will be successful only if analogous cognitive functions are identified and stabilized in animal models. That will require the development of experimental paradigms that can be used to produce, measure, and detect cognitive functions in animal models that are analogous to those cognitive functions disrupted in human schizophrenics. The advantage of animal models is that they allow investigators to intervene in cellular and molecular activities in order to identify the mechanisms of cognitive functions and to determine the sources of cognitive dysfunction. They also provide a context in which to test the efficacy of pro-cognitive agents in improving cognitive dysfunctions before testing them on humans with schizophrenia.

However, as I have argued previously (Sullivan 2009), the forms of learning and memory under study in cognitive neurobiology are unstable for at least two reasons. First, similar to cognitive neuroscience, methodological pluralism is widespread in cognitive neurobiology. The experimental paradigms and adjoining protocols used to investigate the cellular and molecular mechanisms of cognitive functions or processes vary from one laboratory to the next. For example, two experimental paradigms that are both used to detect a cognitive function such as social recognition memory may differ with respect to the type of stimuli used, the intensity or duration of the stimuli, and the duration of the interstimulus and intertrial intervals. Such differences could lead to differences in what cognitive functions are required for performance of a task and what cellular and molecular activities are involved. Thus, there are no real grounds upon which to establish that two labs that use different variants of an experimental paradigm are investigating the "same" phenomenon or its mechanisms, and this precludes integration of explanatory claims emanating from the two laboratories into a common explanatory model of the same function.

One reason we encounter what I have referred to as "a multiplicity of experimental protocols" in cognitive neurobiology is that different investigators have different intuitions about which constraints on the experimental process are most important. Some investigators are concerned with ensuring the reliability of the experimental process by using stimulus parameters that they are confident will produce data that will enable them to discriminate between competing claims about the effect under study in the laboratory. Often, however, such investigators sacrifice the external validity of their interpretive claims, because the stimulus parameters they select are not sufficiently similar to "real-world" stimulus parameters. Generally speaking, such methodological pluralism is encouraged in the hope that it may allow for novel findings that could not be achieved if experimental paradigms and protocols were standardized across investigators. However, such freedom is an impediment to the development of multi-level mechanistic explanations of mental disorders.

A second obstacle to stabilizing cognitive functions in cognitive neurobiology has to do with the fact that cognitive neurobiologists do not engage in task analysis when they design experimental paradigms to probe for cognitive functions of interest. As I demonstrated with respect to the cognitive function of spatial memory (Sullivan 2010), investigators are less interested in the cognitive processes that occur when an animal is trained in an experimental learning paradigm than with obtaining data indicating that an observable change in behavior has occurred—data that can be used as a basis for inferring that the cognitive function that the paradigm purportedly individuates has been detected. The trouble with this, however, as I demonstrated with respect to the Morris water maze, is that terms designating cognitive functions are often applied to sets of behavioral effects under study in an experimental paradigm in instances when no investigator is precisely certain what function the paradigm can be used to individuate. This leaves investigators somewhat free to liberally apply different terms to refer to the function under study, to the extent that the term designating the function begins to oscillate. Such oscillations reveal that, at least in cognitive neurobiology, little work is done to understand what model organisms trained in experimental paradigms actually learn. The vast majority of cognitive neurobiologists are interested exclusively in the relationship between molecular changes and observable changes in behavior that they take to be indicative of a cognitive function of interest (e.g., changes in what has been learned or in memory). From the perspective of their immediate research interests, they don't care about the mental lives of their animal subjects. Thus, they don't worry that the experimental paradigms they use to probe for cognitive functions circumscribe many different functions, nor do they spend time worrying about how to modify experimental paradigms so that they track discrete functions. This is in stark contrast to cognitive neuroscience, which regards task analysis as a fundamental component in the interpretation of behavioral and imaging data and in the improvement of experimental paradigms.

I think it is safe to say, however, that neither cognitive neuroscientists nor cognitive neurobiologists are specifically concerned with the mental states of the organisms they study. Although cognitive neuroscientists do engage in task analysis, as far as I know none of them incorporate the potential mental or emotional states of their subjects into their explanatory models.

Given the kinds of differences that exist between cognitive neuroscience and cellular and molecular neurobiology, we can anticipate that the project of stabilizing mental disorders or cognitive functions and integrating results into multi-level explanatory models that reveal suitable targets for therapeutic intervention will fail. Those investigators who have decided to use the investigative tools on offer in cognitive neuroscience and cognitive neurobiology to identify the mechanisms that underlie mental disorders or cognitive dysfunctions will not succeed so long as there is no coordination across laboratories situated at the same and different levels of analysis to "stabilize the phenomena." I turn now to an evaluation of a research initiative that aims to create such coordination in order to assess its prospects and identify potential problems.

The CNTRICS Initiative

In 2007, two cognitive neuroscientists, Deanna Barch and Cameron Carter, described the development of an inter-disciplinary initiative whose ultimate aim was to develop psychopharmacological or "procognitive" agents to "enhance cognition and functional outcome in schizophrenia" (Carter and Barch 2007, 1131). The Cognitive Neuroscience Treatment Research to Improve Cognition in Schizophrenia (CNTRICS) initiative was in part a result of challenges faced by investigators involved in the Measurement of Treatment Effects on Cognition in Schizophrenia (MATRICS) initiative, a separate initiative spearheaded by Steven Marder and Michael Green in 2004. (See Carter and Barch 2007; Carter et al. 2008; Marder and Fenton 2004.) Investigators and pharmaceutical representatives who had participated in the MATRICS initiative, and the U.S. Food and Drug Administration, had the task of developing a battery of cognitive tests for the purposes of testing pharmacological agents to determine whether they improved cognition in schizophrenia. However, the battery of cognitive tasks that they compiled consisted primarily of "pen-and-paper-based" "clinical neuropsychological tests" that had been "developed for and validated in the clinical trials of atypical antipsychotics in the 1990s" (Carter and Barch 2007, p. 1132). Tasks then used in cognitive neuroscience to study cognitive dysfunction in schizophrenia were excluded, primarily because they were not thought to satisfy the criterion of construct validity. The lack of success achieved by MATRICS, primarily because the tasks selected failed to promote the discovery of pro-cognitive treatments, prompted a subset of the investigators familiar with or involved in the initiative to search for cognitive neuroscientific tasks that met the criterion of construct validity.

Cognitive tasks that had been widely used to study cognition and cognitive deficits in schizophrenia, such as the Stroop task and the Wisconsin Card Sorting Task, were acknowledged as involving multiple cognitive processes and were thus deemed "less helpful for understanding the specific nature of cognitive deficits, for identifying useful drug targets, [and] for assessing change in specific cognitive functions" (Carter and Barch 2007, 1133). As Carter and Barch note (ibid.), one ongoing aim of CNTRICS is to develop "process pure" tasks better capable of tracking single cognitive processes or subcomponents of more general processes.

In one of the initial research paper specifying the aims of CNTRICS, Barch et al. (2008) identified three other desiderata for candidate cognitive tasks—criteria that also correspond directly to the issues of "individuating" and "stabilizing" cognitive processes as scientific kinds. The first was consensus among cognitive neuroscientists as to which cognitive functions to investigate. They identified five broad categories of processes: "(1) executive control, (2) working memory, (3) long-term learning and memory (including reinforcement learning), (4) attention, (5) perception, and

(6) social and emotional processing" (Barch et al. 2008, p. 614). A working group was assigned to each cognitive function category, and each working group identified a set of sub-processes associated with that category for which experimental tasks that met the criteria already existed or could readily be developed. One subcomponent of attention identified for further study was control of attention, meaning "the ability to guide/change the focus of attention in response to internal representations" (Nuechterlein et al. 2009). One task that was designed to probe for this cognitive process was the "Guided Search Paradigm" (ibid.), a task in which a subject searches for a target in a visual array that differs from other stimuli in the array with respect to one feature (e.g., it is a square rather than a circle, or it is red rather than green). The subject is then presented with sets of visual arrays that contain the target and some distractors. The subject is asked to press a button to indicate whether the target is present. The advantage of such a task over the Stroop task is that it doesn't involve language processing, and hence it is likely that fewer cognitive processes are involved. Therefore, the task comes closer to potentially satisfying the "process pure" requirement and potentially allows for more precise localization of the cognitive function in the brain. Furthermore, the absence of a language component allows for easier translation of the task to animal models (Lustig et al., in press). Taken in combination, these features of the Guided Search Paradigm satisfy some of the conditions that I said had to be met for inter-disciplinary integration to be successful. First, it is important that a cognitive task individuate a discrete cognitive function; the simpler the task, the more likely it will be to serve this function. Second, investigators must agree that the task may be used to measure the function in question so that use of that task for measuring that function—the operationalization of that function—is standardized across investigators.[2] So, generally speaking, paradigms like Guided Search hold some promise for stabilizing the cognitive function of "control of attention." A second requirement, put forward by Carter and Barch (2007), is that the protocols associated with each cognitive task must be standardized across investigators. Carter and Barch acknowledge that this is primarily because different investigators "may use similar but nonidentical tasks to measure the same cognitive construct" and "these tasks . . . could . . . vary widely in potentially important characteristics such as number of trials . . . frequency of different trial types and the types of conditions included" (ibid., p. 1134). Imposing standardization of a task across investigators might eliminate problems associated with the multiplicity of experimental paradigms or protocols to test the same cognitive function at a single level of analysis. Furthermore,

such measures might ensure the stability of the referents of the terms designating specific cognitive processes, at least among cognitive neuroscientists.

The first three CNTRICS meetings yielded a battery of cognitive tasks, but the goal of the fourth through sixth meetings (2011–2012) was to identify imaging biomarkers—"characteristic(s) that are measured objectively as an index of a pathogenic process or a response to treatment" (Carter et al. 2011, p. 7)—that might be used to differentiate the normal brain from the schizophrenic brain by means of fMRI scans or EEG recordings undertaken during performance of the selected cognitive tasks. Investigators would then be able to determine the effects of pro-cognitive agents on the imaging biomarkers and on task performance (See, e.g., Carter et al. 2012a). The ultimate aim of identifying imaging biomarkers was to develop "an optical mechanism for translational research" so that "across levels of analysis . . . a common conceptual framework, language, and set of experimental tools that allows basic science to inform clinical and therapeutic research" could be applied (ibid.). However, so far little progress has been made in identifying imaging biomarkers for the cognitive functions that are of interest to CNTRICS investigators. For example, "basic and preclinical research has not progressed to the point where biomarkers of attentional control are fully ready for use in treatment research" (Luck et al. 2012, p. 59).

Though at least some of the aforementioned measures, taken together, may satisfy the requirements of stabilizing cognitive functions within cognitive neuroscience, they are not sufficient for stabilizing these functions within cognitive neurobiology and across the two areas of neuroscience. However, other criteria put forward by CNTRICS are intended to lay the groundwork for meeting that requirement. In addition to ensuring that the cognitive processes are impaired in schizophrenia and can be individuated in practice via appropriately designed experimental tasks, the CNTRICS working groups sought out tasks that can be used to "establish[] links with known neural circuits and neurotransmitter systems" and that have analogs that can be used in conjunction with animal models (Barch et al. 2008, p. 614).

The aim of the most recent meetings of CNTRICS has been to develop animal models for the purposes of screening drug treatments for the cognitive processes thought to be disrupted in schizophrenia. (See, e.g., Dudchenko et al. in press.) One task is to develop animal models of schizophrenia—in other words, rodent subjects that exhibit behaviors considered analogous to human subjects with schizophrenia. The second aim is to identify tasks that are analogous to the tasks used to study cognitive deficits in schizophrenics. For example, investigators seek to identify a set of experimental paradigms that can be used to delineate "control of attention" in rodent models. Three tasks have been selected to probe for this cognitive function in animal models: the five-choice serial reaction time test, the five-choice continuous performance test, and the distractor-condition sustained-attention task. This third task most closely resembles the task conditions in the Guided Search paradigm (described above) that are designed to test control of attention in human subjects. Lustig et al. (2012, p. 1) provided the following reasons for selecting these three tasks:

[T]he highest priority was given to construct validity, both in terms of the ability of the paradigm to specifically measure the process of interest and evidence that it recruited the neural systems thought to be critical for that process and impaired in schizophrenia. Reliability and the ability to standardize the paradigm across laboratories were also major concerns.

These criteria are exemplary of the kinds of strategies that I suggested could stabilize cognitive functions within cognitive neurobiology. If it can be established that all these paradigms measure the same cognitive function, then they also satisfy Wimsatt's (2007) criterion of robustness or the ability to access the same phenomenon via multiple different experimental procedures. Furthermore, the similarity between the Guided Search Paradigm to be used with human subjects and the distractor-condition sustained-attention task to be used with animal models increases the likelihood of being able to directly relate results across the two areas of neuroscience.

At best, insofar as no perfect animal model of schizophrenia exists, one might imagine the following kind of ideal scenario for stabilizing the phenomenon of "control of attention": Research studies using the Guided Search paradigm are conducted with an experimental group consisting of schizophrenic subjects and a control group consisting of "normal" human subjects. The two groups are compared on the performance of certain tasks, and the data are taken to indicate a deficit in "control of attention" in schizophrenic subjects. The study is replicated in different laboratories by different investigators. The results of those studies match the features of the original study in all relevant respects: the experimental paradigms, the experimental protocols, and the criteria used for recruiting schizophrenic subjects are the same. Meanwhile, a similar study is conducted using rodent subjects. An intervention technique (e.g., a lesion or a pharmacological manipulation) is used to produce a deficit in control of attention in one group of rats. The performance of that experimental group is compared against the performance of a group of "normal" rats on the distractor-condition sustained-attention task. The data are taken to indicate that the rats in the experimental group exhibit a deficit in "control of attention." The experiment is replicated in several laboratories, with all the features standardized. A pharmacological agent is then introduced into the rats exhibiting a deficit in "control of attention." These experiments are also replicated across laboratories. When enough data on the pharmacological agent's efficacy in animal models have been accumulated (that is, when the drug meets FDA requirements), clinical trials using human subjects will begin.

This is my understanding of how investigators think the story will go for each of the functions identified as disrupted in schizophrenia, with candidate pro-cognitive agents being tested for each domain of cognitive function thought to be disrupted.

Prospects for Success of the CNTRICS Initiative

As I noted at the outset of this chapter, there is widespread agreement among philosophers of psychiatry that current categories of mental disorders fail to track stable regularities in nature and thus do not constitute natural kinds. There is also a growing consensus among research scientists that the *DSM*'s categories of mental disorders are not sufficient for grounding the search for causes of mental disorders and that a different classification scheme informed by measurement techniques that produce valid constructs is required. (See, e.g., Insel 2013.) The CNTRICS initiative and related NIMH-sponsored MATRICS initiative are the first such initiatives directed at eventually replacing categories such as schizophrenia and depression with a taxonomy designating cognitive functions as (for example) "control of attention" and "reward-based learning." This move prompts two questions: What will happen to the stability of mental disorders in this new system? How stable will the new scientific kinds that will replace them be?

The aim of the CNTRICS and MATRICS initiatives is not to stabilize current categories of mental disorders. If a new competing classification system of cognitive functions consisting of valid constructs begins to emerge and individuals begin to be diagnosed as having specific cognitive dysfunctions in addition to having mental disorders, we might anticipate that current categories of mental disorders could become wildly unstable and that such instability could compromise the stability of the new classification scheme. In other words, the new classification scheme, even with all its emphasis on the stability of kinds of cognitive functions in the form of valid constructs, may become subject to Hacking's looping effects.

This brings us to the question of whether the kinds of strategies of stabilization put forward by investigators involved in the CNTRICS initiative will ultimately be successful in stabilizing cognitive functions as explanatory targets—which may be considered an advantage over the *DSM*. One problem that we may foresee is, as I have demonstrated, that the areas of neuroscience that are trying to accelerate the stabilization of their explanatory targets (i.e., cognitive functions) are not mature sciences in Hacking's sense. The projects of localizing cognitive functions in the brain and identifying their cellular and molecular mechanisms are still in their infancy. To try to identify a set of cognitive tasks for each broad domain of function and its sub-functions and standardize them across research contexts immediately is likely to impede future scientific progress and prevent positive refinements to current taxonomies of cognitive functions. As philosophers of neuroscience (e.g., Bechtel and Richardson 1993; Bechtel 2008) have correctly pointed out, in the search for the mechanisms of cognitive functions the phenomena are likely to change or be "reconstituted" in light of new discoveries, and it is important that investigators remain open to this possibility. In other words, while stabilizing explanatory targets requires collective multi-disciplinary efforts such stabilization is likely only to emerge very gradually over time, if at all. Furthermore, CNTRICS is not the only interdisciplinary initiative directed at understanding the causes of mental disorders. The moral of the story is that coordination across different laboratories and different levels of analysis is desirable for discovering the causes of mental disorders, but a pluralism that promotes different investigative strategies is preferable. The precise form that such pluralism ought to take will have to be saved for another occasion.[3]

Notes

1. These claims are based on a partial analysis of the experimental literature on the Stroop task that considered nine papers published in eleven years (Thoma et al. 2007; Levy et al. 2004; Kerns et al. 2005; Yücel et al. 2002; Alain et al. 2002; Barch et al. 1999a,b; Perlstein et al. 1998; Carter et al. 1997). I regard this number of research studies as sufficient for establishing differences in subject recruitment across research studies and investigators. A broader analysis of the experimental literature would simply put my claim on stronger footing.

2. The same basic strategy was involved in the development of tasks for each of the five categories of cognitive processes thought to be disrupted in schizophrenia (e.g., long-term memory (Ragland et al. 2009), working memory (Barch et al. 2009a), and executive function (Gilmour et al. in press; Barch et al. 2009b; Carter et al. 2012b),

with a variety of tasks being nominated for research in clinical trials. (See, e.g.,, Barch et al. 2009c, p. 111, table 1.)

3. At least some research scientists appear to be in agreement, insofar as it is indicated in the draft of the NIMH Research Domain Criteria Project, that the constructs that will result from initiatives such as CNTRICS and MATRICS will be "subject to continual refinement with advances in science" (NIMH 2011).

References

Adams, R., and A. David. 2007. Patterns of anterior cingulate activation in schizophrenia: A selective review. *Neuropsychiatric Disease and Treatment* 3 (1): 87–101.

Alain, C., H. McNeely, Y. He, B. Christensen, and R. West. 2002. Neurophysiological evidence of error-monitoring deficits in patients with schizophrenia. *Cerebral Cortex* 12 (8): 840–846.

American Psychiatric Association. 1994. *Diagnostic and Statistical Manual of Mental Disorders*, fourth edition.

American Psychiatric Association. 2000. *Diagnostic and Statistical Manual of Mental Disorders*, fourth edition, revised (*DSM*-IV-TR).

Barch, D., C. Carter, P. Hachten, M. Usher, and J. Cohen. 1999a. The "benefits" of distractability: mechanisms underlying increased Stroop effects in schizophrenia. *Schizophrenia Bulletin* 25 (4): 749–762.

Barch, D., C. Carter, W. Perlstein, J. Baird, J. Cohen, and N. Schooler. 1999b. Increased Stroop facilitation effects in schizophrenia are not due to increased automatic spreading activation. *Schizophrenia Research* 39 (1): 51–64.

Barch, D., C. Carter, and J. Cohen. 2004. Factors influencing Stroop performance in schizophrenia. *Neuropsychology* 18 (3): 477–484.

Barch, D., C. Carter, A. Arnsten, R. Buchanan, J. Cohen, M. Geyer, et al. 2008. Measurement issues in the use of cognitive neuroscience tasks in drug development for impaired cognition in schizophrenia: A report of the second consensus building conference of the CNTRICS initiative. *Schizophrenia Bulletin* 34: 613–618.

Barch, D., M. Berman, R. Engle, J. Jones, J. Jonides, A. Macdonald 3rd, et al. 2009a. CNTRICS final task selection: working memory. *Schizophrenia Bulletin* 35 (1): 136–152.

Barch, D., T. Braver, C. Carter, R. Poldrack, and T. Robins. 2009b. CNTRICS final task selection: executive control. *Schizophrenia Bulletin* 35 (1): 115–135.

Barch, D., C. Carter, A. Arnsten, R. Buchanan, J. Cohen, M. Geyer, et al. 2009c. Selecting paradigms from cognitive neuroscience for translation into use in clinical trials: Proceedings of the third CNTRICS meeting. *Schizophrenia Bulletin* 35: 109–114.

Barch, D., H. Moore, D. Nee, D. Manoach, and S. Luck. 2012. CNTRICS imaging biomarkers selection: Working memory. *Schizophrenia Bulletin* 38 (1): 43–52.

Bechtel, W. 2008. *Mental Mechanisms: Philosophical Perspectives on Cognitive Neuroscience*. Erlbaum.

Bechtel, W., and R. Richardson. 1993. *Discovering Complexity: Decomposition and Localization as Strategies in Scientific Research*. MIT Press.

Belger, A., and D. Barch. 2009. Cognitive neuroscience and neuroimaging in schizophrenia. In *Neurobiology of Mental Illness*, third edition, ed. D. Charney and E. Nestler. Oxford University Press.

Bogen, J. 1988. Comments. *Noûs* 22: 65–66.

Carter, C., et al. 1997. Anterior cingulate gyrus dysfunction and selective attention deficits in schizophrenia: [150]H2O PET study during single-trial Stroop task performance. *American Journal of Psychiatry* 154 (12): 1670–1675.

Carter, C., and D. Barch. 2007. Cognitive neuroscience-based approaches to measuring and improving treatment effects on cognition in schizophrenia: The CNTRICS initiative. *Schizophrenia Bulletin* 33 (5): 1131–1137.

Carter, C., D. Barch, R. Buchanan, E. Bullmore, J. Krystal, J. Cohen, et al. 2008. Identifying cognitive mechanisms targeted for treatment development in schizophrenia: An overview of the first meeting of the Cognitive Neuroscience Treatment Research to Improve Cognition in Schizophrenia Initiative. *Biological Psychiatry* 64: 4–10.

Carter, C., J. Kerns, and J. Cohen. 2009. Cognitive neuroscience: bridging thinking and feeling to the brain, and its implications for psychiatry. In *Neurobiology of Mental Illness*, third edition, ed. D. Charney and E. Nestler. Oxford University Press.

Carter, C., D. Barch, and E. Bullmore. 2011. Cognitive neuroscience treatment research to improve cognition in schizophrenia and related disorders. *Biological Psychiatry* 70: 7–12.

Carter, C., D. Barch, and the CNTRICS Executive Committee. 2012a. Imaging biomarkers for treatment development for impaired cognition: Report of the sixth CNTRICS meeting: Biomarkers recommended for further development. *Schizophrenia Bulletin* 38 (1): 26–33.

Carter, C., M. Minzenberg, R. West, and A. Macdonald 3rd. 2012b. CNTRICS imaging biomarker selections: Executive control paradigms. *Schizophrenia Bulletin* 38 (1): 34–42.

Cohen, J., D. Barch, C. Carter, and D. Servan-Schreiber. 1999. Context-processing deficits in schizophrenia: Converging evidence from three theoretically motivated cognitive tasks. *Journal of Abnormal Psychology* 108 (1): 120–133.

Cooper, R. 2004. Why Hacking is wrong about human kinds. *British Journal for the Philosophy of Science* 55: 73–85.

Craver, C. 2007. *Explaining the Brain: Mechanisms and the Mosaic Unity of Neuroscience.* Oxford University Press.

Craver, C. 2009. Mechanisms and natural kinds. *Philosophical Psychology* 22: 575–594.

Cronbach, L., and P. Meehl. 1955. Construct validity in psychological tests. *Psychological Bulletin* 52: 281–302.

Dudchenko, P., J. Talpos, J. Young, and M. Baxter. In press. Animal models of working memory: A review of tasks that might be used in screening drug treatments for the memory impairments found in schizophrenia. *Neuroscience and Biobehavioral Reviews.*

Gilmour, G., A. Arguello, A. Bari, B. Brown, C. Carter, S. Floresco, et al. In press. Measuring the construct of executive control in schizophrenia.

Green, M., J. Lee, and R. Kern. 2009. Neurocognitive Assessment for Psychiatric Disorders. In *Neurobiology of Mental Illness*, third edition, ed. D. Charney and E. Nestler. Oxford University Press.

Hacking, I. 1983. *Representing and Intervening.* Cambridge University Press.

Hacking, I. 1988. On the stability of the laboratory sciences. *Journal of Philosophy* 85 (10): 507–514.

Hacking, I. 1989. The life of instruments. *Studies in History and Philosophy of Science* 20: 265–270.

Hacking, I. 1992. The self-vindication of the laboratory sciences. In *Science as Practice and Culture*, ed. A. Pickering. University of Chicago Press.

Hacking, I. 1995a. *Rewriting the Soul: Multiple Personality and the Sciences of Memory.* Princeton University Press.

Hacking, I. 1995b. The looping effects of human kinds. In *Causal Cognition: A Multidisciplinary Debate*, ed. D. Sperber, D. Premack, and A. Premack. Clarendon.

Hacking, I. 1998. *Mad Travelers: Reflections on the Reality of Transient Mental Illness.* University of Virginia.

Hacking, I. 2007. Kinds of people: moving targets. *Proceedings of the British Academy* 151: 285–318.

Haslam, N. 2000. Psychiatric categories as natural kinds: Essentialist thinking about mental disorders. *Social Research* 67: 1031–1058.

Haslam, N. 2002. Kinds of kinds: A conceptual taxonomy of psychiatric categories. *Philosophy, Psychiatry, & Psychology* 9: 203–217.

Hor, K., and M. Taylor. 2010. Suicide and schizophrenia: A systematic review of rates and risk factors. *Journal of Psychopharmacology (Oxford, England)* 24 (4): 81–90.

Insel, T. 2013. Transforming diagnosis. At http://www.nimh.nih.gov/about/director/index.shtml.

Kendler, K. S., P. Zachar, and C. Craver. 2011. What kinds of things are psychiatric disorders? *Psychological Medicine* 22: 1–8.

Kerns, J., J. Cohen, A. Macdonald 3rd, M. Johnson, V. Stenger, H. Aizenstein, and C. Carter. 2005. Decreased conflict and error-related activity in the anterior cingulate cortex in schizophrenia. *American Journal of Psychiatry* 162 (10): 1833–1839.

Khalidi, M. A. 2010. Interactive kinds. *British Journal for the Philosophy of Science* 61: 335–360.

Kincaid, H. 2008. Do we need theory to study disease? Lessons from cancer research and their implications for mental illness. *Perspectives in Biology and Medicine* 51: 367–378.

Levy, D., N. Mendell, and P. Holzman. 2004. The antisaccade task and neuropsychological tests of prefrontal cortical integrity in schizophrenia: Empirical findings and interpretative consideration. *World Psychiatry; Official Journal of the World Psychiatric Association (WPA)* 3 (1): 32–40.

Luck, S., J. Ford, M. Sarter, and C. Lustig. 2012. CNTRICS final biomarker selection: Control of attention. *Schizophrenia Bulletin* 38 (1): 53–61.

Lustig, C., R. Kozak, M. Sarter, J. Young, and T. Robbins. In press. CNTRICS final animal model task selection: control of attention. *Neuroscience and Biobehavioral Reviews*.

Marder, S., and W. Fenton. 2004. Measurement and treatment research to improve cognition in schizophrenia: NIMH MATRICS initiative to support the development of agents for improving cognition in schizophrenia. *Schizophrenia Research* 72: 5–9.

NIMH. 2011. NIMH Research Domain Criteria (draft). Available at http://www.nimh.nih.gov.

Nuechterlein, K., S. Luck, C. Lustig, and M. Sarter. 2009. CNTRICS final task selection: Control of attention. *Schizophrenia Bulletin* 35 (1): 182–196.

Nuechterlein, K., K. Subotnik, J. Ventura, M. Green, D. Gretchen-Doorly, and R. Asarnow. 2012. The puzzle of schizophrenia: Tracking the core role of cognitive deficits. *Development and Psychopathology* 24 (2): 529–536.

Perlstein, W., C. Carter, D. Barch, and J. Baird. 1998. The Stroop task and attention deficits in schizophrenia: A critical evaluation of card and single-trial Stroop methodologies. *Neuropsychology* 12 (3): 414–425.

Ragland, J., N. Cohen, R. Cools, M. Frank, D. Hannula, and C. Ranganath. 2012. CNTRICS imaging biomarkers final task selection: Long-term memory and reinforcement learning. *Schizophrenia Bulletin* 38 (1): 62–72.

Rush, J., M. First, and D. Blacker. 2008. *Handbook of Psychiatric Measures*, second edition. American Psychiatric Publishing.

Sullivan, J. 2009. The multiplicity of experimental protocols: A challenge to reductionist and non-reductionist models of the unity of neuroscience. *Synthese* 167: 511–539.

Sullivan, J. 2010. Reconsidering "spatial memory" and the Morris water maze. *Synthese* 177: 261–283.

Sullivan, J., and E. Thiels. 2011. The place of the mind in contemporary neuroscience. Presented at annual meeting of Society for Neuroscience, Washington.

Taylor, S., and A. MacDonald 3rd. 2011. Brain mapping biomarkers of socio-emotional processing in schizophrenia. *Schizophrenia Bulletin* 38 (1): 73–80.

Thoma, P., D. Zoppelt, B. Wibel, and I. Daum. 2007. Context processing and negative symptoms in schizophrenia. *Journal of Clinical and Experimental Neuropsychology* 29 (4): 428–435.

Uttal, W. 2003. *The New Phrenology: The Limits of Localizing Cognitive Processes in the Brain*. MIT Press.

Wimsatt, W. 2007. *Reengineering Philosophy for Limited Beings: Piecewise Approximations to Reality*. Harvard University Press.

Yücel, M., C. Pantelis, G. Stuart, S. Wood, P. Maruff, D. Velakoulis, et al. 2002. Anterior cingulate activation during Stroop task performance: A PET to MRI coregistration study of individual patients with schizophrenia. *American Journal of Psychiatry* 159 (2): 251–254.

Zachar, P. 2000. Psychiatric disorders are not natural kinds. *Philosophy, Psychiatry, & Psychology* 7: 167–182.

Contributors

George Graham   Department of Philosophy, Georgia State University

Nick Haslam   School of Behavioural Science, University of Melbourne

Allan Horwitz   Department of Sociology, Rutgers University

Harold Kincaid   School of Economics, University of Cape Town

Dominic Murphy   Department of History and Philosophy of Science, University of Sydney

Jeffrey Poland   Department of History, Philosophy, and the Social Sciences, Rhode Island School of Design; Department of Molecular Biology, Cell Biology, and Biochemistry, Alpert Medical School, Brown University

Nancy Nyquist Potter   Department of Philosophy, University of Louisville

Don Ross   Center for Economic Analysis of Risk, Georgia State University

Dan Stein   Department of Psychiatry and Mental Health, University of Cape Town

Jacqueline Sullivan   Department of Philosophy and Rotman Institute of Philosophy, University of Western Ontario

Şerife Tekin   Department of Philosophy, Daemen College

Peter Zachar   Department of Psychology, Auburn University, Montgomery

Index